"There's a world between these covers—a world of truth, grace, and beauty where gravity keeps your feet on the ground and levity lifts your spirit high. This world exists because Douglas Wood has the experience and the gifts required to bring it to life, giving his readers a chance to dwell in it for a while and return refreshed, even healed, to their own lives."

—**Parker J. Palmer**, author of *On the Brink of Everything, Let Your Life Speak, The Courage to Teach,* and *Healing the Heart of Democracy*

"Douglas Wood writes with bravery and honesty about childhood traumas, learning difficulties, bouts with depression, and how the 'therapy of wilderness' brought peace, perspective, and feelings of self-worth. You'll find yourself laughing, crying, and breathing in the forest air while reading Doug's stories. You might even discover yourself in these essays, through his gentle, understanding, and insightful words."

—**Patsy Mogush**, president, Listening Point Foundation

"In this compelling collection of essays, Douglas Wood provides an intimate and revealing portrait of his relationship with nature, and the family and friends who are part of his life's journey. Wood's love of wild nature is expressed in every page and essay."

—**Chris Knopf**, executive director, Friends of the Boundary Waters Wilderness

"Ever the expert naturalist, guide, and storyteller, Douglas Wood alternates between captivating prose and lyrical poetry in *A Wild Path*. One moment Doug takes us on a strenuous paddle across big water and in the next, a gentle stroll under towering pines. Every essay connects, or reconnects, us with family and friends, flora and fauna, and all the beauties of this vast and vibrant world."

—**Buddy Huffaker**, executive director, Aldo Leopold Foundation

"Douglas Wood's *A Wild Path* reaches deep into the heart—his, mine, and surely yours as well. His stories reflect the lives of our generation drawn to the woods and lakes of the North and toward a simpler life. They are stories of a life well lived, told in such vivid detail they will give you pause to reflect on the stories and meanings of your own life."

—**Steve Piragis**, co-owner, Piragis Northwoods Company

"In *A Wild Path*, Douglas Wood captures the magic, wonder, and awe of experiencing the wilderness. This collection of essays is honest, authentic, and laugh-out-loud funny. A real treat."

—**Rebecca Otto**, executive director, Ernest C. Oberholtzer Foundation

"Douglas Wood has always been able to express the magic in this world like no one else I know. Every essay in this book, from raucous hilarity to serious contemplation—the ironies, the wisdom, the guffaws, and the tears from those beautiful places in Doug's heart—seems a personal gift to me. I suspect that will be the case for all who read it."

—**Denny Olson**, writer, teacher, actor, and naturalist

"Douglas Wood's stories help us perceive the worlds within and beyond the surfaces of Earth—and there, 'in the company of trees,' as he puts it, to discover health and hope."

—**Richard Louv**, author of *Last Child in the Woods* and *Our Wild Calling*

"As a writer, Douglas Wood is like John Burroughs in his vivid descriptions of the natural world. But in his delightful storytelling style and mastery of his craft, he is akin to Mark Twain."

—**Marlene Warren Ehresman**, founder and executive director, Iowa Wildlife Center

"This is a book filled with fun and fascinating tales, but it also contains lessons that, once learned, are as valuable outside the wilderness as within it. *A Wild Path* is far more than a journey into wild places. It is a journey into living a full life, written with skill and insight."

—**Michael Furtman**, outdoor writer and photographer

"*A Wild Path* is as good as it gets for capturing the essence of the wilderness experience and inspiring us all to explore our own pathways into the wild."

—**Stuart Osthoff**, publisher, *Boundary Waters Journal*

A WILD PATH

Also by Douglas Wood Published by the
University of Minnesota Press

Deep Woods, Wild Waters
Paddle Whispers
Fawn Island

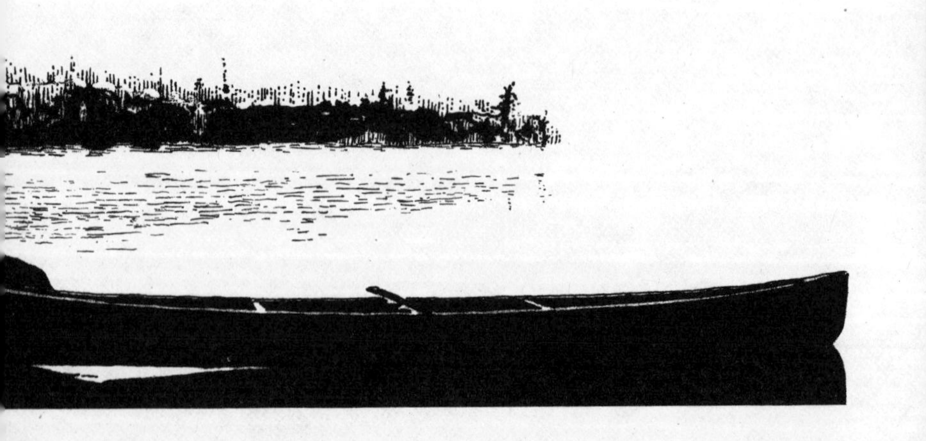

A WILD PATH

Douglas Wood

With Illustrations by the Author

University of Minnesota Press
Minneapolis
London

MINNESOTA

The article included in “Dreams of the Lonely Land” was first published in *Canoe Magazine* in 1988.

Published by the University of Minnesota Press
111 Third Avenue South, Suite 290
Minneapolis, MN 55401-2520
http://www.upress.umn.edu

ISBN 978-1-5179-0594-1 (hc)
ISBN 978-1-5179-1815-6 (pb)

A Cataloging-in-Publication record for this book is available from the Library of Congress.

Printed in Canada on acid-free paper

30 29 28 27 26 25 24 23 10 9 8 7 6 5 4 3 2 1

CONTENTS

vii *Introduction: A Wild Path*

1 Nature Boy: A Story of Wilderness Therapy

13 Toward the Wisdom of Trees

22 To Sleep by the Sundown Sea

28 Dreams of the Lonely Land

42 No Such Thing as Beauty

52 Famous Grouse

58 Bad Weather

65 The Sky Dwellers

71 A Woodland Warning

77 The Grand Tour

83 A Cabin in the Woods

93 Sparky's Close Call

98 Morning Gratitude: A Turtle's Radio Debut

102 Theater of the Wild

112 Making Camp

120 If You're Gonna Be Dumb

126 The Arrowhead Maker, the Tiger, and Me

129 A Valley of Light: Tramping the Hills with the Holy Trinity

143 The First and Only Naturalist-Guided Motorcycle Tour of Northern Minnesota

154 Beethoven in the Pines

159 A Christmas Walk
166 Nemesis
173 A Changing of the Guard
179 Computer Class for the Bronze Age
185 A Circle of Souls
193 From the Wild Horizons
203 Boulders in the River
211 Slowing Down?
217 Three Trout and a Boy
223 A Flower on the Far Side of the World
231 The Fragrance of Jasmine Tea

239 *Acknowledgments*

INTRODUCTION

A Wild Path

These stories and reflections are gathered from a path through the landscape of life. Because I love wild places and wild things, it is largely a wild path. And because I am *in* love with the North Woods—the river-laced, lake-studded Canoe Country that is sometimes more water than land—it is also a path of waters. Sometimes this path has been traveled solo, but more often in the company of friends, family, and people I was guiding through the wilderness. So although these are my stories, these folks are here as well, if only between the lines.

These essays span many years, and because I often like to step off the path, to wander, to smell a flower, or to look at something interesting, they do not tell a linear tale. But they do begin, and end, with a shy boy who had troubles in school and in life, and who took a while to find his way. He had help. Teachers with two legs and four legs, and roots and branches and blossoms, and often just the beautiful land and the living Earth: all assisted and guided the boy on the path, as it always is for those who travel with open eyes and ears and heart.

A cabin under the pines, a lonely granite outcrop under the stars, millrace rapids and wilderness sunsets, ocean lullabies and a circle of souls around a campfire, the scarlet song of a cardinal, the wail of a loon, the howl of a wolf and the warning of a chickadee—all are here and are never further away than a thought, a memory. To revisit them has been a joy and a reeducation, a return to the many times, people, and places I have loved.

Lest a reader fear that this may be a bit much in terms of heartfelt reflections and serious intentions, be reassured. This writer's mind does not work that way, whether for good or ill. There are too many missteps and jokes, too much goofy banter along the way to remain serious for too long. Besides, as any traveler knows, humor is a balm and laughter a blessing on any trail, any cruise down a river, or any crossing of a wide lake.

Perhaps you'd like to traipse along. We won't go too fast. We'll stop when we need to—to rest, to smile, to gaze into the distance from an island or an overlook. Let's go.

NATURE BOY

A Story of Wilderness Therapy

He learned that through the simplicity of wilderness travel and experience—paddling and portaging a canoe, carving a simple home for the night out of the bush, starting a campfire beneath a sheltering ledge while night winds howled in the pine tops overhead, successfully traversing a windswept lake filled with whitecaps, or shooting a wild rapids—through these experiences and a thousand more he was able to encounter the real world. . . . And there to find his place.

I am an ADHD person. Attention Deficit Hyperactivity Disorder. Rather severely. This means that I am by nature scattered and disorganized, forgetful and unfocused, have a difficult time reading or following directions or completing tasks or remembering what the tasks were in the first place. It means that I notice and am interested in nearly everything but have a hard time zeroing in and concentrating on any one thing. It means that I am sometimes overwhelmed by too much information, too many people, too much stimulation, or too much time sitting still in a chair, trying to do whatever it was that I was supposed to do. And other stuff.

I have been this way all my life but was not diagnosed until my fifties. This condition was a problem in many ways, especially in school, or in any situation where paying attention, following directions, and behaving appropriately were important. In other words, many situations. (My wife, Kathy, informs that I still do not know how to behave appropriately.) I, and my parents, were constantly reminded that "Douglas is smart, or he seems to be, but he is not living up to his potential." Which comments were inevitably followed on report cards by a cascade of *N*s (needs improvement) with very few *S*s (satisfactory) and almost no *E*s (excellent.) Which were then followed by lectures and talking-to's at home, and other unpleasant consequences.

I learned that a visit to the principal's office was not a good thing. I learned what it was like to sit in a chair in the school hallway, and I became intimately familiar with the details of the back corner of the classroom, where a special stool was kept. Along with a similarly undiagnosed case of dyslexia (a subject for another day perhaps) this made it very hard to learn how to read (which I eventually was able to do) and virtually impossible to follow or understand math—a goal still not accomplished, but not given up on yet. It was, in short, a vicious cycle that was repeated quarter after quarter, year after year, decade after decade, in one way or another, all the way through my school years and far beyond.

Of course, I would find innumerable opportunities to fall short or get into trouble at home as well, in ways large and small—never anything ruinously terrible but unacceptable enough that I often felt in some way *bad*. Bad about myself. Somehow wrong or different, like a black sheep, so that sometimes I gravitated to the wrong sorts of friends. Or more often, just didn't make any—as we moved over and over again, to a new school and a new neighborhood, where I was once again the new kid. Also, invariably the littlest kid and the youngest kid in every class.

With a prominent, dark birthmark by my mouth, I was constantly told by each new adult I met, and many kids, that "your face is dirty—you need to go wash it." "No, that's just a birthmark," I was taught to say and told not to let it bother me. I had severe environmental allergies, to the extent that our pediatrician half-jokingly told my mother, "Your child does not belong on this planet." Along the way, when I was a young boy, there was also an episode of sexual abuse, a fact I never told *anyone* until many years later—to Kathy, and to a therapist. Again, from what I have since studied and learned and deduced on my own, that was enough all by itself to cause lasting trauma and a mysterious, deep-down feeling of "There's something wrong with me."

THERE WERE SILVER LININGS. Through all the puzzlement and considerable frustration over why Dougie didn't meet expectations, couldn't try harder and succeed in school; couldn't mind and behave himself at home—still I was loved. The one great essential. There was a wonderful relationship with my granddad. No matter how often I got into trouble at school or at home, I don't remember ever getting in trouble with Granddad. (Except once, when I mentioned the location of a secret fishing hole to a stranger—not done!) Granddad instead took a great interest in me, educating me on the arts of bait casting and angling, sharpening hooks and repainting lures, planting and watering trees and roses, and throwing a curveball and fielding a grounder, and, best of all, how to gently tease and get teased. Mostly I remember how Granddad and Grandmother reported back to my parents (during the first summer I stayed with them) on what a good boy Douglas was, so helpful with every task and chore, and "How did we ever get along without him?" I was shocked. It was almost like I was hearing about a different person or had become a new person. Until I went home and back to school.

In parallel with the relationship with my grandparents (Granddad died when I was only twelve, but Grandmother lived to my forty-seventh year), there was perhaps the most important silver lining of all, my relationship with and feeling for the natural world, which has lasted all my life. Claiming the catbird seat in the bow of a fishing boat Up North, gazing back at my dad and granddad, blue sky and blue water and green forests all around us, seemed like heaven to me. I was good at fishing. I won the family fishing derby nearly every year. It was a simple task—cast a lure well or watch a bobber, catch a fish, all the while surrounded by the glories of the North Woods. Cattails, rocky shores, tall pines, yodeling loons, clear deep waters. It was indeed heaven, and always will be to me. And although the stay was always too short—a week or two—the feeling, the experience, of being successful and okay in a beautiful setting remained safely tucked into a secret place in my heart. A sanctuary that the lost feeling and failures in school and the outside world could not touch.

But even beyond that spiritual refuge of the heart, the family fishing vacations opened a door to the whole wild world of Nature. My earliest childhood memories are all of the natural world—or glimpses of it. Green trees outside a window in North Carolina, waving their limbs in a silent breeze as my mother leaned over me, maybe changing a diaper. Looking out an airplane window as we flew through white, billowing clouds when I was barely three. Gazing over the ghostly, shrouded Smoky Mountains from a high overlook, and later building a campfire for a family picnic. Feeding the ducks and geese at Silver Lake Park near my Aunt Mary's house in Rochester, Minnesota, and following a fawn through the woods at nearby Whitewater State Park. Climbing a mulberry tree and coming in with my pockets stuffed with berries and my pants hopelessly stained. One after another, nearly every early memory that was strong enough to take root and remain was of some sort of encounter with Nature. The yearly trips up north made that feeling grow ever deeper, made it as solid as Canadian Shield granite, and evoked a yearning that eventually led me to a lifetime of exploring wild paths and wild places, particularly on that legendary Shield—and eventually the unexpected joy of guiding and sharing such experiences with others.

And it was in that process of sharing, of leading other people to a hidden waterfall or down a stair-step rapids, of carrying heavy loads on a portage trail or battling whitecaps on a stormy lake, of simply pointing out the differences between a white and a red pine, a hair-cap moss and a creeping club moss, a piece of granite and a hunk of schist that I began to see and understand the *therapy of wilderness.* The psychology of green things. The counseling of rocks. As I saw and sensed the powerful effect such experiences of immersion and connection with nature had on the people I guided—nearly all of them, I gradually learned, carrying in some form their own private scars or doubts or insecurities—I began to really understand the healing and restorative power of Nature.

My own journey through failure and trauma seemed to make me exquisitely attuned to the needs and frailties of others; each small victory I witnessed or encouraged in participants—"I can carry a canoe! I can start a campfire! I can run a rapids!"—felt like a cause for celebration. A small but significant milestone in someone's journey. Mother Nature, through the whispering of aspen leaves, the roaring of rapids, the golden silence of a sunset, was healing and gently transforming lives.

Of course, I was far from the first person to make this discovery. Jesus and Buddha both found themselves by spending time in the wilderness or simply sitting under a tree. Other religious figures, from St. Francis of Assisi to St. Bernard de Clairvaux, spoke of the wisdom and benevolent properties of nature. Shakespeare and poets like Shelley and Bryant, Emerson and Longfellow, wrote of finding "books in the running brooks, sermons in stones, and good in everything" (Shakespeare, *As You Like It*). In Eastern cultures the connection is at least as strong. Traditional Hinduism, Buddhism, Zen, and Taoism all derive wisdom teachings from the natural world. A favorite Zen saying poses this question: "Green trees, fragrant grasses: a place not sacred? Where?" And the Buddha imparted perhaps his most famous teaching by silently holding up a single lotus blossom.

Indigenous cultures, prominently including the Native people of this continent, have had no doubts about the essential ties between humanity and our first mentor, Nature. The teachings and quotes are innumerable. Perhaps my favorite is from Black Elk, who said it so beautifully: "The first peace, and the most important, is that which comes within the souls of people when they realize their connection, their oneness with the universe and all its powers. And that at the center of the universe dwells the Great Spirit. And that this center is really everywhere—it is within each of us." The simple Lakota ceremonial acknowledgment Mitakuye Oyasin—all my relations—is deeply and endlessly meaningful. So the original idea of Nature as guide, healer, teacher, even comforter is a very old one—perhaps one of the oldest—and is known in virtually every corner of the Earth.

Even simple representations of nature can have a therapeutic effect. When my mother was in an assisted care facility, all the halls were adorned with large-scale outdoor paintings and photographs. She loved for me to push her in her wheelchair to see the paintings as we talked and visited and wandered down the long and winding corridors. "Oh, I remember this one," she would say. "I love these birch trees—they remind me of Lake Wabedo when I was a little girl. And I *love* that island in the sunset!" Recently it was I who needed health care and time in the hospital. When I was allowed to get up and walk, I found that all the halls of my wing were similarly decorated with lovely outdoor scenes. And sure enough, I found myself shuffling along, admiring them all, picking out favorites, even snapping photos of the art with my smart phone so I could gaze at the pictures while back in bed. Surrounded by stainless steel and plastic and linen, I felt just a little bit connected to the outdoor world. Countless studies now confirm that even a touch of nature in a school or workplace—a view of trees or green space from a window, green plants indoors, paintings, or photographs—can reduce stress, improve moods, and enhance productiveness.

Other research demonstrates that even a little bit of time scheduled outdoors in a park or green space can markedly improve the functioning of kids with ADHD or behavioral disorders, significantly lowering anxiety, anger, depression, and oppositional defiant disorder. Richard Louv writes movingly of such things in his classic book *Last Child in the Woods* as he speaks of saving children from "nature-deficit disorder."

Sometimes, of course, more than a painting or a view out the window or a bit of time on a grassy playground is required. My son, Bryan, runs Osprey Wilds Environmental Learning Center near Sandstone, Minnesota, where schoolkids come from near and far, some even taking ten-hour bus trips, to be immersed in Nature, in the woods, by a stream and a lake, for several days and nights. For many, it is unfortunately the first time in their lives they have been in such a place, connected to what was for eons our common human heritage. Their first time to actually see the stars at night, to sit by a campfire, to hold a garter snake or a crayfish in their hands, to hear owls hooting in the dark, to be challenged on a high ropes course, to paddle a canoe. It is a powerful experience. For some who come back and report years later, it is transformative and life-changing.

There is another level of therapeutic outdoor experience as well. A young friend of mine named Ellie has worked for several years as a guide, lately for an organization that specializes in wilderness therapy. Set in the high desert, the program takes at-risk young people out of their normal daily lives, away from comfort zones, temptations, and addictions, sometimes away from abusive family situations, and places them in the context of wilderness. There, over the course of two to three months, an intensive process of therapy takes place. Through backpacking, rock climbing and canyoneering, mountain biking, simple camping-out, and learning primitive skills, barriers are broken. Each week a new challenge, a new itinerary, is encountered. Through negotiating rocky trails on a bike, students experience being in something called a flow state. Carrying a heavy pack up a long ascent, they learn firsthand (the only way to truly learn) about grit and gumption and resiliency. In an arched and awe-inspiring place of streaming sunlight known as the Golden Cathedral, mystical environmental elements combine with the mastery of practical skills such as rappelling, problem solving, and group cohesion. Trust is discovered. Personal awareness and self-efficacy are developed.

In a recent conversation, Ellie told me of simply sitting with her kids on a rocky overlook after a long day of backpacking, gazing across Lake Powell at the most beautiful sunset ever. Doing nothing but soaking it in. She spoke of the importance of such things as stability and routine, getting up each morning and going to bed each night, with simple tasks—predictable and stable—far removed from the chaos many experienced at home. She talked about the process of striving for a condition of simple well-being, in a place where a clean slate and a fresh start are possible.

Ellie told me of a teenaged girl, Andrea, depressed and sometimes suicidal, from a successful family of high achievers, who felt like she never measured up, was never good enough. During counseling at the program, she was diagnosed for the first time with ADHD. At one point she had been trying to absorb the day's in-the-field geology lesson and gave up in frustration, the old feelings of inadequacy returning. "If I can't do this simple lesson, how am I ever going to do anything with my life!" she sobbed. Sitting on a rock away from the group campsite, in the company of stones and desert plants that offered nothing in the way of judgment, Ellie comforted her. The wilderness guide, seemingly uber-confident and competent, able to master any situation, disclosed problems and insecurities from her own life. She spoke of her own doubts and failures and told how difficult but vital it had been to discover her own unique strengths and skills and abilities—along with the lesson to forgive herself for things that were not her strengths. In the high desert, under the stars and the silent grace of the universe, the message was powerful. Andrea heard. She tried again. She completed the geology lesson. It was no small thing.

Ellie told me that such instances happen regularly in one form or another with her groups in the wild. As I listened, I remembered my own years of wilderness guiding—of people who broke through and discovered something, who changed jobs and careers, who left abusive relationships, who got married or divorced, who left the convent or made new vows and decisions. Who simply grew a little stronger.

Nowadays in my own work, I visit a great many schools. Because of my children's picture books, many of them elementary grades. I talk about the importance of taking care of the Earth. I sing songs about our "Little Blue Ball" and tell stories about rabbits reaching for the moon, mosquitoes the size of 747s, and woodland *windigos* who gobble up unsuspecting travelers. Along the way, I also tell my story of the boy who had ADHD, who was the worst reader in the class and had many other troubles, but who one day became a writer of books. Sometimes, interesting things happen.

ONE DAY AFTER A PROGRAM, as the kids filed out and I was packing up quickly for the next school, I heard a small voice behind me. "Mr. Wood, would you please shake my hand?" I turned around. There stood a little boy, a little over three feet tall.

"Why, sure, buddy," I said as I knelt down. "What's your name?"

"My name is Jack. I'm in first grade, and I have ADHD, too. And . . . I'm not a very good reader."

"Well, hi, Jack," I said. "Sure, I'll shake your hand. Come here. Put 'er there, pardner." And we shook. And we talked for a few moments about first grade. And reading. And life. And the beautiful, green world we live in. "You're going to do just fine, Jack," I said. "Sometimes things are a little bit hard, but it's a big club, this ADHD, poor-readers' club. It has lots of members, and you and I are members together. Remember, everybody's different in this world and we don't all learn the same way or at the same time. But you're gonna learn to read, Jack, just like I did, and you are going to have a *wonderful* life."

Then I told Jack he'd better hurry up and get back to class before his teacher worried, and off he went as I resumed packing. Five minutes later, just as I was ready to leave, I heard a female voice shouting in the hallway, to the accompaniment of running footsteps. "Special delivery for Mr. Wood! Special delivery for Mr. Wood!" And into the gym ran a teacher. "I'm Jack's teacher," she said breathlessly, "and he wanted me to give you this. It was very important to him." She held out a little, three-by-three-inch Post-It note. On the note was a child's writing: "I lov you, Meister Wod." Beneath the writing were two pictures of round-circle faces—one had a turned-down mouth, with tears coming down its cheeks, and one had a smile, with two hearts for eyes. "Jack said your stories made him sad but then made him happy," said the teacher. "And he wanted to say thank-you."

I took the little note and for a long time kept it stuck to the computer monitor in my office, so I could see it when I needed to and remember that life is composed of unpredictable ripples and connections; we don't always know where these little puffs of air we call words will go or what their effect may be. Or what a new day may bring. I will never know how many Jacks may have read my books or heard me tell a story in their school that may have somehow made a small difference. But I have hope.

AND WHAT OF the desperately shy young boy of years ago, who could barely work up the courage to say hello; the introverted, forgetful, daydreaming, disorganized ADD-dyslexic who felt like a failure at school and nearly everywhere and had the rock-bottom self-esteem to match?

Well, he was rescued. He was rescued not solely but largely through the process of loving—and learning to share his love of—wild places and wild things, of the Zen poet's shorelines "lined with green trees and fragrant grasses" and the sacredness of everywhere. He rescued himself: he found himself in the wilderness. In the company of "all his relations." With their help and guidance, he met a very important person—his own true self—on the trail.

He learned that through the simplicity of wilderness travel and experience—paddling or portaging a canoe, carving a simple home for the night out of the bush, starting a campfire beneath a sheltering ledge while night winds howled in the pine tops overhead, successfully traversing a windswept lake filled with whitecaps, or shooting a wild rapids—through these experiences and a thousand more, he was able to encounter the real world. A natural world that made sense, that evolved slowly, through natural processes. In this world he was able to reduce the confusion and anxiety and complexity of life to something manageable, to something like its bare essentials. And there to find his place. A beautiful place. A place he could share with others and, through their eyes and ears and experiences, learn to see it even more clearly.

The boy was gradually able to become less shy, starting with the most important day of his life, when after several years of longing and admiring from a distance, he was finally able to find the courage to say hello to a beautiful girl he knew. It turned out she had been waiting for the hello, had even had a dream about it. And eventually, together, they found two old woodland cabins to take care of, raised two wonderful boys, and even discovered the joy of grandchildren. Along the way, the boy found some success with writing, another way to share the beautiful, natural things he loved. He became, in many ways, a Nature Boy. The same boy he was in youth, but with a little bit of earned confidence, some modest triumphs, and a lifetime of love from the pretty girl and his family added to the recipe. He learned—I learned—that life is difficult for everyone, and everyone has their trials, but that just like hiking a rough portage trail, if you keep taking the steps through the mud and the bog, eventually you'll find an overlook. And a chance to see what it's all about. And how grand the view is.

I still struggle, every day, with ADHD and disorganization. With dyslexia. With forgetting stuff—some of it important. With completing simple tasks. With prioritizing them. With filling out stupid forms. With remembering why I came into a room or even walked five feet across the kitchen; with making lists on top of lists and never quite getting any of them finished; with trying to understand why this thing I'm doing (whatever it is) seems so hard, when everybody else seems able to accomplish it easily. I still worry about failing. I still get down on myself. I can still be shy—although a recent participant in a north woods trip I was guiding insisted, with some indignation, "You are *not* an introvert! No way!" I calmly replied that I am, but I've learned that I can smile and say hello and step out when I need to. Usually.

Some days are still tough, and sometimes life kind of gets away from me. But I now have a lifetime of days to look back on, to know that I somehow made it through them. All of them. And that I'll probably get through this one, too. And sometimes, when it all still seems to be a bit much, and I need a little peace and comfort and a return to the real world, I just go out the cabin door with Great-Great-Grandfather Caleb Emery's hickory walking stick. And I say hi to the chickadees. And wander off for a walk in the woods. It is, I have learned, good therapy.

TOWARD THE WISDOM OF TREES

There is inspiration to be found in the company of trees—strength and perspective and a sense of belonging to a world more timeless and less scattered, less harried and senseless than the one we inhabit on a daily basis.

One late evening as a young man I went out for a walk in the countryside, near where we lived. I was feeling very low. It was late fall, probably November. The stars were out, shining brightly, but I barely saw them. To me the night seemed black, as most of the nights had for quite some time, with the days not much brighter. Words like *hope* and *meaning,* words that I believed in, seemed to have lost their meaning. Daily I struggled with a darkness that was more interior than exterior, but that seemed to be nearly all encompassing. Things that had always brought pleasure no longer did. Laughter seemed foreign. Paths that had once been full of promise now seemed to lead nowhere.

I trudged along in the November chill, down a lonely country road beneath stars I couldn't see, toward something I couldn't name. Toward nothing at all. It became a long walk. But then, all of the days and nights had seemed long recently, with little identifiable purpose. So onward I trudged. And trudged.

At some point I looked up from the ground beneath my feet, and saw—not stars—but a tree. A white oak, devoid of leaves. Its winter silhouette spread gracefully, proudly, strongly against the starlight. Its great trunk, its outstretched limbs, its black tracery of branches touching the stars all seemed to embody a sort of visual poem—defiant, aspiring, beautiful beneath the vast vault of the night sky. And in an instant—one single moment—I *knew* something. Something I needed to know. Something important. Something that trees know: when life is hard and you're not sure what to do, reach. Reach up for the light. Reach down for where you're rooted. Reach out into the world around you. Survive and endure. Extend yourself and grow, through whatever hardship comes your way. Stay rooted and strive. Even if you never grasp your goals (what tree actually reaches the distant sun?) you will attain something greater: your true self. Your true form. Your own

silhouette beneath the stars. You will somehow fulfill yourself, become yourself, and add something of value to the world.

Did I hear all those words in that moment? No. But words are words. I absorbed the message. The meaning. And after standing there for a long while beneath the oak, I began to walk once more. My gait had somehow changed, my stride lengthened. And I noticed I had turned for home, without even really thinking about it. Arriving there, the boys already in bed, Kathy met me at the door—worried, as she had been for some time. I hugged her. Hard. And I did something I hadn't done for a long time. I laughed. My body shook with laughter, as if it was shaking off a great weight, the heavy cloak of darkness. As I'd walked home, I had finally noticed the stars shining above me. And I had seen more trees, trees in the starlight, many beautiful trees.

That walk seems a long time ago now. And yet not. The starlight walk was not the end of my depression. I saw a counselor. A good one. I studied psychology and learned much about human thinking and emotions and personal growth. I came to better understand my childhood and formative years and some of the wounds many of us suffer along the way that can leave scars. I read more widely than ever before. I *reached.* But I also remembered my tree.

Of all the teachers I have known, I have found very few more wise or helpful than trees. Their patience knows no bounds. They don't get bored. They don't run off. They don't seem to long for more interesting company or a brighter student. Their lessons are clear, beautifully illustrated, and easily understood.

If I were to write a course description for a class titled "The Wisdom of Trees," it might go like this:

> Having a rough time? Trouble coping with all that Life is throwing at you—storms, drought, discouragement, hardship, loss? Need a little inspiration? Some advice? Go sit under a tree. An old one, gnarled, with missing limbs, twists, turns, and knotholes.

Still haven't got it? Sit some more. Lay your head against a great root and fall asleep. (Yes, it's okay to sleep in class.) Drift off to a lullaby of birdsongs, the gentle sighing of wind through leaves or needles. Wake up to the sight of blue sky—or clouds or sun or moon—through a tracery of branches.

If your troubles remain, try the same thing tomorrow, and as often as you can. You will find a generous measure of wisdom and of peace. It worked for the Buddha under his bodhi tree after all, and for countless seekers of many cultures and many times.

AS MY OWN LIFELONG STUDY in my private Woodland University went on, I eventually began to keep a log of little things I'd learned or discovered or had been taught through endless, patient repetition from the tall professors, until an idea finally sunk in. I included some of my favorites in a little book I illustrated with pen-and-ink drawings, which has long been carried in a small shop beneath the California redwoods in Muir Woods. A fine place for it. Among the lessons: Reach down as well as up—no roots, no branches. . . . Stand tall but bend when you need to. . . . Be a shelter to someone. . . . Grow—from the bottom up, from the inside out. . . . Welcome rainy days. . . . Reach for the light. . . . Respect your elders. . . . Make fresh air, not hot air. . . . Know that the brightest blossoms are not always on the tallest trees. . . . Keep your head in the clouds and your feet on the ground. . . . Remember that big trees are just little trees that kept going. . . . Know that dreams are the seedlings of realities, and it is often from the fertile soil of failure that they grow. . . . Grow where you're planted. . . . Give your fruits freely. . . .

Along the way, I gathered thoughts from others who also sought the wisdom of trees. One of my favorite soliloquies came from my old friend Sigurd Olson, who as an old man, a beloved elder of the conservation movement, stood on a place in the north woods called Pine Island, in a grove of three-hundred-year-old pines. There he put his hand out and leaned against the trunk of a towering red pine, swaying in a gentle breeze. He spoke of how it gave him a feeling of belonging to the past, how the proud old trees had become a part of him. Then he walked over to a young seedling, maybe four feet tall. Standing beside it he said, "A great many people—young people—come to see me. They ask me, 'What is your hope for the world?' I always answer them, 'The hope for the world is in you. You are the new generation. I'm the old generation.'" Then taking the little tree in his hand, shaking its topknot gently, he continued: "Just like this little tree here . . . right beside one of these enormous red pines. This sapling epitomizes you, the hope of the world. . . . You have your task to do. You've got to carry on the battle to preserve such beautiful places as this. The battle goes on endlessly. It's your task—you've got to see that you keep the flame alive—no matter what the obstacles. The whole world depends upon you. The whole world depends on this little pine, in a sense, just as at one time it depended on these enormous trees here."

There is inspiration to be found in the company of trees—strength and perspective and a sense of belonging to a world more timeless and less scattered, less harried and senseless than the one we inhabit on a daily basis. In observing the way a white cedar, caught beneath a deadfall, bends and struggles, then finding an opening, reaches upward for its place in the sun, one can absorb a lesson in overcoming obstacles. In seeing the twisted, broken contours of an old oak or maple, one can learn something about surviving the storms of life—not intact perhaps but with a singular beauty enhanced by scars and imperfections. In a fire scar on an old pine trunk is written a story of survival and regeneration. And an old mossy trunk on the woodland floor contains a message of immortality and transformation, the lesson that even in death there is life, that the fallen tree keeps giving and, in all that grows from it and around it, rises once more.

GROWING UP IN SIOUX CITY on the Iowa prairie, I felt a deep longing for trees. Occasionally, we would go for an outing or a family picnic to the forested limestone hills of Stone Park. There, I felt I was in a sort of heaven, breathing air that was fragrant, moist, and cool, walking in the shade of benevolent beings whose blessings were distributed generously and freely to anyone who had an ear, an eye, and a heart to appreciate them. Traveling for the first time as a child to northern Minnesota and finding myself beneath pines taller and more beautiful than any trees I'd ever seen, I found that the feeling was magnified, and I knew that someday, somehow forests must be a part of my life. Finally, after a lifetime of being in love with trees, and long after my transformative, solitary night walk on the country road, I found myself by great good fortune the owner and caretaker of a beautiful Minnesota woods along the Mississippi River, living in an old cabin nestled under tall white pines.

There, I had the opportunity to get to know trees, individual trees, on a daily, personal basis. To care for them. To plant them. To find repose among their great trunks and under sheltering branches, and to feel grief when they fell. To share the seasonal changes and the evolution of the forest. I learned the habits, characteristics, and preferences of many different species—who liked their feet wet and who liked to keep them dry; who liked open sunlight and who preferred dappled shade; which species tolerated close quarters and which valued personal space. I helped to battle their enemies, from white pine blister rust to pine bark beetles to emerald ash borer and butternut canker. Countless times I've stood like Sig Olson did, with my hand upon an old pine trunk, and tried to imagine the world of its youth, a world before automobiles, telephones, televisions, or computers, a world before my grandfather was born. I've listened to the various forms of music in their branches, from summer gales to autumn whispers; listened to the groans and sighs of living beings rooted to a small piece of earth, the same piece I became rooted to myself. And in making the acquaintance of so many trees, along with the many other plants and beings they shelter and nurture, I have sensed their wisdom and absorbed something of their perspective.

Human beings, as we know, are not blessed with an abundance of "natural" wisdom, the seemingly intrinsic abilities of species from pasque flowers to tundra swans to wild geese, redwoods and red squirrels to ants to grizzly bears, all of whom possess in some varying degree marvelous and mysterious understandings of how to be who they are and how to live in the world. These understandings we refer to knowingly with the shorthand of *instinct,* as if by this label we have somehow defined or comprehended the entire subject. Human beings, on the other hand, possess very little in the way of such instinct or innate knowledge. Rather, with our radically extended childhoods and our outsized brains, we are required to *learn* how to survive and what it means to be human.

Luckily, we have teachers—and not just among our own species. A favorite old book in my library rests on an easily accessed shelf. Worn and dog-eared, it contains a large collection of American Indian tales and traditions from the Plains tribes. A passage on a sacred legend of the Arikaras deals with the cedar tree. It tells of a time when the human beings were new to the world, tells of their pitiful state, their bewilderment, and the terrible hardships they faced as they struggled to live. But they heard the friendly Voice of Vegetation telling them to seek aid and comfort from the cedar, in whose strong boughs they would find shelter from the storm, which would also give them medicine and incense. As a mark of gratitude, the cedar has long been referred to as Grandmother.

Such stories are known around the world among cultures who still live near the world of trees and wild things—or among their descendants who at some level also remember. But it is not just among traditional peoples that such an understanding exists. Modern science has long known that animal and human hemoglobin and the chlorophyll of plants and trees—the two substances most closely associated with life processes—are nearly identical. The main difference lies simply in the fact that the porphyrin ring in the hemoglobin molecule is built around a single atom of iron while that of chlorophyll is built around an atom of magnesium. The circulatory systems of trees and humans are thus intimately related. Further, ingested chlorophyll, the traditional building block of life, is useful to humans in many ways, from its powerful antioxidant and cleansing properties to the treatment of wounds, infections, hemoglobin regeneration, immunization therapy, cancer fighting, digestion, liver detoxification, and many others.

Of course, the salt water of the Earth's seas is also remarkably similar to the blood plasma coursing through our veins. In fact, within the family tree of life on Earth, one can quite accurately say that other mammals—including primates—are our parents;

that plants and trees (the latter here for about 369 million years longer than we have been) are our grandparents; and that the sea and the sun are our great-grandparents. We are all quite literally related—one family of life sharing one planet. The Arikara story of Grandmother Cedar Tree is thus in no way far-fetched, but an intuitive recognition of a simple, timeless truth.

Modern research also indicates the profound discovery that trees, through an elaborate network of soil fungi known as filigrees and other means not yet understood, are able to communicate, to literally talk to one another in a manner somewhat comparable to the neural networks in human brains. This discovery indicates that the use of phrases like *mother tree* and *forest wisdom* are in no way outside the bounds of scientific discourse. Let alone human empathy and understanding.

And so perhaps for many reasons, it should be no great surprise when a young man in turmoil, on a late-night walk beneath the stars of a vast, mysterious universe, or any other person in distress or need of comfort, or even a tribe or community or young species as a whole, uncertain in its prospects and in need of guidance and protection, should turn to wise elders. Should turn to those who understand so much about living on planet Earth—about growing, enduring, reaching, and surviving. It is no surprise that we should turn to the wisdom of trees.

TO SLEEP BY THE SUNDOWN SEA

Then suddenly, as I topped the last dune, there it was. An endless, enormous, unimaginable expanse of blue. Wild, free, boundless. Stretching forever. Reaching to the farthest limits of the sky, reaching to the other side of the world.

I was thirty-three years old and had never seen the ocean. Although that's not right exactly. I was born in Manhattan. Which is technically a coastal island, bordered by the Hudson, East, and Harlem rivers as they enter New York Harbor and empty into the Atlantic Ocean. But I don't know if I saw the Atlantic Ocean then. My parents moved to Durham, North Carolina, when I was six months old. Durham is about three hours from the Atlantic coast, and it is possible my parents took me there, but again I have no memory of it, nor have I ever seen any family photos of young Douglas frolicking on the beach.

When I was three, we moved from Durham to Louisville, Kentucky, where my younger brother Bruce was born, and when I was seven, we moved to Sioux City, Iowa, where Tom was born and where I lived until the age of twenty-one. Then after I married my college sweetheart, we lived in Cherokee, Iowa; Morris, Minnesota; and eventually Sartell, Minnesota.

Through all these years and changes of address, a constant was my love for and fascination with waters, nurtured by Little Lake near my grandparents' home in Alton, Illinois; the annual family vacation to Lake Kabetogama in Minnesota's north woods;

along with time spent near whatever stream, lake, river, or pond was nearby at a given time; and finally through the beginning years of guiding wilderness canoe trips throughout the Canoe Country of Minnesota and Ontario.

But I was thirty-three, a child of the Heartland, and had never experienced the ocean. And that bothered me. A lot. More and more I felt the call, the tidal pull, and more and more I felt the irony—a person in love with waters who had never seen, or heard, or smelled, or felt the ocean. How could that be? We had a young family, and dollars were always tight, and my summers were full of guiding, and as the years went along, a trip to the coast—either coast, any coast—never quite happened.

So when the call came—"How would you like to come to San Francisco to perform your *EarthSongs* for a major event and visit John Muir's home, and we'll pay you and cover the airfare?"—I didn't have to be asked twice. The date went onto the calendar, circled in red, and the closer it got the more excited I got. Yes, the event would be fun. But I had sung before many a nice audience at many interesting events. This time I was going to the ocean!

I HAD EVERYTHING PACKED a week early. I would take my guitar and clothing and travel kit, of course. But I was also taking my canoe-trip Duluth pack, loaded with tent and sleeping bag and pad. I would do my performance and then I would head for the beach. And camp there. And watch the sun set over the great Pacific. And listen all night to the waves washing the shore. How perfect would that be?

I did some research and discovered I would be only a short drive from Point Reyes National Seashore, with which I was vaguely familiar from books. The Muir Woods Redwood Grove was nearby, too, and I would go there first and get my first glimpse of some of the most magnificent trees in the world. California, here I come!

The big day arrived, and I drug my gear into the airport and climbed onto the plane. At this point I had flown very little, and the flight itself was an adventure. I sat in my window seat with my nose pressed against the glass like a six-year-old, watching the cultured squares of midwestern farm country below gradually morph into open prairie, then mountains and deserts and more mountains, then finally the incredible expanse of blue reaching into the west. After touching down in San Francisco, I rented a car and found my venue. I don't really remember the event at all. I recall the thrill of visiting the great naturalist John Muir's home, seeing the lovely grounds and Muir's beautifully preserved Victorian house and his writing desk. But mostly I remember quickly saying goodbye to my hosts, getting back into the car, and heading for the coast.

Redwoods first. And for a lifelong tree lover they were a revelation. There were really trees this big? This wide, this thick, this tall? They are *real*? I loved the big pines of my canoe country, but these were beings of an entirely different order of magnitude. I got a crick in my neck, straining to see the tops. And I breathed deeply, over and over again, entranced by the scent, the misty fragrance of the primeval forest. Sunbeams streamed down through the limbs of the great monarchs—as if through stained glass windows, searchlights trying to find the ferns far below. I sat on an enormous fallen log and listened to the trickling of a tiny stream. I thought of some words I'd read from William Cullen Bryant, "The groves were God's first temples," and although I thought I had understood them before, now I knew I did. I felt in my bones that the great grove was indeed a holy place, a doorway into the sacred story of life on Earth, and the mysterious dimensions of the eons. It is a feeling I still retain today.

But the ocean was calling.

So back into my little rental car with my Duluth pack, tent, and sleeping bag, and on to Point Reyes. It was getting late in the day, and I couldn't miss the sunset. Along the way I stopped at a little roadside stand for famous San Francisco sourdough bread and a box of strawberries. On my tight budget, that would be supper.

Arriving at the park, I chose a narrow, winding road that kept meandering west, figuring that it would be difficult to miss the Pacific Ocean entirely. Eventually, bypassing other distractions, I came to a small parking lot. The end of the line. And there, at the edge of the lot, by a little trail that led down to the beach, I was confronted with a difficulty. A sign: ABSOLUTELY NO OVERNIGHT CAMPING. The sign looked serious. It looked like it meant what it said.

I looked at the sign for a long time. Except for my little rental car, the parking lot was empty. The sun would be setting soon. I could hear the waves rolling in on the beach just a couple hundred yards away. Bigger, slower swells than I had ever heard on any canoe country lake. I could smell the sea air—or at least I thought I could, having never smelled sea air before. I heard gulls crying and mewling. I thought about all the years I had been waiting to see the ocean. I thought about all the recent months I had dreamed of sleeping by the sea, with the waves as my lullaby. I thought about the sign. I imagined all the bad things that might happen to a person if they ignored it. I picked up my Duluth pack—tent and sleeping bag inside—slung it over my shoulder and headed down the sandy trail toward the beach. The sign stood there, silent and accusatory, as I walked past.

The trail, lined with small, leathery seaside plants I did not know, wound teasingly, seductively over a series of grassy dunes. The sound of the waves grew steadily louder. Then suddenly, as I topped the last dune, there it was. An endless, enormous, unimaginable expanse of blue. Wild, free, boundless. Stretching forever. Reaching to the farthest limits of the sky, reaching to the other side of the world. I plunged down the dune toward the beach, tears in my eyes.

The Duluth pack was tossed to the ground, shoes kicked away, and shirt skinned off as I ran across the wide, sandy flats. I had to get into the water. I had to touch the sea! Somehow, although I had never been to such a place before, I had the unmistakable, heart-aching feeling of coming home. And because I was there all alone, the whole scene felt completely personal, private, my own sweet and tender reunion. The water was cool, salty to the taste, the swells enormous but slow and gentle, patient, inexorable. Timeless.

But sunset was coming, and I had preparations to make. Back across the beach I eventually trudged to my pack, my faithful old friend that had accompanied me on so many expeditions, to so many campsites. I toted it over to a likely spot—perhaps—beyond the reach of any incoming tide, I wasn't sure. I pulled out the little one-person tent, the sleeping bag, and pad, smoothed out a spot, and quickly set everything up. Then out came the strawberries and the San Francisco sourdough bread.

I sat on the beach—the beach I had completely to myself because I was now an outlaw—and watched the sunset. Red. Pulsating. Fiery. Exactly the same sort of sunset that has happened billions of times on countless beaches all around the world. Observed, no doubt, by billions of people. But it was unlike any sunset I had ever known. And so I watched, fascinated as the great, flaming globe sank into the sea, and I ate my little feast. It was, I thought, just about the finest dinner I had ever had.

Slowly the sky darkened. Eventually stars were strewn across the heavens, the same stars I knew from the North Country but different somehow, because they were reflected by an ocean. After a long time, I crawled into the tent and zipped myself into my bag, the sea air grown chilly. I would rise early in the morning, I thought, the better to escape arrest and possible incarceration. The dawn crying of the gulls would wake me. And then I would explore the coastline, looking over the great kelp beds, watching for whales or sea lions, familiarizing myself with the magnificent park. But for tonight my goals and plans were simple. I would fall asleep by the ocean, that was all, lullabied by the ancient song of the waves, watched over by the stars that had guided seafarers for centuries.

That evening seems long ago now. And I have since visited the ocean many times—many different oceans on different coasts on different continents. I've traveled to every major U.S. city, many of them coastal, on many a book tour. I've camped in a survival shelter of leaves and boughs on the shore of Chesapeake Bay. Have beachcombed on Florida's Redneck Riviera, where a marvelous old lady who lived in a beach house on stilts gave me a left-handed whelk that rests in my writing office yet today, next to a wave-washed egg of rose quartz from Northumberland's Holy Island on the North Sea. I have a speckled globe of schist from near Katharine Hepburn's Fenwick estate on Long Island Sound, and sand dollars and shells from Fort Lauderdale and Sanibel Island. I have ridden the waves in tall sailing ships and have leapt from rock to rock and pool to pool admiring starfish and brightly colored sea anemones among the fabulous sea stacks of Oregon. I've gazed across the North Atlantic from the rocky coast of Mount Desert Island in Maine, and across the Caribbean from the last ledge of coral at the tip of Key West. I've winged across the wide Pacific to China, and there seen sights I never imagined I would. I have stood on the beach with grandchildren in my arms, laughing with delight as the waves tried to push us over, and squinting as we tried to spot the Canary Islands four thousand miles away. And still, I look forward with excitement and anticipation to every new chance to visit the ocean and breathe the salt air.

But there is one memory different from the rest, somehow clearer and more profound, for it is the one that led to all the others. It was the time I first saw the ocean. The time I had strawberries and sourdough bread for dinner as the sun descended in a brilliant ball of fire. When the deepening sky came alive with stars, and the waves sang their ceaseless, age-old lullaby, just for me. I will always remember the night I fell asleep by the sundown sea.

DREAMS OF THE LONELY LAND

The trip sounded formidable, even frightening, with its huge sprawling lakes and roaring rapids. . . . I vowed someday I'd go there, run the same rapids, camp on the same campsites.

In the thirty or so years that I have been writing and publishing books, and speaking and occasionally traveling on book tours, I have often been asked a version of the question, "How did you become an author?" People often assume the story will have something to do with the publication of my first book, *Old Turtle.*

And indeed it does. I well remember writing the short but deeply imagined manuscript. How it fell out of my head in about half an hour at the end of a day visiting a school, after many years of pondering the themes within it. How I gently toyed with the words for another month, trying to make the ideas shine brightly as if through clear glass. How after finally typing it up—slowly and carefully with two fingers—and showing it to Kathy, she looked up with tears in her eyes and said, "It's wonderful!" I remember then taking the manuscript along to a meeting with the small Minnesota publishing house with whom I was working on another modest, spoken-word project yet to come to fruition. As I went into the meeting with the publisher, Don, and two or three assistants, I casually dropped it on his wife Nancy's desk and asked her to give it a look.

Ten minutes into our meeting she burst into the room and said, "Whatever you're talking about, put it away—we're publishing *this!*" I remember how after a few minutes of discussion and a serious verbal offer, I excused myself and ambled casually down the long hallway to the small bathroom, where I jumped up and down inside. I had an offer on a book—my first book! And I remember the many triumphs and travails that followed, as I tried to learn the ropes of the publishing world. All of that is still clear in my mind, as if it happened last week, as well as the exciting process of finally getting the book out into the world via WCCO radio, and the further media efforts and book tours that followed. It is all still there in my mind's eye.

But that is not how becoming an author happened. Not really. Instead, it was a canoe trip and a magazine.

I had been writing and performing my *EarthSongs* for about ten years—hard years of bars and late nights and occasional good gigs. At the same time, I had my summers—my canoe trip guiding—to provide grounding and nature study and joy to my life. I finally reached a time when I thought that the years of paddling and guiding in the BWCA and the Quetico-Superior country had prepared me for the next step, a major northern expedition. And the one I wanted to try was a 520-mile journey down Saskatchewan's Churchill River, connecting near the end to the Sturgeon Weir, the same trip that Sigurd Olson had taken in 1955 and written about in his book *The Lonely Land.* It was my second favorite Olson book, after *Listening Point.* But this book was different—not simply the beautiful, contemplative essays for which Sig was famed, but a real adventure. I had read and reread it several times. I imagined the huge lakes, the vast distances and wild rapids of the Canadian bush, and I wondered if I would ever feel ready to take on such a journey. There came a time when I did.

Months of planning ensued. Logistics and equipment, strategizing with my friend Jim Fitzpatrick, with whom I'd done a number of canoe country trips. The recruiting of a band of voyageurs. The barely containable rise of excitement and anticipation. When the trip was nearly upon us, perhaps a week beforehand, an idea occurred to me. I was perusing a favorite periodical, *Canoe Magazine* (more recently *Canoe/Kayak*), in my basement office. Suddenly I thought, "I wonder how a person gets an article published in here?" Then I wondered if an article about a group retracing Sig Olson's famous journey might be publishable. Then I wondered if I could actually write it. I flipped through the magazine to the masthead page listing all the publishing info. There was a phone number there. I walked around my office twice—maybe three times—screwed up my courage, and called it.

A voice answered: "Hello, this is David Harrison, publisher of *Canoe Magazine.*" Ooops. I was expecting—I don't know—maybe a secretary. Certainly not the publisher! "Umm, uhhh . . ." I struggled for words. Finally, I got my name out. Then I began trying to explain why I'd called. I managed to mention Sigurd Olson, Lake Île-à-la-Crosse, the Sturgeon Weir, Cumberland House, how we planned to paddle five hundred miles, and read from Sig Olson and the great eighteenth-century explorers by the campfire each night, as we compared and contrasted the country we saw to the land that Sig and the early voyageurs knew. Harrison stopped me. "Yeah, I get it—you're retracing the *Lonely Land* trip. Sounds great: send it in when you get back." Click.

I wasn't sure what that meant—what the *click* meant. Was he actually interested, or just trying to get rid of me? I had no idea.

IN ANY CASE, it was time to take the trip. And it was grand. In every way, living up to my dreams and exceeding them. When I arrived home, I sat down to write the article—what would be my first published work, not counting songs. I wrote a word, crossed it out. Wrote another word, crossed that one out. I wrote a sentence. Crossed it out. Caught my breath, paused for a few moments, and wrote a paragraph. And crossed it out. Clearly, this was not going to be easy. Everything I wrote sounded either unoriginal or forced or stupid. Certainly not Olson-esque. I told myself, "I'll do this tomorrow," and tried again three days later. No better. "Maybe next week." That wasn't any better either. "Next month." Nope.

At this point, I thought, "Christmas. During Christmas vacation, after the thoughts and ideas have had time to simmer."

Christmas came, and I locked myself in the basement at Kathy's parents' farm, sat down at a big oak table, and tried to write my article. Nothing. I could barely start, let alone finish. I was lacking what so many beginning authors lack—confidence. As in any, whatsoever. Years later, I would find, scribbled in the margins of one of Ernest Oberholtzer's thousands of books on Mallard Island, a frustrated note to himself. "The beginning writer," wrote Ober, "can find a thousand reasons not to write, and not a single one to get started." I knew that Ober had always wanted to write a book, and he was a good writer. But he never did, and it haunted him. I could relate.

But back to my own article-writing struggle: I found a sensible solution. I simply gave up. "I don't need to write the stupid article," I told myself. "Nobody in the world will ever care or know the difference. I'm a songwriter and composer, and I'm fine with that." It was a neat solution. But inside I was disappointed with myself. Very.

Months went by. Many months. One day in July the phone rang. "Hello?"

"Yes, hello—is this Douglas Wood?"

"Yes."

"Is this the Douglas Wood who was going to write the article about the Churchill River trip?"

"Uhh, yes."

"Did you take the trip?"

"Yes."

"Well, this is David Harrison of *Canoe Magazine,* and we've been waiting for your article. We thought it sounded like the perfect centerfold feature for our fifteenth anniversary special edition."

A few seconds went by. I tried to think of something clever. Nothing came to mind. "Oh."

"Have you finished the article yet?"

My mind raced. “Umm, it’s not *quite* finished yet.” (Not a single word was written.) “When would you need it?”

“Well, we’re getting close to deadline—we’d need it by next Tuesday. Can you do that?” (It was now Friday.)

“Oh sure, sure, it’s almost done.” (Not a single solitary word.)

“Okay, we’ll watch for it!”

“Okay, bye.”

And that’s how I became an author. By lying. And then by sitting down and in one burst writing the article and sending it off. Somebody actually wanted it. I had promised it. I did it. With no time to second-guess or agonize over each word and sentence. I found a scrap of paper from the canoe trip on which I had begun a letter to Sigurd Olson, who had passed away six years before, trying to imagine talking to him and telling him all about our journey. I simply finished the letter. And indeed, *Canoe Magazine* published it as their centerfold feature, just as David had promised. And it was a thrill to see my words in print.

Did I ever get rejection letters after that? Zillions of ’em. Did I ever suffer a loss of confidence? All the time. But deep inside I knew I could do it. I had done it once, and somebody really liked and published what I wrote. That was enough to get me over most of the humps. I have told the story to many young or aspiring authors at many a workshop or conference. I still have the article—my letter to Sig. I still like it.

It speaks of a dream—two dreams, really. The dream of a wild and wonderful journey, and the dream of writing about it. It is, I suppose, a sort of love letter. To a beloved mentor, perhaps a second grandfather. To a vast, forested carapace of land that had called to me since childhood and would call me back many more times to come. And to a way of travel, a way of being that spoke of history, freedom, and a sense of completeness inaccessible without long vistas and the great silences they encompassed. It was a letter to all of that—which is why I could finally write it, and why in the end it was not difficult to write at all.

Here then is the letter to Sigurd, my first published article:

The Night Is Beautiful, Sig. The lake is wine, and the sky . . . well, these colors don't have names, do they? If they do, I don't know them. The loons are launching songs at the stars, and the air smells just like air was meant to smell. I am sitting here on a long finger of granite reminiscing on a dream, Sig, in your Lonely Land, camped exactly where you camped 32 years ago.

I don't think I ever told you how the dream began. Years ago—I remember as if it were yesterday—I was in bed with a howling case of the flu, charting new adventures in misery. Kathy came in to check on me. I tried to speak without moving my lips and asked if she could please read something to me. Something to quell misery. She chose a book I'd recently brought home from the library, by a fellow named Olson. She started to read:

I believe that I have known one of the oldest satisfactions of man, that when he gazed upon the earth and sky with wonder, when he sensed the first vague glimmerings of meaning in the universe, the world of knowledge and spirit was opened to him. While we are born with curiosity and wonder, and our early years full of the adventure they bring, I know such inherent joys are often lost. I also know that being deep within us, their latent flow can be fanned to flame again by awareness and an open mind.

I closed my eyes while she read and focused on the flow of words and images. I didn't realize it yet, but I was in the hands of a master. You somehow wove philosophy and recollection, prose and poetry and science together into a tapestry as rich and beautiful as the wild North you wrote about. At some point in her reading, Kathy paused, and I was suddenly aware that my cheeks were wet with tears. She thought they were tears of misery.

They were not.

A new window had been thrown open upon my understanding of the world. That book was *Listening Point*. The others followed in quick succession, until I had read them all. Out of those pages you poured the songs of white-throated sparrows and loons; scenes of looming pines and islands and moonlit ridges spangled with spruce; and of course, the poetry of a canoe moving upon the water:

The movement of a canoe is like a reed in the wind. Silence is part of it, and the sounds of lapping water, bird songs, and wind in the trees. It is part of the medium through which it floats, the sky, the water and the shores. A man is part of his canoe and therefore part of all it knows. The instant he dips his paddle, he flows as it flows, the canoe yielding to his slightest touch and responsive to his every whim and thought.

One book stood out as different from all the rest, Sig. In place of your usual meticulously crafted essays was an adventure story, the tale of a journey down a brawling river far to

the north—highway of the voyageurs, explored by Thompson, MacKenzie and Simpson—the Churchill River.

To a novice like me, the trip sounded formidable, even frightening, with its huge sprawling lakes and roaring rapids. But I couldn't put the book down, and your writing made the places come alive. Valley of the Snake. The Chimneys of Namew. Lake of the Dead.

I vowed someday I'd go there, run the same rapids, camp on the same campsites. Now, here I am, and the water is wine.

We have a good group, Sig—one of the best I've had in years of guiding. Oh, we're not a match for your six seasoned "voyageurs." Even though we're twenty to thirty years younger than your over-the-hill gang, we can't quite equal your pace. Sometimes it's a mix of inspiration and humiliation! A couple of times Ted has sworn he could see the flash of your paddle down at the end of the lake. Still, as the trip goes on we're beginning to develop that cohesiveness and efficiency your group had mastered over years of adventures together.

There has been magic along the way, Sig. Sometimes it seems we must be only an hour or a day behind you rather than thirty years, so little has changed. Our first full day, a sparkling, sapphire day on big Isle la Crosse—a day just like yours—we were sailing with a big tail wind. Riding those hissing rollers down that forty-mile sweep, canoes lashed together, we began to catch our first glimpse of the grand scale of this country. About half-way down the lake, while Bear and Jim ruddered, and Gail and Mary manned the sail, I began to read aloud from your *Lonely Land*:

A little rocky island ahead seemed to be covered with white, and had it been late fall we would have guessed it was a mantle of snow. As we neared, however, we saw it was completely hidden by the closely packed bodies of pelicans, so close together that nowhere did the rocks show through. Suddenly the far edge of the mantle began to lift and peeled off slowly to the other end. For a moment sunlight glittered on a milling confusion of snowy wings, and then the great birds took off in sedate formation toward the far shore.

Just as I finished reading, Bear shouted, "Look over there!" and there it was, a little island outcrop covered with white. About a mile away, virtually the only rock on forty miles of low, sandy lake. It had to be the same one. As we drew near, the pelicans rose like a billowing blanket and spiraled away. Not a detail had changed since your trip, Sig, nor probably in thousands of years before. There was magic in the air. But oh, the smell . . .

Look at this sky, Sig. The sunset seems to go on forever, stretching to infinity. Our little point feels like a vantage point on the entire cosmos, a place to eavesdrop on the universe. I wonder what your thoughts were here. At such a place you often wrote you could hear the echoes of the old voyageurs' chansons, reverberating off the rocks down the river of time. We hear your echoes.

Over and over again, Sig, our experiences mimic your own right down to the wind direction or the weather. And that feeling of magic sets in. One of our favorite spots was your old camp on the pink granite ledge at Crooked Rapids. We caught a batch of big walleyes there, just where you'd said they'd be, and brewed up a big pot of fish chowder, using your old recipe. A bear and a moose swam across the river and a family of eagles was nested on the far side. Later on I played my harmonica while Mike and Marlene waltzed on the granite in the moonlight, and before we went to bed, Mary read us our evening passage from your book:

There to our joy at the head of another rapids was a broad shelf of pink granite . . . . What a wild and lovely spot! The clouds were breaking up and through a rift we could see the promise of a good day tomorrow. Ducks were constantly in the air for this was a flyway between their feeding grounds. The river gurgled past the ledge, and below us were the rapids we would have to shoot in the morning. There was plenty of room for tents. The fire would be on a flat shelf close enough to the water so I could dip up what I needed without having to make a trip to the river's edge.

That night we felt especially close to you, Sig. But there's more to our experience than an occasional wave of déjà vu. There's a more subtle, gradual magic at work—a deepening awareness. Of self. Of the world. Of mystery. It is your old "singing wilderness" at work. As the days pass, old ways of looking at the world—preoccupation with measurement, acquisition and achievement—imperceptibly begin to fall away. In their place grows a more accepting, more free-flowing subjective way of seeing one's self and the world around. Overtones of poetry and myth, long stored in the dusty back-rooms of the mind, emerge and blossom, and experiences become tinged with shades and hues of meaning.

You know the portage around Trout Lake Falls, Sig . . . . Well, the other day Marlene was standing in the water on a sloping shelf next to one of the canoes. As she stood there she just began sliding inexorably down that slope, until she was neck-deep. The rest of us started laughing and hollering, "The Mammaygwessy pulled you in, the Mammaygwessy pulled you in!" You see, we'd been reading your tale of the canoe you'd lost one morning, then rediscovered on the far side of Dipper Lake. Later you learned of the Cree legends of the Mammaygwessy, the little people with six fingers and six toes and no noses, who hide among the rocks and waterways and cause mischief—tipping over canoes or untying them, taking little things from around camp and misplacing them. So, when Marlene took her swim, it was just one in a series of incidents confirming their presence.

We left a tobacco offering on the pictograph ledge beneath Silent Rapids, as ancient travelers would have done, and we found a marvelous mural farther down Black Bear Island Lake. It towered high above the water, on a smooth cliff face, the images staring down as they had for centuries. We recognized a Water Serpent, Thunderbird, a sacred wheel and a shamanic face, in addition to the figure of the Mammaygwessy. Atop the cliff, on a sheltered ledge, was an aerie. We sat there a long time, with a sense of awe and timelessness—what the Lakota would have called "Hambeday," or mysterious feeling.

Speaking of Black Bear Island Lake, Sig, what a hauntingly beautiful body of water. It is easy to see how you were moved to ponder the quote by Sir James Jeans that you set on your Duluth pack as you paddled: "The universe begins to look more like a great thought than a machine." And the passage you so loved from Dostoevsky: "Love all God's creation, the whole and every grain of sand in it. Love every leaf, every ray of God's light. Love the animals, love the plants, love everything. If you love everything you will perceive the divine mystery in things."

You wrote: *There was no difference between his thought and that of Sir James Jeans, for what they both found was the same. Here before me on Black Bear Island Lake was all life, here the great thought, here the order of the universe and the divine mystery. I need look no further.*

That night we had a special gathering around the campfire circle, mirroring each other, acknowledging our ties to one another and to the four quarters of the world. The lake glowed softly in the last light and a loon wailed at the stars, its call echoing from the rocky shores. An evening to be long remembered.

As we were leaving the island the next morning, heading toward Birch Portage, we saw another group of three canoes approaching, the only other canoe party we'd seen on our long journey. They hailed us over, and a scruffy-looking chap in the stern of one of the canoes began to ply us with questions. His name, we would learn, was Milow Worel.

"Where are all you folks from?" he asked. "What do you

do down in the states? How'd you all get together?" Then he asked us about our route.

I answered, "Well, we began two hundred miles to the west on Isle la Crosse, and we're heading toward Frog Portage and the Sturgeon-Weir River, ending up at Cumberland House. We're retracing—"

"Oh, I know," he piped up. "You're retracing Sigurd Olson's trip, the one he wrote up in his book *The Lonely Land.*"

"Well, that's right," I said. "How'd you happen to know that?"

"Oh, I corresponded with Sig about that trip. He had some questions about the country I was able to answer. You see, we're all members of the Saskatchewan Historic Trails Canoe Club, and we paddle the old routes all over Canada. This is my sixth time on the Churchill," he replied.

As Milow was talking, I glanced down at the cover of my river guide-book. I looked up at Milow, then glanced down again. Pointing to the photo on the cover, I asked, "Is this you?"

"Well, it used to be," he answered. "That picture was taken in 1967." He went on to say that he and his friends had written all the Ministry of Natural Resources pamphlets we were using on our trip.

We had a grand morning with Milow and his crew—portaged together, ran the lower rapids, and shared lunch on Trout Lake. There Milow sat down and, free hand, without referring to notes or maps, proceeded to draw out for us the rest of the rapids we'd encounter on the remaining three hundred miles of our journey—ledges to dodge, holes to avoid, where to follow the conservative directions in the guide-books and where to ignore them. Quite an impressive performance.

When I think about the odds of such an encounter, Sig, I still feel the goose-bumps. We had chosen this particular time for a trip I'd been planning for years, a trip expressly dedicated to retracing your paddle strokes. Out of hundreds of thousands of square miles of wilderness, our paths crossed as they were coming down from the north on their route and we were heading east on ours. What if we had broken camp an hour earlier, or half an hour later—or they had?

So much more has happened along the way, Sig. There was the morning we could almost see your old friend Father Moraud approaching through the rising mists of Knee Lake, black cassock billowing out behind. I understand his memory is still much revered by the Cree people of this area.

There was our stop by the 135-year-old wilderness church at Stanley Mission, and the haunting sounds drifting over the forest as Gail and Marlene played the old push-pedal organ.

There was the harrowing traverse of big Mirond Lake, into the teeth of a howling Nor'easter, and our wild runs down Knee and Snake Rapids.

Especially, there's been the pervasive feeling of the shrinking of the world; the sure sense that, for a few weeks at least, I know everyone in the world, and they know me. I can look around in a circle and see all their faces. Each of us knows that everything we do and everything we say has a real and tangible effect on all the other people in our world. It's a wonderfully empowering and humbling experience. In the midst of communion with the immensity of nature, we are brought into contact with the most intimate and personal of worlds.

But it has grown late now. The sunset has faded and the moon has laid a path of quicksilver across the lake. Everyone else is asleep, and even the loons are quiet.

Our trip is nearly over. You had written:

By the time I reached home the whole expedition had begun to seem a little unreal. I spread the equipment out in the yard to give it a final airing before putting it away. . . . As I worked over the outfit, the Churchill River seemed far away, and the rapids of the Drum, the Leaf, and the Sturgeon Weir and the great storms on Dead and Amisk only a soft rushing in the dusk. . . . I knew there were some things that would never be dimmed by distance or time, compounded of values that would not be forgotten; the joy and challenge of the wilderness, the sense of being part of the country and an era that was gone, the freedom we had known, silence, timelessness, beauty, companionship and loyalty, and the feeling of fullness and completion that was ours at the end.

I re-packed the outfit and placed each item carefully away. It would not rest too long. Sooner or later it would all come out again. The Reindeer country was waiting: Athabasca, Great Slave, Great Bear, and the vast barren lands beyond them all. Another year perhaps and the Lonely Land would claim us once again.

Now nine months have passed, Sig, since I began this letter. And I am thinking again about dreams and journeys, and thinking that perhaps I understand—that the realization of a dream is not the closing of one door so much as the opening of another. And maybe the point is that there's always another door, another horizon, and that in the end, it is all one trip.

AND SO, THIRTY-FIVE YEARS AGO, my first article was complete. And I was indeed about to begin a new journey, or another part of the same one. As a writer. I'm still on it. The rapids still whisper in the distance. And there are more dreams ahead. Always more dreams ahead.

NO SUCH THING AS BEAUTY

The booming challenge of a barred owl over a marshland chorus of frogs and the low, rumbling pedal point of a distant rapid. The sweet, pure song of a white-throated sparrow piercing the evening gloom. Or a wilderness waterfall, untrammeled and unconstrained, roaring its voice to the listening rocks and trees. And, perhaps, to a human being.

It was before sunrise. There was a soft glow in the east, over the mast-like sentinel pines on a nearby island. I had paddled out from camp with a water jug and the old, dinged-up coffeepot to gather water for breakfast and for the lunch pack. We always gathered water far offshore, where the water was deep and clear, with any impurities settled out. It remains one of the small but significant pleasures of Canoe Country, to be able to dip a cup or a hand into the water and drink it. It was, I always thought, the way that water ought to be on planet Earth.

The rest of the camp was still asleep, no movement, no voices, no sound of zippers opening or tent poles coming down. No camp axe splitting firewood. A few last, blessed moments of sleep in the warmth of the bags, before the breaking of camp and the launching of the day's journey. It felt to me as if I had the whole lake and the entire North Woods to myself. A few rags of mist hung over the still waters. A loon began a half-hearted wail and then stopped. The call echoed off the rock shore of the island. Sitting there alone, I was struck—as I often was in such moments—by the profound beauty of it all. As if every component, from sky to trees to rocks to water, to loon to canoe to paddle to me, somehow fit together perfectly. And as I thought about beauty, about the mystery of it, about things fitting together, another thought came unbidden, unexpected. It was a memory, from college days, decades before.

I remembered sitting at my desk in one of the classrooms of Eppley Fine Arts Building, on the campus of Morningside College in Sioux City, Iowa. I was a freshman music major, taking a required class called Music Appreciation. This was a general sort of overview of the history and theories of Western music, encompassing all that we should know and why it was important. The professor, Dr. Lawrence DeWitt, was holding forth.

He was speaking about twelve-tone music, and atonal music, and aleatoric music, modern, twentieth-century forms relying on intellectual constructs or random chance, all of which he thought were terrific. There was, said Professor DeWitt, no such thing as music that was intrinsically beautiful, of its own accord. Such considerations were merely manifestations of our own prejudices and preconceptions—the way our ears had been trained since infancy to accept and to like certain sets of sounds that were culturally

accepted and preferred. He sounded very smart. And very certain. But I raised my hand.

"That's not true," I said.

"I beg your pardon."

"That's not true, what you're saying."

"Oh, really, Mr. Wood? Please continue. I'm sure we will all benefit from your wisdom."

"Well, it, it just isn't true. I think there are certain pieces of music, certain compositions, that are actually good, that sound beautiful to anyone with ears, and other ones that are ugly. That just sound bad."

"I see," said Dr. DeWitt. "Do you realize that I am the head of this music department? And that I have this position because I have studied extensively, and that I have a doctorate—a PhD from Indiana University, one of the finest music schools in the country? What is your degree, Mr. Wood?"

"I—I don't have one."

"No, you don't. You are a freshman. And if you make it through the next four years of study—and that is by no means a given—you may receive a bachelor's degree. So I think it might just be possible that I know a little bit more about this subject than you do. Would you agree?"

"Umm, yes."

"Now, do you have anything further to add?"

"Well, I just don't think it's true, what you're saying. I think that some music is beautiful and some isn't. And that's just what I think."

Well. These many years later, I really don't remember any more of the conversation. I wasn't banished from the department, but I certainly didn't become one of Dr. DeWitt's favorite students either. I remember not agreeing to his proposition. I remember his withering gaze and his commanding, condescending tone of voice. I remember feeling totally outgunned. And I remember other students after class asking me if I was completely nuts.

Maybe.

But I simply couldn't accept what he was saying—that essentially there is no real difference between beauty and ugliness. That such considerations or judgments are just tricks that our brains play on us, based on what we have been conditioned to accept or appreciate. Might there be *some* truth to that? Of course. The old saying that "Beauty is in the eye of the beholder" is pertinent. I will go to my death believing that Monet paintings like *The Water Lily Pond* or *Impression, Sunrise* are beautiful and worthwhile in a way that a fabric wall hanging of Elvis in a two-dollar frame is not, although its owner may love it. And maybe that is just a reflection of cultural training and opportunity. Partly. But maybe, in all humility, it's a function of good taste as well. And the fact that some things really are beautiful, and some are not. I know I wish that during the time of my youthful confrontation with Dr. DeWitt, I had known Charles Schwartz. And Scooter the Cat. And Duke Ellington.

I MET CHARLES SCHWARTZ at an environmental conference once and never forgot what I heard him say. Schwartz, a Missouri native, was a wonderful artist and Aldo Leopold's illustrator for *A Sand County Almanac.* He was also a fine naturalist in his own right. He was teaching a little workshop about nature and wildlife drawing and began to speak about his concept of beauty. In Charles's accounting, real beauty and aesthetic value all depended on something. Something more than just superficial appearance, more than being pretty. Genuine beauty and quality depended on things *fitting.* That things had to fit, to belong, one with the other—or, rather, a whole community of things belonging together, in a real, organic sense, supporting one another in a sort of sustainable and harmonious balance. The sort of balance that might take millennia to evolve, like a patiently and tenderly created work of art. Charles believed that with care and interest, we humans are able—intuitively and instinctively—to perceive and appreciate that sort of *fit-ness* in nature. And that when we do, we call it beautiful. And maybe we are even able to draw it or paint it or re-create it in some artistic form. Schwartz's words made me recall my long-ago class with Professor DeWitt, and my intuitive sense that musical notes have to fit together as well, in a way that they support each other and make a comprehensible, artistic whole. I remember a warm feeling of validation and smiling at the thought of it.

Of course, one of the keys to perceiving beauty is a predisposition to care about it to begin with. To recognize it as a possibility. To even believe it exists. I remember Sig Olson speaking about an encounter in the late 1950s with a professional forester who spoke disparagingly of old-growth forests (a relatively new term) as *cellulose cemeteries.* The remark cut Olson to the quick, shocking him, even causing him to briefly doubt his own ecological philosophy and deep affinity for ancient trees. He lay awake nights trying to sort it out and wondering how he should have responded. But Sig soon recovered his equilibrium and remembered his vision and understanding of a forest—especially an old-growth forest—as a place of intangible values, an entire, complex community of life, each part interconnected with and dependent on the others, and the profound elegance and balance of the whole. All of it fitting together, even in ways we do not completely understand.

In such a place beauty and meaning are to be found within all the smells, sights, and sounds of the woods, precisely because of their interconnections and relationships with one another, in a way that a monoculture plantation or tree farm cannot replicate. The beauty of the forest lies in the interrelationships of all its parts, just as the beauty and meaning of a piece of music lie in the interrelationships of the notes and even the spaces between the notes. Sculptors, painters, and visual artists know this and take great care in the use of materials, colors, textures, balance, and perspectives in order to create the visual effects they are after. Even in a modern work of abstract art, the care is taken in order to achieve the vision of the artist.

In my many years since college, I have had countless occasions to ponder the meaning of beauty in a wide variety of contexts, from artistic ventures in music, art, and writing to simple moments in the outdoors. Moments like a midnight paddle on a soft, summer night on a lake sprinkled with reflections of the starry heavens. Or a first November snowfall, gentle as a benediction among a grove of cedars and balsam firs. The booming challenge of a barred owl over a marshland chorus of frogs and the low, rumbling pedal point of a distant rapid. The sweet, pure song of a white-throated sparrow piercing the evening gloom. Or a wilderness waterfall, untrammeled and unconstrained, roaring its voice to the listening rocks and trees. And, perhaps, to a human being.

Out of all my searching and exploring and pondering I have found that it is those moments—and sometimes the artistic attempts that follow them—that are most important. We live in a modern world in which beauty, it seems, is ever more readily discounted or discarded. Products and artifacts are made with only convenience, profit, or practicality in mind, with precious few thoughts given to the aesthetic considerations on which artisans once prided themselves. The very idea of beauty as a consideration was largely mocked and demeaned in much of music, poetry, and art throughout the twentieth century, particularly after the Great War, World War I, with its merciless, mechanized obliteration of so many of the ideals and illusions that preceded it. Professor DeWitt was no doubt aware of this and attempted, in his ever-so-gentle way, to point out to me the new "truths" that resulted.

But some of us are holdouts. Backsliders. Some of us prefer Claude Debussy to John Cage. The Hudson River School of painters to Wassily Kandinsky or Kazimir Malevich. Robert Frost to poetry slams. Not simply because we are old-fashioned. Not really. More because of a stubborn aesthetic sense that we cannot discard or abandon.

SCOOTER WAS A HOLDOUT. Scooter was a cat. A very fine cat of unusual wit and perception and personality, who graced us with his life for eighteen years. Scooter delighted and entertained us in countless ways. And Scooter, we learned, was also a music critic, one who was not shy about making his feelings known. In our house music was always important, and as the boys grew up and played their instruments, and Kathy rehearsed for musicals and taught her piano lessons, and I played my guitar and mandolin and banjo, music was almost always in the air. One evening, I was showing my son Bryan how to play his new harmonica. By chance, as we played together we stumbled upon a dissonance—two notes, a minor second, which do not go very well together. We thought it sounded funny and kept repeating the dissonance. Across the room, Scooter woke up from one of his naps. Suddenly, his eyes were wide open, head raised, back arched. Then the ears started. Back and forth they went, like furry radar dishes, searching for something. Or trying to escape from it.

Finally, the ears went straight back, laid tight against his head. At that moment, Scooter made a decision. He took off, the whites of his eyes showing, ears flattened. He dashed up the stairs and disappeared from sight. We laughed and laughed and, of course, decided we could not let this wonderful entertainment go to waste. Thereafter, for several evenings, the harmonicas would come out and we would serenade Scooter. He soon became more assertive in his disapproval and would come over and swat at the harmonica with his paw, attempting to alleviate the source of his vexation. Bryan and I learned that harmonicas were not even necessary—that the same effect could be accomplished with our voices, softly humming a dissonant interval and holding it for an annoying length of time. The effect was always hilariously the same. After a few nights, however, Kathy would no longer allow this auditory aggravation to continue, pronouncing it cruel and unusual. She was right, of course. We apologized to Scooter and gave him extra catnip. I think he forgave us. Maybe.

Now, Scooter was smart. He knew. He never went to college or studied Music Appreciation. Yet he clearly knew that some notes sound good together and some definitely do not. And he was not about to tolerate the latter. I admired him for his good taste and firm resolve.

And he was right.

THERE IS ANOTHER MUSICAL MEMORY—perhaps my favorite one of all—that also inspires thoughts about the meaning of beauty. It also involves a harmonica. Many years ago, I was attending a national environmental conference, having been invited to share my *Earth-Songs* in concert. The night before that event, I read something in the program notes about an open-fire, "black powder reenactors" session under the stars. Intrigued, I decided to go. I found a fairly large group of folks in a broad, open meadow. Many were dressed in fringes and buckskins, some carrying long rifles and possibles pouches, all gathering around a beautifully laid fire. There was a ring of skin-and-fur-covered ground chairs in the circle nearest the fire, and it was evidently here that the organizers would sit.

The chairs filled in, until finally there was only one empty seat left, buckskin draped over the wooden frame. The fire crackled away. The scents of the moist evening ground rose into the air. After a while, the time came to begin the evening's activities, and a bearded mountain man stood up and began to speak. "You all know whose seat this is," he said softly, motioning to the empty chair. "Bill helped to plan this conference, poured his heart into it for two years. He knew he didn't have much time left, but he wanted to make it. Make it to this night, to this one last campfire under the stars. But, unfortunately . . ." His voice caught and trailed off. Everything was silence, only the gentle crackling of the fire. Then the man gathered himself. "Well," he said, "Bill had a favorite song, one that he loved more than any other on this Earth. So . . . I'm going to play it for him now."

And the mountain man reached into his buckskin pouch and pulled out a harmonica. He put it to his lips and began to play. And he could play. After four notes, I knew the song—one of my own favorites—the American folk classic "Shenandoah." Beneath the stars, beneath Pegasus and Bootes, Draco and Cassiopeia, and the Great Bear and Little Bear, before a rapt audience of firelit faces, the notes rang into the night. Pure. Sweet. Simple. Inexpressibly beautiful and deeply moving. The sound of a simple harmonica, unaccompanied.

And I wept.

I did not know the man with the harmonica. I did not know Bill for whom the song was played, or any of the other folks there. But I felt the moment. And I knew the single most beautiful performance of a piece of music I had ever heard. Or have heard since.

There were many components to this profound moment, this expression of beauty. There were the stars above and the leaping flames of the fire. There were the solemn faces and the romance of the long rifles and the buckskins, hearkening back to another time. There were the heartfelt words and the gesture toward the empty seat by the fire, a seat that all had hoped would be filled. Everything seemed to fit together in such a way that the almost human voice of a harmonica, lofted hauntingly into the night sky, could touch the heart and kindle the deepest sort of response. But that is always the point with beauty. It is about things fitting together. *Together.* Notes. Colors. Moments. Sights. Sounds. Landscapes. Feelings.

Some things are fitting, are pleasing and comforting and delightful to the eye and the ear and the mind and the heart, simply because they harmonize with one another, with the world at large, and with something deep inside of us. An internal something that can comprehend loveliness, elegance, and grace. Proportion and symmetry. Fitting-ness.

The philosopher George Santayana said that beauty cannot be described in words. Still, he defined the *sense of beauty,* in his book of the same name, as "a pledge of the possible conformity between the soul and nature, and consequently a ground of faith in the supremacy of the good." I think I agree, as much as a backwoods philosopher like me can understand such high-toned language. I wish I had known the quote as a freshman in Dr. DeWitt's class. I would have tossed it out—casually, carelessly—and maybe impressed the professor. But in the end, for me Duke Ellington said it more simply and perhaps said it best. "If it sounds good," declared the great American jazzman, "it is good." Yes. That will do.

My old college music professor was not alone. There will always be those who say there is no such thing as beauty. Or that it doesn't matter. Or that it is an illusion, a matter of chance, or simply born of the customs of the day. But I have heard Yo-Yo Ma play "Gabriel's Oboe" by Ennio Morricone. And I have heard Peter Ostroushko play his "Heart of the Heartland" on the mandolin. I have heard white-throats singing at dusk beside a murmuring river wrapped in mist. I have seen a wood duck at dawn on a woodland pond, rising trout dimpling the water. And I have heard a harmonica under the stars. And I know all I need to know about beauty. I know that it exists. And either a person can see that and hear that and know that, or they can't.

OUT ON THE LAKE in the morning light, with the sun just beginning to rise in a flaming ball behind the pines and with the water gathered, I dipped the paddle and pulled. Guided the bow back toward camp. I heard the familiar soft whisper and gurgle, the tinkling fall of droplets as the paddle lifted and came forward, again and again. The sound was a kind of music, of course, a soft melody I had heard a million times. It inserted itself gently into the great silence of the North, the sort of encompassing silence that allows small and gentle things to be heard.

Then there was the distant, lonesome wail of the loon, a note that was finished this time, reverberating down the lake. It was altogether fitting. All of it was fitting. And it was beautiful.

FAMOUS GROUSE

Who was I to ruin the moment, to dispel the notion of a guide so completely at home in the wilderness that he goes hunting with a rock?

The group I was guiding stopped behind me as I held up my hand. We were exploring a beautifully forested, emerald green island in Quetico Provincial Park—a maze of lakes, streams, and bogs punctuated by the rugged rock outcrops of the Canadian Shield. This particular island, one of my favorites, was bigger than most, heavily forested with pine, spruce, and balsam fir, lush with ferns, mosses, and shade-loving midsummer wildflowers. I had taken the group on a bushwhacking, cross-country hike, pointing out the plants and lichens, cradle knolls, blueberry patches, and colonies of Labrador tea along the way. We weren't being particularly quiet: in fact, after I pointed out old man's beard, a gray-green lichen that dangles from dead spruce branches, one of our gang had grabbed a handful of the long, stringy stuff and jammed it up under his cap. He looked like a crazy old man indeed, and everyone got a good laugh.

Earlier on a portage trail, the same adventurer, possessing a lively interest in wild animal scat, had picked up and thoughtfully fondled something he had found on the trail. Wolf scat, he assumed. It wasn't. "Aaaaaach!" came the rueful exclamation from the back of the group, where our scatologist had paused. "This is dog shit!" It is always good to have comedic relief on a wilderness journey. And so our crew, as is often the case, was alert to moments of fun and hilarity, not taking great care with silent voices or footsteps.

But now as I held up my hand, the group grew quiet. Up ahead on the ground, perhaps twenty-five yards away, was a spruce grouse. It moseyed along slowly, head bobbing, pecking at this and that on the forest floor. Spruce grouse are not nearly as clever and wary as their cousins, the better-known ruffed grouse, who have made many a hunter look like an idiot as they explode into flight with a great thundering of wings, dodging and darting among the trunks of pines and aspens. The spruce grouse is a more pedestrian bird, uncommonly trusting and unconcerned, so much so that it is sometimes referred to in the North as the fool hen.

I thought I would demonstrate to my crew just how placid and imperturbable a fool hen was. I looked around. I saw a small rock. I picked it up. "Watch this," I said and nothing more, thinking I would throw the rock near the grouse and show how it would stand stock-still. Placid. Imperturbable. Foolish.

I threw the rock. The grouse, struck in the head, fell over. Dead.

There were gasps. There were exclamations. There was dismay.

At that point, of course, I had no choice. I sauntered casually over to the deceased fowl and picked it up. As though it was the most common, ordinary thing in the world. As though I went hunting every day for wild game in the forest. With a rock. Not even bothering to bring one, just picking up whatever might be lying around, handy to the moment. And then dispatching with easy efficiency any prey that might be nearby. Which was all true, of course. Mostly.

In any case, as I say, I had no choice. The words "Watch this," which I had meant simply to call attention to a harmless, scientific experiment, could just as easily have been taken to mean "Now I'm going to demonstrate how we go hunting in the North Woods. Here comes dinner." In fact, that was very clearly how they were taken. Who was I to ruin the moment, to dispel the notion of a guide so completely at home in the wilderness that he goes hunting with a rock? And provides dinner to his hungry companions.

Clearly, Lewis and Clark should have had such accomplished scouts along on the Corps of Discovery Expedition. They'd have eaten better.

So over I walked. I picked up the grouse. I admired it modestly for a moment, then showed it off to the gang. We would take it back to camp, I said, pluck it and dress it, and roast it on a spit over the evening campfire under the stars, just the way it's always done. It would make a small meal to be sure, but we weren't bloodthirsty—moderation and reserve should be employed, as in any ethical hunt. I wasn't going to rampage around the forest, killing everything in sight, without a proper license. No. One grouse would have to do—a little taste for everybody. Which is what we got.

For the rest of the trip, I heard about that grouse. Not to my face so much, but in undertones and murmurs whenever my back was turned, or when people thought I wasn't listening. They were soft, tentative comments, tinged with awe and perhaps a little fear. More than a touch of disapproval as well, sometimes, especially from a few of the women. But I said nothing to defend myself against such obloquy. I was above it, living as a natural-man-in-the-wilderness, accepting nourishment as the forest provided it. We were picking berries and fruits and making sweet gale and wintergreen and Labrador tea, after all, and fishing for walleye and bass and pike. A grouse was just a small step up the food chain.

Needless to say, I never threw another rock at anything either. There was nothing to gain and much to lose, in terms of perception. I couldn't hit another grouse again if I tried, and in fact that was the point—I hadn't tried. I could throw another hundred rocks at another hundred grouse—or tree trunks or boulders—and not hit a one. So we were left with the one moment, the one instance, emblematic to the casual observer of countless assumed instances, where the guide went hunting for food with a Stone Age lapidary implement and succeeded. It was not my fault if people took that inference. Of course, I may not have said anything to actually discourage such impressions either. One has to protect the reputation, image, and aura of the brotherhood of guides.

Being a wilderness guide, I learned through scores of trips over thousands of rugged miles, is a combination of many things. And like other such callings, it is more an art than a science. To explain exactly how it is done would seem virtually impossible, as it depends on the particular character of the landscape traveled and of the guide him- or or herself. Certain consistent principles always pertain, no matter the circumstances. Safety would be at the top of any list. The guide is responsible for the safety, and safe return, of all the participants—and that is a large responsibility. Many times it is top of mind—during a rough lake crossing, a thunderstorm, running a challenging rapids. But it is never out of mind entirely. And things one might do on one's own are considered in an entirely different light with the safety of others involved. I've heard old-timers say that they were scared most of the time on big wilderness trips—whenever poised at the lip of a rapids, for sure. But it was always fear laced with exhilaration. And that is surely another part of guiding. To pass on the idea, wordlessly perhaps, that life should be more than the constant striving to be safe and comfortable. That it should be, at some level at least, an adventure.

My old friend and guiding partner Jim Fitzpatrick liked to say: "We don't have adventures. We have *experiences.* An adventure is what you have when something goes wrong." I love that idea and have often repeated it. Explorer and northern cartographer David Thompson, capsizing on a northern river, saving his canoe by cutting the bow line with his pocketknife, capsizing again, then plunging over a waterfall, losing almost all the group provisions, nearly starving, and barely making it out alive—now that's an adventure. One I would never want to replicate. But there are such things as adventures of the spirit, wherein each day can be encountered with anticipation and enthusiasm, charged with the thought of unseen islands and headlands and skylines up ahead, the testing of one's skills and abilities, the thrill of learning new things, the deepening of knowledge and companionship, the discovery of new campsites—each ingredient a part of the adventure of living.

The teaching of those skills and knowledge is a big part of guiding. In my earliest trips I thought it was important that I do everything for the group. Keep them comfortable and happy and do virtually all the work. I soon learned that was an exhausting and in the end impractical approach. But more than that, it didn't work very well for the participants. In my efforts to keep folks comfortable and give them a happy experience, I was in fact taking away one of the great pleasures of any trip and one of the main reasons people take such an excursion—the opportunity to learn. Yes, I could start a fire with flint and steel, flip a canoe onto my shoulders, hang a food pack, or set up a rain tarp, but that was to be expected. The real question was, could I show Bill or Joe or Nancy how to do it, so that they could head into the wilderness on their own next time or eventually lead others? With each new skill acquired, confidence and self-assurance grow, and hopefully at the end of any wilderness trip not only are muscles and sinews a little stronger, but psyches as well.

The opportunities for sharing and learning in the wilds are limitless. From the geological history of the planet and the Canadian Shield, to the story of the woods written in fire ecology, to the use of map and compass, to learning the difference between a J-stroke and a cross-draw, to how to read a rapids, to the knack of catching a walleye in a deep pool (and afterwards filleting it)—all these things and a thousand more are available to anyone who has a natural curiosity and wants to learn. And the sharing of them is for me the greatest pleasure of guiding.

There is something else, though, that has always been of prime importance on my trips, and that is simply having fun. I know, it doesn't seem as vital as staying safe. And it's not. But it's pretty darned important. I've had participants write me after a trip that their "face still hurts" from smiling and laughing so much. Nothing could make me happier. This quest for the pure joy of living has led to such moments as waltzing to harmonica music on a pink granite outcrop beside a wild rapids beneath a full moon; to food fights involving fish chowder and chocolate pudding; to endless Ole and Lena jokes and countless silly nicknames; to gunnel-jumping races and stolen shoes and underwear worn as hats. And also, to a rock thrown a little too well that provided an unexpected dinner.

That night, after our exploration of Emerald Island, after a peach-colored sunset and a glorious moonrise, as we sat in a circle around our campfire and savored the aroma of woodsmoke and roasting grouse on a spit, then passed it around and shared a wild taste—on that night we tasted more than the grouse. We tasted freedom. Companionship. A connection to other generations around other campfires. We tasted adventure and mystery. And when someone asked me how I knew I was going to hit that grouse with that rock, I just smiled. And let the aura of mystery remain. That's part of being a guide, too.

BAD WEATHER

The skies will change. The clouds will blow off. The sun will come out again.

We had been out for nearly three weeks on the big wilderness river system. Had begun in the height of summer, with temps in the upper eighties under a towering midday sun. Many were the times we leaned over the gunwales of the canoes and dipped our hats or neckerchiefs or T-shirts into the water, then put them back on, in an attempt to remain cool. At night the sunlight lingered until nearly midnight, and we slept in light clothing, our bags unzipped to welcome an evening breeze through the mosquito netting.

The weather, although warm, had been grand. True, we were drenched by the skirts of a few thundershowers roaming the big country of northwest Saskatchewan and were once chased across a stretch of open water by approaching lightning bolts, racing to shelter barely in time. But for the most part we experienced the rare treat of unbroken good weather for more than two weeks and were able to soak up all the beauties and good tidings of the wilderness under blue skies, with ball caps and sunglasses always close by, while wool mackinaws, rain suits, and stocking caps remained stuffed into the bottoms of the Duluth packs. We became, as my grandmother used to say, "brown as berries" and gloried in our good fortune.

But summers are short in the North Country. And with the arrival of a stiff nor'easter, with buffeting winds and rain and rolling whitecaps, we got an early foretaste of fall. The temperatures plunged and stayed down for days. Lake crossings in the big winds were a fierce challenge. The rains did not quit. And all the heavy clothing that had been safely tucked away was pulled out, put on, and eventually became damp, soggy, or soaked. Although experienced wilderness travelers, we felt our moods changing as well, from the sunny dispositions that had reflected sunny skies, to something more akin to gray, gloomy, and irritable. All a part of a wilderness trip perhaps, but not our favorite part.

After weeks in untraveled country, we now found ourselves in slightly closer proximity to a far northern town and a railroad, with a few more signs of human impact, including portage trails just a bit more heavily used than before. We were on such a trail during a break in the rain, pushing through mud, wet grass, and wet alders and going back for our second load when we met Charlie. Charlie was a Cree fishing guide, out with his two sportsmen in their big motorboat, crossing the portage to another boat cached on the other side. Charlie seemed to be in good spirits. But he seemed more than a little concerned about us.

"You guys okay?" he asked. "You look pretty wet and cold." I replied that we were doing okay. Charlie seemed unconvinced.

"Looks like you need a good fire to dry out," he said. I answered something along the lines of the woods are too wet and it would take forever to get one going.

"Naw, naw," said Charlie. "I can get you one going in no time. Hey guys, go and gather up some wood, will you?" he said to his fishermen. I made a slight protest but quickly gave in, knowing we did indeed need to warm up and dry out and wondering what Cree Indian woodcraft magic Charlie was about to employ to accomplish the mission so quickly. I could sense that he was wise and knowledgeable as well as helpful, and I was ready to learn. And get warm.

MY OPINION OF CHARLIE quickly changed. He had no idea what he was doing. He and his guys gathered up anything and everything that might charitably be described as wood, all shapes and sizes, and dumped it into an ever-growing pile by the side of the trail. There seemed to be very little in the way of planning or forethought in the construction. Accustomed as I was to laying a careful fire—usually in the log-cabin style of crisscrossed sticks and logs with smaller tinder placed just so under the larger pieces, with just enough space to allow for oxygen and breathing but close enough so that the flames would catch and grow—I thought the entire slapdash construction looked foredoomed. Especially considering it was wet. There was not a chance in the world that that sodden heap of brush was going to become anything other than a smoldering, smoky mess. Indian woodcraft indeed! But I kept my mouth shut out of embarrassment and common courtesy and kept watching.

When the pile was about four feet tall, Charlie disappeared and went back to the boat. He returned with an empty coffee can, poured a fair amount of white gas into it, slid it under the pile, and dropped a match into it. Hmmm. It made a fine, steady torch. The torch quickly began to dry out the nearest twigs and branches, then the next ones, and the next and the next, with each successive layer catching fire, drying out more of the pile and spreading the flame. In minutes we had a crackling, roaring bonfire.

Indian woodcraft indeed.

We thanked Charlie profusely, pretending that we had had total confidence all along. Which of course we had. Mostly. And after he had left with his fishermen, we stayed a good long while by his bonfire, getting thoroughly dried out. And warm. And happy. And in an unexpected, welcome bit of serendipity the bad weather ceased, the clouds cleared, and although the temps remained chilly and the stocking caps stayed on, for the remainder of our trip we paddled once again under sunny skies.

I have used old Charlie's trick many times since, when a three-day low has stretched into four or five days, when even the small, dry twigs on the underside of balsams and spruces become soaked, and when emotions become gloomy and soggy as well. Then a warm crackling fire, seemingly produced by magic out of nowhere, can be just what the doctor ordered. Woodcraft, Charlie reminded me, does not necessarily require flint and steel—with which I have indeed started many a fire—or other arcane knowledge but simply involves figuring out what works, what you've got, and what needs to be done.

Bad weather can call forth such situations. And life is full of bad weather. In Canoe Country, much of what we do and the way we pack is an acknowledgment of the certainty of bad weather. If not now, then an hour from now, if not today then tomorrow, if not this week then the next. The old Minnesota saying—"There's no such thing as bad weather, only bad clothing"—has much truth to it. The entire camping equipment industry is nothing so much as our eternal human attempt to stay ahead of bad weather. From breathable, waterproof rain suits and hats to good old wool and all its modern iterations, to fleece to ripstop nylon tarps and tents to lined, impermeable Duluth packs to lightweight boots and mukluks and sleeping bags, to camp stoves that you can light in a hurricane, to duct tape—everything is better, lighter, and more effective than anything that Daniel Boone or the voyageurs or legendary outdoor writers Sigurd Olson or Calvin Rutstrum could have dreamed of. And it all helps us to stay safe and comfortable in the wilds.

But there is still the human component. We still need to use our own wits and manage our own emotions. Simply accepting the reality of hardship, of bad weather, is a part of it. I still remember a Quetico Provincial Park trip I guided many years ago. Everybody arrived in the rain. We made our introductions in the rain. We unloaded the cars and loaded the packs and canoes in the rain. We paddled in the rain, we portaged in the rain, and we arrived at camp in the rain. Unfortunately, this was the group's introduction to the Canoe Country, to what a real canoe trip was all about. It was an unusually harsh one, and to first-timers the whole thing didn't seem like much fun. I have never seen a more morose group of human beings in my life, as they huddled under the rain tarp I had set up, grumbling among themselves, waiting for me to get the campfire going and produce something warm to eat. I had mentioned the necessity of setting up tents, gathering more wood, and other camp chores. There were no obvious moves in any of those directions. But I was reluctant to be too assertive or to get annoyed and add to the emotional distress. So I kept working away as cheerfully as possible.

Suddenly Julie spoke up. "Hey, guys," she said in a somewhat exasperated tone, "Doug didn't make it rain! He's doing everything he can for us, and it's not going to rain forever. We've got to chip in and help. Haven't you ever been wet before?!" And she began bustling around, getting out the packs and tents, helping with the dinner. Soon everyone was in motion, camp was set up, dinner was prepared and eaten, and dishes cleaned up. It was just what needed to be said, and done, but I couldn't have said it. It had to be someone from the group, taking the initiative, shaking off the lethargy. In the morning the skies were clear, the canoes sliced through blue waters, and we had a dandy week in the Quetico wilderness. Needless to say, I had a soft spot for Julie for the rest of the trip, and she went on to join us in some of our most memorable expeditions in the far north.

SOMETIMES IT'S JUST COMMON SENSE that's missing. On another Quetico Park trip, I led my group down a long stretch of open lake on a cold and windy day. One rocky island loomed in the distance, and as we approached, we saw someone waving an orange life jacket from the shore. Fearing the worst, we rushed over, quartering the waves, and arrived to find a number of young men standing around, their tents pitched on an open campsite in the teeth of the wind. One of the fellows spoke up. "Hey, can you guys loan us some Coleman fuel? We ran out, and we're really cold!"

I tried to appraise the situation, which didn't make much sense. They were clearly able-bodied and should have been able to start a fire with a little wind protection. "I can give you some fuel," I said, "but we're just starting our own trip and we need to save most of it. Why don't you move your camp around to the other side of the island? Pitch your tents there. It's a nice little campsite, and you'll be out of the wind and twenty degrees warmer. That will help more than anything." He said something about being worried about mosquitoes if they camped out of the wind. I came up on shore, poured out some gas, grabbed their hatchet, split a little wood, got a fire started, and once again mentioned the importance of getting out of the wind on the lee side of the island. They assured me they would.

Toward the end of the week we met another group coming into the park and stopped to visit for a bit. They mentioned being flagged down by a group of guys on a little rocky island who were cold and wanted to buy camp stove gas. "How were they doing?" I inquired. "Pretty miserable," was the answer. "Where were they camped—which side of the island?" I asked. "On the west side, right out in the wind!" was the answer. I shook my head.

The real challenge with bad weather—other than the truly life-threatening sort—is almost always emotional. The bottom line is you've got to deal with it. How do we manage the gray skies, the buffeting winds, the cold, the rain, the discomfort? Can we improve our situation? If not, how do we get through it? Adopting what I call *Minnesota fish position*—head down, shoulders hunched, no neck, hands shoved into pockets, immobile—is seldom a useful response.

As the years have gone by, I have come to think of emotions themselves as a sort of weather—the weather of our own inward skies. Unpredictable, beyond our conscious control, always there in one form or another. Clouds drift over and drift away again. Storm fronts arrive, sometimes seemingly out of the blue. There are occasional blowdowns. Or blowups. We learn to be prepared, to accept the reality of discomfort and bad weather, of sadness and anger and frustration, as a part of life, and perhaps not to invest quite so much in whether the skies are blue or gray in any particular hour on any particular day. The skies will change. The clouds will blow off. The sun will come out again.

When I was a little boy out in the fishing boat or otherwise spending time with my Uncle Wilbur, he delighted in gently teasing me. In teasing me particularly—more than any of the other sons or nephews, it seemed. He had a fine sense of humor and employed certain standard nicknames and bromides that he trotted out whenever the occasion was appropriate. Whenever I might be irritated or upset or "down in the mouth," or when the weather was simply crummy and we couldn't go fishing, one of his favorites was, "Dougie, into each life a little rain must fall." And then he'd wink and chuckle at his own wisdom. Again. And I would groan.

But he was right of course. That's why sayings become bromides. And I've employed Uncle Wilbur's wisdom more than once while sitting out a thunderstorm with sons and nephews and nieces, or many a group of wet campers. Or when, if it's really needed, sliding a coffee can of white gas under a pile of wet wood and then watching as the sunshine returns to a circle of smiling faces.

THE SKY DWELLERS

We live in a beautiful and mysterious world, bound and inhabited by forces beyond our understanding and control.

It was early spring, and the river was calling. It was a call, a summons, with notes of excitement and anticipation, the scents and sounds and sensations of open water. And another feeling too. As with any summons too long ignored, there was an itch of restlessness, of something forgotten but important, left undone. The feeling—almost—of guilt. Of literally missing the boat. The river was calling. An answer was overdue.

And so on an evening when the robins chirped their merry "Cheer-i-o" from the backyard apple tree, as a blue sky faded to pinks and purples, and a sliver of moon slid away to the west, six-year-old Bryan and I grabbed the paddles from their corner in the garage. I flipped the Pistachio Princess, lonely through the long winter months, onto my shoulders. And we traipsed down to the riverbank.

We knew it would be a fine evening paddle. Muskrats, geese, ducks, the first evening stars: all our friends of the dusk would be there. But we were unprepared for the extraordinary beauty that awaited us.

As the last stains of sunset faded from the water, as the moon slipped away and the sky darkened to indigo, the first subtle hints of another unexpected light began to brighten the upstream horizon. "Look, Bryan, the Northern Lights," I whispered, as if to speak aloud might cause them to flee from sight. We glimpsed only a few brief columns at first, like searchlights appearing and disappearing, scanning the heavens for an answer to some essential question. Gradually, the individual beams merged into a single gauzy curtain, light green in color, wafting and waving in a silent wind.

It was a lovely display, like those I'd often seen before but Bryan had not. So we sat there in the canoe, eyes focused northward, up the silver ribbon of the Mississippi, watching the green curtain blow. We watched for a long time.

It was Bryan who first noticed the change. "Look, Dad," he whispered in excitement, also unwilling to speak aloud. "Across the river." And there it was. Another curtain. Or a tattered fragment of the same one. Billowing in the east. Then rising straight up, over our heads toward the stars. Soon another curtain joined from the west. A few more minutes and the picture was complete. We were surrounded, enfolded, afloat beneath a great pyramid of light. Again it was Bryan, with the poetic sensibility of a child, who saw the obvious, the true nature of the scene. "It's a teepee, Dad, and we're right in the middle!"

And indeed we were. No longer did we see separate curtains but, rather, a single shimmering cone, rising on all sides around us, with a small, dark opening, a smoke hole—a portal to the universe—at the top. And no longer was the color light green, the shade I had always seen before and pointed out confidently to canoe trippers from some granite point or island observatory in the far north. Now all the colors of the sunset we had witnessed earlier were released once more. Violets and pinks and reds and blues and some shades I couldn't name. The scene was spectacular.

Again Bryan whispered, "We've gotta show Mom and Eric!" And again he was right. Of course we must show them. Never had I seen the Aurora Borealis like this, and who knew when another chance might arise. So we dipped our paddles into the reflective waters and raced back to shore, fearing that at any moment the dancing lights might leave. But they did not, if anything growing stronger and brighter as the minutes passed. Arriving at the house, Bryan dashed inside, all attempts at whispering abandoned within the familiar walls, and called the other members of the family. "Guys, guys, you've got to see this!"

And so we watched together, barely speaking, on our backs in the front yard in a lodge made of light. Eric particularly seemed delighted and transfixed. How long the display lasted I cannot recall. Long enough to soak it all up, to fill our imaginations, and to remember as a family decades later. It is the sort of memory many families share, if they are fortunate to spend times out of doors together. Times that bind us together in wonder and remind us that a family is a small yet vital thing, the first and still essential human community, beneath and within the vastness of an inexplicable universe.

THE NORTHERN LIGHTS symbolize all the forces of nature that long pointed human beings in humility and awe toward the world of mystery and spirit. Ephemeral, beautiful, unpredictable, and baffling, they were the enigmatic night dancers of the North, a shimmering curtain of color and radiance, separating the realm of the known and understood from all that was not. And much was not. The explanations and legends surrounding these strange phenomena were often hauntingly beautiful, from ancient times until more recent days. In many versions, the departed spirits of the dead were involved.

In his 1914 book *The Labrador Eskimo,* explorer Ernest W. Hawkes relays a traditional story in which the ends of land and sea are bounded by a great abyss, through which a dangerous passageway leads to the heavens. The spirit beings who live there light torches to guide the footsteps of new arrivals. The strange voices of the sky dwellers—*selamiut*—can sometimes be heard whistling and crackling with the dancing lights, as they try to communicate with the human beings still on Earth. And the only appropriate human voice in response, according to tradition, is a whisper—just as Bryan had sensed beneath our lodge of light.

There is a lovely old tale of the Anishinaabe (Ojibwe) people in which a young girl travels urgently on a cold winter night, desperately seeking medicine for her people. Returning, she flounders in the deep snow, losing her moccasins, and must finish her journey barefooted. She is guided through the darkness, through bogs and woods and over frozen lakes, by the bright, dancing spirits of the dead, high above the pines and spruces. In the spring, after her feet have healed, the girl and her people return to the spot where her moccasins had been lost. There, and in each place where her bloody footprints were left upon the snow, they find moccasin flowers (lady slippers) blooming in the forest.

Such tales of intimacy and wonder are found in abundance around the world in the northern latitudes, legends and myths that speak to the deep human need for narrative, for stories that help us make some sense of who we are and where we live. Are the stories accurate in any scientific, factual sense? Almost never. But that does not mean there is no truth to them. They often contain many truths, including the great truth that we live in a beautiful and mysterious world, bound and inhabited by forces beyond our understanding and control.

Poets too are irresistibly attracted to the task. Few have written of the sky dwellers more evocatively than the legendary bard of the North, Robert Service, in "The Ballad of the Northern Lights":

Oh, it was wild and weird and wan,
 And ever in camp o' nights
We would watch and watch the silver dance
 Of the mystic Northern Lights.
And soft they danced from the Polar sky
 And swept in primrose haze;
And swift they pranced with their silver feet,
 And pierced with a blinding blaze.
They danced a cotillion in the sky;
 They were rose and silver shod;
It was not good for the eyes of man—
 'Twas a sight for the eyes of God.

In that last line, Service touches on the ancient and intuitive response to the unexplained and the unknown: the humble human reach toward deity, toward spirit. Nowadays we no longer think of the Aurora as dancing spirits, fit only for the eyes of God. We know that the scientific explanation involves something called the solar wind, as charged particles of plasma are hurled from disturbances on the sun far into space. Some are trapped by the Earth's magnetic field lines, which become more dense and dip toward the Earth's surface near the poles. When the charged particles, accumulating in regions called the Van Allen Belts, strike atoms in the Earth's atmosphere, they cause electrons within the atoms to move into a higher energy state. In returning to a low energy state, they release a photon—light. Certain by-products of the process, however, need no explanation. Beauty. Fascination. Awe.

Seldom have I led a crew on a wilderness expedition without repeatedly getting these questions: Do you think we'll see the Northern Lights on this trip? Will the Northern Lights be out tonight? And seldom are the questions asked in hopes that a purely practical explanation might be given, a science lesson taught. On a granite point beneath the constellations, or in a canoe floating on a reflecting sea of light, the most natural, most appropriate response seems to be to gaze in silence or in awe, to speak in whispers. And maybe to hope for a story to be told. A story to connect us to the past, to ancestors, to the beauty that surrounds us, and perhaps to the world of spirit.

Today, we are warned by theologians and scientists alike to be wary of teleological arguments for a "God of the gaps," in which gaps in scientific knowledge are assumed to be evidence for God's existence. In other words, God becomes the explanation for anything not currently explained by science. The warnings are well founded. For the gaps in understanding of the physical universe, everything from evolution to the Big Bang, keep getting explained, and in the process God and the dimension of the spirit are pushed further and further from the consciousness of responsible humans, who rightly believe in facts and truth and verifiable knowledge.

From the hellish confines of a Nazi prison during World War II, theologian Dietrich Bonhoeffer wrote: "How wrong it is to use God as a stop-gap for the incompleteness of our knowledge. If in fact the frontiers of knowledge are being pushed further and further back (and that is bound to be the case), then God is being pushed back with them, and is therefore continually in retreat. We are to find God in what we know, not in what we don't know." Mathematician and Methodist theologian Charles Coulson wrote: "There is no 'God of the gaps' to take over at those strategic places where science fails; and the reason is that gaps of this sort have the unpreventable habit of shrinking."

Now decades later, the gaps in our cosmological knowledge have indeed shrunken, with new facts and truths tumbling one upon the other in ever growing rapidity. But paradoxically, the discovery of quanta and quasars and black holes and Earth-like planets in impossibly remote solar systems are matched (almost balanced, it seems) by the discovery of new unknowns and "yet unprovens"—string theory, multiverses, dark matter, and dark energy.

One is left, finally, with the sense that all the unknowns will never be pierced and proven altogether. Or, rather, with each one that is, another one—or two or ten—will be encountered, leading ever onward on a journey of unending exploration and discovery. A journey perhaps taken in the company of an abiding dimension of the spirit—the sacred—within and above and beyond it all.

That spring night on the Mississippi was cause for awe, humility, and a profound appreciation of mystery. The exact responses humans have always felt from time immemorial. Responses that are manifested in stories of spirits, of blooming flowers and dancing ancestors in the sky. In the intuitive need of a father and son to speak in whispers while floating in a canoe on a great river, beneath a shimmering lodge of light.

A WOODLAND WARNING

The sky had suddenly grown dark, and the dull and distant rumble of thunder was quickly becoming a steady growl.

It had been a long day. In fact, a series of long days: speaking engagements, hectic appointments, rush hour driving. It was March, early spring, and the weather was unseasonably warm and beautiful. What I needed was to sit under a tree. And I knew just the one.

Arriving home at the Pine Point cabin, I ditched the sports jacket, threw on jeans and some old shoes, and grabbed Caleb Emery's walking stick. I sauntered down the trail to the little footbridge I'd built years before, spanning a small, stagnant, unnavigable back channel that at one time had intended to become a miniature oxbow. I had dropped two large red pines across it, connected them with crosspieces at four-foot intervals, layered two-by-six-foot walking boards over the top, then added handrails. It was a very fine bridge, I thought, and I liked to congratulate myself (and occasionally mention to others who might walk the trail with me) that I was the only person I knew who had personally, and single-handedly, built a bridge across the Mississippi River. This was technically true of course, if not the whole truth and nothing but the truth, as most of the Mississippi rolled by a hundred yards away, unconcerned with my modest engineering efforts.

In any case, I crossed the bridge, turned right, and moseyed along the bank toward the tree I had in mind—a favorite white cedar, a century and a half or more in age. Its drooping, green canopy created a natural blind, under which I had constructed a simple log bench. I liked to sit there on occasion—listening, watching, breathing the sweet cedar-scented air. And that was my plan for this day.

But such was my weariness that I remained on the bench for only a minute or two, then found myself on the ground, scraping together a small mound of fallen cedar fronds. When I had a suitable pillow I lay down, saying to myself that I now had a bed, and an aromatic pillow, fit for a king. Or at least for a lumberjack.

For a short while I lay there, watching the red pines above the cedar toss their heads in the March breezes. The gentle whoosh of the wind through the pines, the swaying trunks, the cedar-scented air all created an effect that was comforting and soothing, and I quickly felt the stress of the past few days melt away. Eventually I saw and heard nothing at all, and I drifted off.

I was suddenly awakened by insistent voices—voices I realized that I'd been hearing for some time. "Tsk, tsk, tsk. Chick-a-dee-dee-dee," they repeated over and over.

This was not unusual, for we regularly feed the chickadees and other birds, and I often "talk" to them in our woods. But this time their voices seemed much louder than usual, and I saw that they were very close, only a few feet above my head in the cedar. I answered them softly, thinking I might startle them now that I was awake. But instead they came down from the branches, to barely an arm's length away, chattering more and more insistently. "Chick-a-dee! Chick-a-dee-Dee-Dee-DEE!"

I enjoyed our little conversation but couldn't help thinking something was amiss. Our dialogue continued for another minute or so. I noticed the pines, which had been swaying gently as I fell asleep, were now tossing their heads ever more wildly. The sky had suddenly grown dark, and the dull and distant rumble of thunder was quickly becoming a steady growl. Still the little birds continued in their strangely determined way. "Chick-a-dee! Chick-a-dee!! Chick-a-DEE-DEE-DEE-DEE!"

"Okay, okay, I'm going," I answered, chuckling as I stood up and headed back toward the cabin. "Thanks for the heads-up," I said playfully over my shoulder.

It is about a five-minute walk from the cedar to the cabin at the usual pace. I did not walk at the usual pace. After just a minute, the wind was roaring up the river valley. At three minutes, just before I reached the cabin yard, it slammed like a fist into our woods, followed moments later by hail and sheets of rain, bending the trees nearly double and whipsawing them violently. By this time I was running. I made it to the old carriage house garage and watched out the window, fascinated but fearful at what I might witness, and unsure of the strength of the garage roof. The storm became even more furious, the sounds of trunks and limbs rending and crashing becoming a part of the great cacophony of thunder, wind, and hail. It was hard to see much, but what I could see was alarming.

As is so often the case with such storms, it passed relatively quickly, and after twenty minutes or so I was standing on the riverbank, watching the black, roiling monster disappear to the east, admiring the glowing hoops of a double rainbow that signaled the all-clear.

A short walk revealed that we had lost a century pine that fell across our lane, shattering into pieces. Many limbs had fallen in the cabin yard and onto the deck. I grabbed the chainsaw and chaps and got to work. Later that evening we learned that a tornado had dropped out of the same storm, just twenty or so miles to the east, only minutes after my emergence from the garage.

The next day I had to leave early in the morning to visit a school, to tell stories, and to share books and songs, and I was away for most of the day. During the day, especially on the long drive home, I found my thoughts returning to the little chickadees and to their strange behavior. Arriving at the cabin in the late afternoon I took the time for a more extensive walk than the day before, to check the extent of the damage in our forest. I slowly navigated the trails, clearing windfalls here and there, breathing in the familiar, resinous scent of pine. Overall things were not as bad as I had feared.

Eventually I ended up at my favorite old cedar and was relieved to find it unscathed. I sat down on my log bench. I looked around for my chickadee friends, but none appeared. Then I noticed. About twenty feet from the cedar, a large box elder lay broken and twisted on the ground. It would not have struck me, nor were any of the larger pines around it fallen or uprooted. But I remembered how soundly I had been sleeping the afternoon before. Remembered the ferocity of the storm, the wind, the hail. Remembered the tornado that had come to ground just a few miles and minutes from our woods, the earliest spring tornado in Minnesota history. It had been a dangerous storm. It would not have been a good thing to be caught out in it unsheltered, asleep on the ground. And I remembered the strangely insistent voices that had awakened me.

For the first time I also remembered something else—something I had not noticed or pondered until that moment. No other birds had been singing in the woods as the storm had approached. They never do. The calm before a storm is just that. Not only is the air often still and quiet, but so is the normal music and conversation of the forest. Everybody is buttoned up and tucked in—in thickets, in tree holes, under sheltering overhangs. The woods are silent in the minutes before a violent storm because everyone is safely hiding.

My chickadees should have been hiding too.

Instead they were—what? Warning a sleeping woodsman? One who feeds them and often talks gently with them while on a forest walk? Alerting someone who does not share their ability to feel a storm coming or to sense a change in barometric pressure? Insisting that the sleeping man on the ground wake up!!? Wake up and get to shelter!

I don't know. I don't pretend to know. But such things make me wonder. They make me aware from time to time that we live in a world alive with mystery. Alive with connections and intimations and invisible bonds. Bonds that our more ancient or primitive ancestors easily acknowledged and never questioned.

I have long believed that the world is filled with teachings and teachers, messengers perhaps—if we are awake and aware and prepared to listen. It is also worth noting perhaps that for more than thirty years the chickadee has been my favorite woodland creature, a sort of personal talisman or totem animal, and also that my nickname among those who have traveled the wilderness with me has long been Chickadee. I also once wrote a children's book, based on a favorite Plains Indian legend, titled *Chickadee's Message.*

The story says that in long ago days, the Evil Powers of the universe are vexed, seeing the human beings learning to survive and thrive on the Earth. They decide to teach the People a lesson, to break their spirit, perhaps destroy them. And so they set malignant forces loose on the land: disease and famine, storm drought, flood and fire. After a spell the Evil Powers are curious as to how the People are doing and decide to send a scout or messenger to find out and to bring word back. The messenger chosen is the chickadee—small but brave and resourceful. Arriving at the People's village the little messenger is treated with honor and respect, then asked the purpose of its visit. When told, the People remove themselves to hold council. Upon returning they tell Chickadee to return to the Evil Ones and tell them that the human beings are still alive and hopeful and ever will be, that no amount of discouragement or hardship will ever break their spirit, and that they will always live upon the Earth, remembering its goodness and beauty.

This is the message the chickadees of the world have been proclaiming ever since, from firs and pines and cedars, in winter and in summer. And it is why, the old story says, that to hear a chickadee is to feel just a little braver, a little stronger, and to discover a smile on your face.

This is what the old story says. Like many such stories it has layers of meaning and exists on a different plane accessible only to the heart. I have known the story for a long time, have told it around many a campfire. I have often seen the dawning of recognition and connection, have seen the smiles appear on faces illuminated in the flickering light.

But nowadays I think of the story in a slightly different way. Because now I know. Sometimes chickadees come, as ever, to bring a warm and friendly greeting, a smile, and a message of hope. But sometimes, encountering a sleeping friend in a moment of danger perhaps, they bring a different sort of help. Sometimes they bring an insistent call to pay attention, to wake up! Sometimes they bring a warning.

THE GRAND TOUR

With the legendary bird on the cliffs above, with the spring-swollen Mississippi River rolling by just a few hundred yards away, draining fully a third of a continent, I wondered, as I so often have, at the spirit and meaning of place.

When I think of my younger cousin Terry, with whom I spent most of two boyhood summers and countless other times, all the recollections and images are always right there, clear and bright in my mind's eye, although from decades ago. Teaching Terry to swim at the lake. Fishing together, netting a big northern pike. Feeding chipmunks or chasing frogs. Throwing a Frisbee. Teasing and being teased, expertly and mercilessly, by his dad, my Uncle Wilbur. Grilling in the backyard on a hot summer evening. Playing catch, baseball, or Wiffle ball, just the two of us perhaps, with a whole imaginary ball club behind us on the bases and in the outfield. And on some special occasion for two young baseball fanatics, going to a St. Louis Cardinals' ballgame at old Busch Stadium.

Now it was time to share another sort of experience—saying goodbye to his mother, my Aunt Mary.

The call came at 7:30 on a spring morning. Terry on the line, calling from Edwardsville, Illinois, his hometown. I had received an email from Terry just the day before, saying he was visiting his mother, who was in nursing care and dealing with a variety of health problems. Terry, a Naval Academy graduate and career intelligence expert, has long lived in the Washington, D.C. area.

But he would be in Illinois for several days, he said, helping his mother—who had lost most of her hearing and sight and had trouble typing or writing—with some new kind of computer setup so she could stay in touch. And a few other odds and ends.

But on the phone Terry was saying his mother had passed away during the night. They had spent the afternoon and evening, his first day back home, visiting and dining together. Mary had forgotten he was coming and was so delighted with his "surprise" visit. Then Mary had wanted to play cards, and they had a rousing game of gin rummy and laughed and chatted until late in the evening. Terry fell asleep on a couch just down the hall from her room. And early the next morning he was awakened by the nursing home staff and told that his mother had slipped away gently in the hours before dawn.

Terry was matter-of-fact on the phone, as he usually is. But I could hear the stress in his voice: he had so many things to take care of and not much time. Could I come down, he was asking, to the Alton-Edwardsville area and attend the funeral? The unspoken request: could I play catcher to his pitcher as in the old days, maybe back up any errant throws down the first base line? Of course, I said. I'll be there.

I grew up with two younger brothers, Bruce and Tom. But Terry was an only child, and as we grew up it turned out I was his de facto older brother, too—particularly with the two summers I had spent in southern Illinois with our grandparents, his family nearby, my own brothers far away. All those days together, many of them outdoors, many of them free-range and doing nothing in particular, added up to a deep bond. In his adult years, Terry had also accompanied me on several wilderness canoe trips, one in the far north. It had been, his dad had written me, the "trip of a lifetime" for Terry, who "won't stop talking about it." He still talks about it to this day. But the years and the miles had intervened, and we had lately not had the chance to spend much time together. And the childhood days now seemed long ago.

Until I got his call. And it all came flooding back.

TERRY PICKED ME UP at the airport. As it turned out, he had, with a naval officer's knack for efficiency and organization, already taken care of virtually everything. Turned out there wasn't much in a practical sense left for me to do. But that wasn't really why I was there. At such times, brothers are supposed to be together. And particularly, older brothers are supposed to be there for younger ones. After spending a bit of time with the minister and going over a few details at the funeral home, and taking care of this and that, we ended up spending the rest of the day in an unexpected way. We went on a sort of Grand Tour. Revisiting childhood. Revisiting our favorite old haunts. Revisiting who we were so many years ago.

One of our first stops was at the foot of the famed Piasa Bird, a re-creation, carefully repainted and renewed decade after decade, of an ancient American Indian creature of myth and legend. Painted high on the limestone cliffs above the Mississippi River near Alton, the great bird—appearing to be part-dragon, part-deer, part-cougar, and part-eagle—was described by Father Jacques Marquette and Louis Joliet in 1673. According to Marquette's diary, the Piasa "was as large as a calf with horns like a deer, red eyes, a beard like a tiger's, a face like a man, the body covered with green, red, and black scales and a tail so long it passed around and over the body, over the head and between the legs." The fearsome creature had reportedly been given its name by the Illini Indians—*Piasa* meaning "the bird that devours men." As a boy, I had often seen the great dragon-bird on the white cliffs as Grandmother, Granddad, and I had driven past but in all that time had never been allowed to stop and explore.

This time we stopped. And found to our delight enormous water-carved limestone caves beneath the bird. Skirting a fence and a NO TRESPASSING sign or two, I found a way inside. It smelled wet and earthy and cool on a warm spring day. The ceilings arched and towered eighty to one hundred feet in height, supported by great limestone columns as in an ancient stone cathedral. The sun streamed in between two arches and the effect was breathtaking. With the legendary bird on the cliffs above, with the spring-swollen Mississippi River rolling by just a few hundred yards away, draining fully a third of a continent, I wondered, as I so often have, at the spirit and meaning of place. How long had the original painting been there when Marquette and Joliet first encountered it? What had those red eyes seen? How different was the world it had known, before and during those days of continental exploration? The answers to those questions were not forthcoming. But with the timeless trickling of icy cold spring water down the ancient walls, it was the asking, and the time to ponder, that seemed important.

We left the mysterious Piasa and its questions behind us in the river valley and headed uptown, to visit the old house on the quiet brick street in Alton where our grandparents had lived and where I spent two summers with them so long ago. Many a Wiffle ball had been swung at and missed in the front yard beneath the big cherry tree—the largest in Illinois—or occasionally launched toward the second story of the Perrys' house next door. The grand old tree, whose wide trunk made a fine backstop, was gone now. At the end of the street had been a small ravine and a shady woodlot, where in my solitary times I had retreated into the cool shadows from the heat of many a steamy afternoon and imagined a great wilderness. Had listened to the cooing of mourning doves and the singing of cardinals, watched the quivering ears of a shy cottontail, and found the nighttime tracks of the raccoon. Now the woodlot was gone, the ravine filled, a housing development occupying the area.

At the other end of the street there had been a green grassy space we used for a ballfield when we could get our hands on a real baseball and a wooden bat. Now gone. The graceful old elms that once arched over the length of the street? Gone.

We drove an hour north toward "Little Lake," as we called it, a small pond where our grandparents once had a tiny cottage, and where Terry and I had fished with cane poles for bluegills, crappies, and catfish. It was difficult finding the right crossroads and the old gravel lane, executing the proper turns, and trying to remember the way. But remember we did and found to our delight the *L*-shaped pond, the cottage still perched beside it. All locked up of course. But to stand there and listen to the catbirds and brown thrashers from the woods, to see the sparkle of the water and almost hear the squeaking of the oarlocks from the old rowboat were reward enough. We took photos of one another beside "our" old cottage, before "our" old lake, and we felt the swelling of appreciation and gratitude—mixed with bittersweet nostalgia—that we had been granted such childhood experiences.

Later we had lunch at a small diner neither of us supposed still existed, a place my Granddad called the Greasy Spoon, in Uptown Alton. The menu had changed, the walls and booths were more run-down. But the hamburgers were good, and so were the memories.

Of all the places and times Terry and I remembered, it seemed only a few remained. So much was gone. A whole world gone. In the booth of the Greasy Spoon, we talked about such things. And we talked about Terry's mom, now gone as well. In the years of our childhood, she had been a graceful, constant, gentle presence. Not loud and funny and filling the room, like her husband, my Uncle Wilbur. But always there, watching out for Terry's welfare and my own, insisting that homework be done and done well, preparing Thanksgiving and Christmas dinners, caring graciously for everyone, a vital part of the foundation of our lives. Especially Terry, the only child. It is not easy to lose a mother. It is not easy to lose a world.

The next day the service went well, the attendance small as we knew it would be. The day was a bright, clear blue gem of Illinois spring. The small cemetery with the family plots looked its finest. It was a good day for saying goodbyes. They were said, and I patted the headstones of my granddad and Uncle Wilbur as well and said a few quiet words to them. It had been a long time since I'd stood in that cemetery, on the green grass under the blue sky. Come tomorrow we would be off to our respective homes, Terry and I.

But there was one more stop to make on our Grand Tour. We checked the schedule in the sports page. There was a ballgame tomorrow, before our flights left. We would go. We'd make a pilgrimage to Busch Stadium—the glorious, new Busch Stadium—to watch our boyhood heroes, the St. Louis Cardinals. For about a third of the country, the Cardinals are and have been for a century the focus, definition, and very embodiment of baseball and all its meanings and traditions. And they were all of that to two young boys in the 1960s.

Terry and I arrived early to take it all in, knowing we would have to leave before the game ended to catch our flights. We didn't mind. It was being there that was important. The huge stadium, its enclosed concourses lined with hot dog and Budweiser and souvenir stands, was all gleaming and fine and lovely, but a bit dark inside, rather like the rock-bound cave beneath the Piasa Bird, with light streaming in here and there from arched entrances to the ballfield. After a bit of wandering and exploring, grabbing a dog and a Bud, Terry and I ambled over to the entrance leading to our seat section. There we stepped through the portal and suddenly found ourselves in the bright, open air high above the ball field—and nearly blinded by blue sky and sunlight. A sea of Cardinal red surrounded an emerald green diamond. White-uniformed ballplayers with red caps cavorted on the field—warming up, throwing, catching, running—all the old, familiar, perennial motions of baseball.

It all looked perfect. Timeless. Eternal. The resurrection of all our boyhood dreams.

At that moment the public address announcer spoke for the first time, in booming stentorian tones, a reverberating voice that seemed to come from the very sky itself. "Hello, everybody," he said. "And welcome . . . to Baseball Heaven."

A CABIN IN THE WOODS

It was dark within the massive log walls, and gloomy, but the effect was magical.

I have lived for a long time now in cabins. This is a fact that has been useful in keeping me happy and, for the most part, sane. A psychologist once told me that my personality type was such—creative and imaginative and highly sensitive—that I might have simply spiraled off "into space" had I not intuited early on how deeply tied and rooted I was to the natural world and to "earthy" things. I am not sure if he meant *earthy* in terms of cosmological, planetary things or dirt-growing things, or both. It is about the same, I guess. And the fact that I remember that comment almost forty years later probably indicates its accuracy and resonance for me. A college friend's father had earlier said that "Doug always has both feet firmly planted in midair." Well, I can't argue. Thus the world of rocks and dirt and trees and grass and creatures was always important to me. It literally kept me grounded.

I strongly suspect that I am not alone in this regard and that many of our troubles—individually and as a species—are caused or exacerbated by an ever more tenuous and distant relationship to nature. In its thesis on "nature deficit disorder," Richard Louv's marvelous book *Last Child in the Woods* makes this point beautifully. In my own life, readings, and travels, in observing the work of my younger son's nature education center, and in my countless visits to schools and with professional educators, I have seen and heard a simple truth over and over again: that children (and adults) who are separated from nature—for whom green spaces and living, growing things, fresh breezes, and singing birds are not frequent components of a daily life—often become stunted and warped, self-referential and anxious. And burdened by pathologies large and small. Who really knows what psychological vultures with Latin names pick at the insides of people who simply feel that they don't belong here, that they aren't connected to the Earth in some profound and meaningful way? All factors that a simple and regular touch of nature can do much to alleviate.

For me (and fortunately and separately for my wife, Kathy) there was from early childhood the simple and deep desire to one day live in a cabin. It was just about that basic. For many of our generation, growing up reading and watching television programs about Daniel Boone and Davy Crockett, about Hoss Cartwright and Matt Dillon and dozens of other Western or frontier heroes, there was probably a similar subconscious sentiment. For most folks it went away, at least to some extent. For the two of us, it never did. There was also the common generational childhood experience of growing up "free-range"—Kathy on an Iowa farm and I near the edges of an Iowa town—wherein we were often told to go outside and play and return in time for supper. There was never a thought given, so far as I know, to the dark and desperate threats to children that are now constantly reported and sometimes exaggerated by our hyperconnected social media world. I grew up feeling safe and at home in the outdoors. In neighborhood woodlots and ravines, near creeks and seeps and rolling hills, under blue skies. In the world of nature. And completely unknown to me on her Iowa farm, so did Kathy.

For me there was also the transformative, life-giving experience of getting out of town, away from the small local woodlots and the backyard and neighborhood, traveling to my grandparents' tiny cottage at what we called the "Little Lake" in southern Illinois; on camping trips with my dad and brothers; and even better and more profoundly, heading up north with the family every summer to stay at a resort for a week or two at Lake Kabetogama. There, to live in a cabin—for a short, blessed time. A small, simple cabin near the water, with windows that opened to the scents of the forest, to the sounds of aspen leaves shivering, pine boughs sighing, and loons yodeling from out on the lake. And a doorstep that led to scenes of pine-masted islands and white granite shores, cattail-rimmed bays, deep forest trails, and wide, wave-tossed vistas. It was a wild and endlessly beautiful place, now become a national park. And it was there that the family was all together, with no distractions or diversions, no TV, no "important" jobs or activities to go to—just each other, with fishing and berry picking and woods roaming in the daytime, and cutthroat rounds of Hearts or Canasta or board games in the evenings. It was in such times for me that the cabin dream was nurtured and took a deep hold.

When I was eighteen, I hopped on a bus from Sioux City, Iowa, to International Falls, Minnesota—leaving home for really the first time—and worked for a summer on Kabetogama as a dock boy. For those who may not know the term, *dock boy* is the kid at the resort, usually somewhere between the ages of thirteen and nineteen, who does, well, everything. Everything, that is, that the resort owners, already busy beyond all reason, have no time to do and must therefore delegate. This everything includes, in no particular order: cleaning fish; scooping minnows; selling worms; pumping gas; carrying and mounting outboard motors; launching boats; swabbing out boats; rustling up seat cushions, life jackets, and minnow buckets; giving fishing and navigation advice; predicting the weather; fixing docks; painting cottages; patching leaky roofs; mowing grass; cutting brush; and generally running around doing whatever needs to be done. And watching girls. At least that's the way it used to be done. At least that's the way I did it.

The girls part was haphazard and catch-as-catch-can and actually took up very little time because there was no time to devote to it. But with families arriving from Chicago or Des Moines or Minneapolis or Omaha or Fort Wayne, and dads and uncles and brothers out fishing all day, oftentimes there were girls (again of certain teenage years) far away from boyfriends and not inclined toward hours of uninterrupted fishing, who might be interested in hanging around watching gas being pumped or fish being cleaned. If you did it in an interesting, charming way. Which I did. At least that's how I remember it, from long, long ago.

While dock-boying might appear to be a strenuous and unglamourous job, I felt it to be by far the best job imaginable. Outdoors, blue skies, fresh air, pine trees, a lake, boats, fish, new families (and girls) every week, week after week. Rinse and repeat. And perhaps best of all, my own cabin to live in. My cabin was just one room, old, more than a little rickety, the roof and walls not perfectly straight or vertical, with no heat, no water, and no electricity. But all of that just made it better. More authentic. More Daniel Boone-ish. And every night, after another sixteen-hour day, with a few candles stuffed into the tops of wine bottles for light, I congratulated myself on my excellent good fortune. How cool was this, living in the North Woods *in my own cabin*? And when the summer was over, a seed was firmly planted. Someday . . . someday . . . maybe . . . I would actually have a cabin of my own. For real.

Someday took a while. Nearly a quarter of a century, to be precise.

BEFORE WE GET TO THAT, Kathy was meanwhile having her own growing-years version of cabin longing. In terms of TV watching, she really had no interest in Hoss or Pa on *Bonanza*, but she was deeply, deeply in love with Little Joe. And so she watched each Sunday night and soaked up the image of the Cartwrights' magnificent log home somewhere in the pine-studded foothills of Wild West–era Nevada. She too was familiar with Disney-esque versions of Daniel Boone and Davy Crockett. And she sometimes imagined the old chicken house on the farm being transformed into a frontier cabin. Perhaps more important, there was a little log cabin replica in the northwest Iowa hills near Smithland, a forested area not far from her family's open-country farm. And every time they drove past on their way to town, she would gaze at it. And dream. Someday . . . maybe . . .

One version of Kathy's someday arrived when she came to her senses and accepted me as a poor substitute for Little Joe and came along with my family to Lake Kabetogama for the first time. It was not like Iowa. At all. She had never experienced anything like the North Woods or spent a week in a cabin by a blue, sparkling lake. And just as I had hoped, she fell in love—not just with me but with the whole package. Of which I was luckily a minor part. A following trip to Itasca Park and grand Douglas Lodge and the CCC log cabins there further cemented the impression.

And so there eventually followed marriage and childrearing and jobs and careers and changes of address and life in general. With never much money. With the vision of someday living in a cabin in the woods flickering weakly in the back of both of our minds. Every summer we would return to Kabetogama and often Itasca—as I was hired to perform my *EarthSongs* in the park—with occasional visits to other beautiful destinations where cabins and cottages were a feature. And the old dream flickered . . . and often seemed impossible. But the flame was never completely extinguished.

And then I wrote a book.

My early career as a schoolteacher had lasted only four years. I took early retirement at the age of twenty-five to "pursue other opportunities." This obviously did not set us up well for life financially. There followed about fifteen years of bar performing, concert touring, magazine writing, speaking/lecturing about nature and the outdoors, visiting public schools, and wilderness canoe trip guiding. And other stuff. And though we managed to stitch things together, with Kathy managing the finances, there was always something "to keep the rabbit's tail short." Quite short.

The idea for my first book, *Old Turtle,* came to me as I drove away from a school I had been visiting for the day. The school was in Owatonna, Minnesota, and was named for a president. Possibly

Washington. Maybe McKinley. In any case, as I got into the car and drove away, I began to hear words as though from dictation: "Once, long, long ago . . . yet somehow not so very long . . . when all the animals, and rocks, and winds and waters . . . and trees, and birds, and fish . . . and all the beings of the world could speak, and understand one another . . . there began . . . an argument."

The words came fast, and it was hard to keep up. Plus, I was driving. I got to my parents' house just outside of town, where I was staying while visiting the schools, waved to my mother, and headed up to the guest room where I sat down in a rocking chair with a yellow legal tablet. And finished writing the story in half an hour. Oh, I kept it on my desk for a few weeks, toying with the language, but essentially it was done.

Not long after, I met with a small, Minnesota publisher (Pfeifer-Hamilton). They liked it, and we were off. New adventures loomed. In two years (the time it took for artist Cheng-Khee Chee to create the grand pictures) the book was published. A radio interview with WCCO was arranged, and more media events followed. Then national tours. Lots of good marketing by the publisher. And lots of sales.

And for the first time in our married life, Kathy and I had some money. Not a lot but some. And the old dream—of a cabin in the woods—flickered back to life.

Not far from our house in Sartell, Minnesota, about four miles up the road and out of town, an old log cabin sat near the river in a grove of tall, century-old pines. It was empty. We had been introduced to it by friends who watched over it for the owners, back east somewhere. They were the remaining family of a St. Cloud State botany professor who had had it built in the early 1930s, after the original pine grove had been cut by loggers. The small, slim younger trees had been left standing, thus they were now more than a century old. And beautiful. We learned from historical archives that a long battle had been fought to preserve the original stand—between the local logging mill that owned the timber rights and local conservationists who wanted to preserve it. An agreement had been struck in which the mill would be paid more money than the timber rights were worth. But the agreement was breached, the mill stating, "The pines of Pine Point are ripe and need to be cut." So in March 1929, noted prominently on the front page of the *St. Cloud Times* under a lead story and picture of Al Capone, cut they were.

But now the pines were tall and proud again, with chickadees and nuthatches and pileated woodpeckers and barred owls dwelling within and watching over them. Once learning of the place, I loved to take Eric and Bryan there for forest walks, identifying and admiring wild ginger, trout lily, hepatica, trillium, bloodroot, bottle gentian, and countless other wildflowers. While in the winter months, we looked for the tracks of deer, otter, mink, gray and red fox. And always, during any month of the year, there was the pleasure of simply listening to the sighing of breezes in the pine tops, as we had so often done in the old groves of Itasca, to which these Pine Point woods had once been compared in the news accounts of the day.

But most interesting of all, within the woods and under the great, dark boles rested the old cabin, designed, we had been told, after a Minnesota Log Cabin displayed at the Chicago World's Fair. The old botany professor had built it from local red pines, with a great double fireplace of St. Cloud granite. It stood proud and empty, like a monument to another time. Once every year or two, the family from out east (the professor had died in 1954 under the pines he loved) would return for a week or so, and we would keep our distance. But the rest of the year, with the blessing of our caretaker friends, we would explore. And dream. And imagine. *What would it be like to have such a place?*

We learned that other folks also visited the cabin, sometimes breaking the door latches to gain entry, starting fires in the fireplace for warmth on cross-country skiing outings (with a few fire scars on the Douglas fir floors to prove it). Keggers were sometimes had by local youths. People came to have their Christmas card photos taken before the picturesque log structure under the pines.

I came too. If the locks were already sprung, I would step tentatively inside, breathing in the cabiny air, absorbing the ambience. It was dark within the massive log walls, and gloomy, but the effect was magical. It seemed amazing to me that after all the years, and unsupervised abuse, the cabin still stood. It stood in an undeveloped stand of the old pines—about twelve acres—after the original sixty or so acres had finally been subdivided, following decades of efforts by local developers to acquire them from the professor's family. The family had finally sold but to a developer who promised the lots would be large, three acres each, and that a covenant would be implemented to protect the remaining woods. Meanwhile, the cabin lot itself was sold to the developer's brother and his wife, who set about restoring the old place into a beautiful summer cottage.

THUS IT WAS that we saw Pine Point begin to be developed. And the cabin cared for and renewed. So we stayed away and went on with life—occasionally stopping by on a bicycle ride, peering down the lane, not wanting to intrude or trespass. Until one day, the year of *Old Turtle*'s publication and on such a ride, we crept halfway down the lane and saw a vehicle there. We hesitated. "Let's go on down," I said to Kathy. "And say hi. No reason we shouldn't."

So down the winding lane among the big pines we went. And met a nice man. Who told us of his own journey to the cabin. How he had bought it from his brother, the developer. How his wife loved the big trees and the woods and the cabin's fine architecture. How they couldn't come very often, or stay for long, but visited as frequently as they could, just to soak up the peace and quiet. And the sighing of the wind in the pines. How they had worked hard to bring the old place back to life and to restore it to its former glory.

I in turn remarked on what a beautiful job they had done, how glad I was that someone who really cared had acquired the old place and not torn it down to build a McMansion. And I spoke of the many years we had known and admired the lovely cabin in the woods, its wildflowers and birds and tall trees and all that it embodied.

And the man said, “Well, would you like to buy it?”

I don’t remember what we said in that moment of shock, but it certainly wasn’t yes. How could we even entertain such a far-fetched idea? But we took the thought, and the phone number, home with us. And talked. And pondered. And remembered the old dreams each of us had nurtured so long ago.

Finally, I called the number. Discussions ensued, with the initial offhand offer becoming more complex. And the man’s wife balking at the whole idea. And the price becoming something of a moving target. Kathy and I were not accomplished wheeler-dealers, or real estate moguls, and eventually we grew weary. And frustrated. I finally decided to give up on the whole thing and began a project of locating and purchasing a true up-north getaway on Rainy Lake—a great adventure in itself.

But through it all, the image of the gorgeous riverside cabin only four miles away, which we had already loved for years, lingered in the backs of our minds. So that when the man called a year later, and said he had made some adjustments and significantly dropped the price, and he really thought we were the people who should have the cabin and take care of it, and asked if we were still interested, I said . . . no. We had already made another purchase and simply couldn’t swing it. Which we couldn’t.

But Kathy was listening. “Who’s that?” she asked. I told her. “Well, just a minute, Doug, can’t we at least think about it? And maybe call him back?” And so the phone call ended, with my promising a call-back. More discussions—this time between the two prospective buyers in the Wood household—ensued. This happened with much agonizing over budgets and future prospects—and questions like, Would there be any more books?—and the small size of the cabin for a four-person family, and all the other uncertainties involved.

Meanwhile, I had given Kathy a rose for our anniversary. A single rose in her little engagement announcement vase from twenty years before. It was a nice rose, a red one, and it lasted. And lasted. And lasted. And eventually began sprouting new leaves and taking on a new life. Kathy said it was a sign. An omen.

How could I argue with that? How does one argue with omens? Or a woman's intuition? So after everything, it came down to a rose and a feeling in Kathy's heart: "That place feels like home. It's where we are supposed to be."

And so it was that after a lifetime of dreaming of having a cabin, we now had two. And still do, nearly thirty years later. Along the way we have learned much. That old cabins require a lot of care and upkeep. That trees fall in the forest and sometimes on the roof. That budgets are tricky things. That when it is 30 degrees below zero, modern windows are better than the old originals. That a tall, piney woods is a fine place to raise two boys. And grandchildren. That every day in a beautiful pace is a beautiful day. That among the chickadees and cardinals and crows and squirrels and otters, we have the finest neighbors one could hope for.

And that Kathy was right. This place—this cabin in the woods—feels like home.

SPARKY'S CLOSE CALL

By the time I got there, the situation seemed dire. The redbird was limp, blood covering his black-masked face and beak.

It was a cold January morning and I was hunched over in my office, trying to write, when I heard thumping from the back door of the cabin. It was irregular, not rhythmic, and it didn't really sound like somebody knocking. But what else could it be? A delivery person probably, arms full, mittens on. I got up, grumbling, imagining that whatever I was writing was brilliant, Hemingway-esque, and irreplaceable, and that to leave my train of thought for a moment might be to lose it forever.

Arriving at the back door and looking out the window I saw nothing. No deliveryperson, no package set inside the door, no mittens. But I opened the door anyway—maybe the package had been set to the side—and beheld a curious sight. There on the sparkling snow a few feet away was a pile of feathers—gray, black, and red. The pile moved. And after a few moments my brain kicked in and I realized what I was seeing. It was a shrike, and pinned beneath the shrike, a cardinal. *My* cardinal.

I grew up spending summers in southern Illinois with my grandparents. It was cardinal country. The St. Louis Cardinals were the local baseball team and I was the biggest Cardinal fan in existence. I fell asleep nearly every night with my grandmother's small transistor radio pressed against my ear, listening to Harry Caray and Jack Buck set the scene and call the plays. Every day

Granddad and I perused the standings to follow the progress of our heroes. And I lived and died with the exploits of Bob Gibson, Curt Flood, Ken Boyer, Stan Musial, and Lou Brock.

But it wasn't just the baseball Cardinals that I loved. This was cardinal country through and through. No doubt the team had originally been named for the prevalence of the brilliant redbirds in the wooded hills of Missouri and southern Illinois. On my grandparents' leafy street alone it seemed there must have been several dozen of them, singing every morning and evening from the tip-top of every walnut, elm, and cherry tree in the neighborhood. Grandmother and Granddad fed the birds and squirrels in the small green patch by the back porch, and while I enjoyed the blue jays and other birds that frequented the feeder, it was the cardinals with their brilliant plumage and bold, scarlet songs that captured my heart. Cardinals were a part of my boyhood. And many years later, when we moved to the woods of Pine Point, despite my love for all our furred and feathered neighbors, I regretted the fact that we had no cardinals.

Until one day we had one. And then two! And they stayed, living and nesting in the northern-hardy kiwi vine that Kathy had planted and that had somehow flourished, climbing up the logs and chinking and over the back door of the cabin. I became happily accustomed to awakening to the song of a cardinal, just as I had so often in my youth. On winter days I watched for a red flash against the snow and through the trunks of the pines. And the cabin in the woods felt more . . . complete.

So it was that I burst out the back door and shooed the shrike away from the cardinal. And so it was that I thought not even for a moment about the welfare of the shrike, a bird more rare even than a northern cardinal, a bird who has his own difficulties in surviving a cold Minnesota winter. I had my loyalties, and they ran very deep—deeper than conscious thought. Something was killing a cardinal—my cardinal—and that could not happen on my watch.

The shrike, a gorgeous, graceful little predator—sometimes called the butcher bird for its habit of impaling its prey on a thorn

bush or a barbed wire fence—flew off into the woods. And after I held the redbird for a few moments it too flew away, into the low yew bushes by the back door. I breathed a sigh of relief and went back indoors. But as I watched through a window, the shrike swooped in once more, swift as death, and took the cardinal to the ground. By the time I got there, the situation seemed dire. The redbird was limp, blood covering his black-masked face and beak. I picked him up and brought him inside.

Placing the bird in a shoebox lined with tissue, I drove him a few miles to the home of my good friend Elaine Thrune, for many years a wildlife rehabilitator and president of their national organization. "Can we save him, Elaine?" I asked anxiously. Opening the box, we found the redbird sitting up, looking a bit more perky.

Elaine gave him a careful examination, which was clearly not appreciated, and wiped away most of the blood, finding no serious injuries. The bird nipped her finger, hard.

"You know," she said, "cardinals have very strong beaks. It's just possible that some of the blood is from the shrike and not the cardinal. Why don't you let me keep him indoors in this nice roomy cage over the weekend, and we'll see how he does."

On Monday morning, after worrying all weekend and listening to the cardinal's mate chipping endlessly from all around the cabin, I called Elaine. "Well, how's our bird?"

"Feisty," she said. "He definitely wants out of here. Why don't I bring him over?"

Soon Elaine and I were standing in the snowy yard opening the shoebox. Our little patient sat there for a few moments, perhaps getting his bearings, then fluttered off into a low cedar at the edge of the woods. He perched there quietly for a long time. I had heard no more chipping from the female for the past twenty-four hours. I worried some more. Maybe she was gone. "I'm going to name him Sparky," I said. "Because he's bright and he's red and he's a fighter. This little guy is Sparky from now on!"

"Well, Sparky sounds good to me," said Elaine. "Let me know what happens."

Eventually I went indoors, leaving Sparky resting in the cedar, seemingly pondering the situation. When I came back outdoors later he was gone. I looked and looked, carefully scanning the trees and shrubbery near the cabin yard. Then I heard it, from down in the hollow a hundred feet away, the bright, metallic chipping of a cardinal. Of two cardinals, calling back and forth! And I raised my hands in triumph.

The months went by, winter became spring, summer, fall. And a curious pattern emerged. Often, when I was out in the woods for a walk, or while lumberjacking and cutting deadfalls, a red streak would come flashing through the trees and there would be Sparky, landing in a branch close over my head, singing his heart out. "What, what, what, what cheer! What cheer! What cheer! Purtily-purtliy-purtily-purtily!" Sometimes he would follow me down the long winding lane, chipping and singing as I went to check the mailbox.

Aww, he remembers me, I would think. He's still grateful that I saved his life. How cool is that? And a warm and happy glow would come over me. "Hi, Sparky," I would say. "Hello, little buddy." And the woods and the entire world seemed just a little happier, a little closer to just right.

Then one day it came to me, as I sat on a log, taking a break from tree work, listening to Sparky sing. Birds really don't sing because they're happy or grateful. They sing to attract a mate, to claim territory, and especially to mark their turf, to proclaim, "Here I am! This is my tree, my woods!" Cardinals particularly are territorial, extremely so. They are pugnacious about defending their turf. And this was Sparky, the little battler, the shrike fighter. Sparky, I belatedly realized, was not saying, "Thank you, thank you, thank you." Far from it. He was more likely saying something like, "You! You're the idiot who put me in a shoebox. A shoebox! What were you thinking? Don't ever do it again!" And saying it over and over again so the message would sink in and I'd remember it.

Now several years later, Sparky and Mrs. Sparky still live in the vine over the back door. Sparky still sings to me occasionally or follows me along the driveway. But not as often as he once did. It's possible he's forgiven me. Mostly. And best of all, we now have more cardinals in the Pine Point woods, singing from more treetops. Sparky's grandchildren and great-grandchildren, I like to think. I smile whenever I hear them. And I feel connected to other cardinals some six hundred miles downstream, part of a neighborhood and a boyhood that seem, for a few moments, not quite so far away and long ago.

MORNING GRATITUDE

A Turtle's Radio Debut

What happened next, I came to understand,
was every author's dream.

I woke up feeling grateful. A global health crisis loomed and the stock markets were crashing, people were isolating and social distancing, and I had gone to bed feeling worried and scared. But I somehow woke up feeling grateful. The March sun streamed in through the windows. "Thank you," I said, to Whomever one says such things from one's heart. "Thank you for my life and my family, for my work and my cabin and my woods, and all my many blessings." And I went down the old split-log cabin stairs, feeling better than when I had climbed them the night before.

I went to the desktop computer in my office overlooking the river to put up a morning Facebook post—something I do on many days for the kind and interested friends who follow me. For the post I took a picture of one of my bonsai trees in the cold window corner of the office, the morning rays lighting it up like a bright green torch. The simple, graceful little tree in the sunlight, the eagle chirping from the river, the chickadees calling "Spring's here!" and Sparky the Cardinal singing his heart out all contributed to the good feeling. And then I heard a little song in my head: "Good Morning, Good morning! It's grand to be on hand. Good morning, good morning to you!" I had heard the song many times before, as had countless Minnesotans, courtesy of radio legends Boone and Erickson, Charlie and Roger, respectively, decades earlier. So I posted the song lyrics with a photo of the bonsai tree in the morning sun.

Someone responded to my post minutes later with an old clip of Boone and Erickson on the air, and suddenly the memories came flooding back, the feeling of gratitude growing even stronger. For I was remembering another morning, from twenty-eight years before.

I had appeared on WCCO radio—back in its glory days—a number of times with Charlie and Roger, as a young musician and songwriter. Roger especially loved my humorous "Minnesota Mosquito Song" and the slightly risqué "Outhouse Blues," and no matter what I might have come to talk about, he would invariably insist that I perform one of those songs as part of the deal. Charlie was always unfailingly kind to an unknown kid from outstate with his blue jeans and plaid shirt and twelve-string guitar. Each time I was on the air with them I watched in awe as they talked to me, *listened* to me, talked to each other, performed their live commercials, produced their bits and their sketches, announced the weather and the news, all the while keeping one eye on the big clock on the wall with the second hand spinning around, and timing everything to the microsecond.

One late October day in 1992, I worked up my courage to call 'CCO once again—it was always a big deal to me, as I was never quite sure they'd actually remember me—and asked to speak to Charlie. I knew Charlie was a big fan of books and literature. He answered the phone.

"Uhhh, Charlie, I wrote a book," I said. "It's called *Old Turtle,* and it just came out."

"A book, huh? Why, that's great! Would you like to come down to the station and talk about it?"

"Wow, that would be wonderful! Thanks!"

And so a date was set for Friday of that week.

I showed up in my jeans and plaid shirt, and Charlie and Rog, on a short break, greeted me in the hallway. I handed the brand-new book to Charlie, as Roger headed down the hall. Charlie stood there, back against the wall, and paged slowly through the whole thing, beginning to end, not saying a word. Then he looked at me. "Would you like to read this on the air?" he asked. I remember the moment as if it were yesterday.

"Oh . . . you mean . . . read it aloud? The whole *thing*?"

"Yes, I think you should, why not?" said Charlie.

Well, "Why not?" was because I had a vague idea what live commercial time on 50,000-watt, clear channel WCCO radio might cost. And getting five to six minutes of it uninterrupted for *free* was . . . extraordinary. But I nonchalantly said something along the lines of, "Sure, that would be great!" And we headed into the studio as I tried to keep my nerves under control.

After getting headphones on and sidling up to the mike and a bit of chit-chat, and a nice introduction about their "good friend, Doug Wood, who has just written a book," it was time. And so I read my book, my first book, *Old Turtle,* live in public for the very first time.

WHAT HAPPENED NEXT, I came to understand later, was every author's dream. By the time I finished, the guys excitedly told me the switchboard was "lit up like a Christmas tree!" People were calling in from everywhere, many in tears, pulling off the road, finding telephones, asking, What *was* that book? Where could they find it? Where was it available? Who was the author? Charlie and Roger kept me on the air for a good while, answering some of the calls personally, asking me more questions about the book and the art by Cheng-Khee Chee, and the little publisher from Duluth. And there in that studio on that day, in that hour, my life changed. I became an author. The rest of my life became something new. Something different. Something better.

The five thousand books the publisher had printed sold out over the weekend. More books were printed, and they sold out as well. And yet more again. *Old Turtle* took off at a speed that turtles seldom if ever display. National book tours and events and awards, many more TV and radio interviews, and countless wonderful things happened, including the opportunity to write thirty-eight more books. I appeared several more times with Charlie and Roger—Boone and Erickson, "legends within their own minds," as they liked to say—and I thanked them every time.

But I could never thank them enough.

Charlie and Roger are both gone now. And I miss them. Many, many Minnesotans of a certain demographic miss them, their wonderful stories and corny jokes and stupid Minnesota Hospital sketches, and their signature "Good Morning" song. But I think I miss them in a special way. In a way that is tinged with enormous gratitude. They made us all smile and laugh and perhaps forget some of our troubles for a while. They made us feel a part of something special and north woodsy, and dairy farm-ish, and Ole and Sven-ish, and made us feel like we shared the experience of starting the day and watching the sun come up together. They gave us a feeling of community. And they gave one young man a rare opportunity—a chance to read a book on the air—that changed his life. I can just hear them now: "Good morning! Good Morning! It's grand to be on hand. Good morning, good morning, to you . . ."

So I will say it here one more time. Thanks, guys. Thanks, Charlie and Rog. Thanks for everything.

THEATER OF THE WILD

Out of the woods he charged like a freight train, saplings toppling before him, broad antlers tossing, then into the lake with a tremendous splash, water thrown in every direction, a momentary rainbow round his great head.

The theater of the wild is limitless, and the stage is vast. Within it something is always happening, some drama large or small. Someone is always living out a story, someone always waiting in the wings. Those of us who are lucky enough to spend much time out of doors, if we are aware and alert, are sometimes witness to extraordinary events. But more often the events are normal, quiet, quotidian, yet somehow still extraordinary—in their wonder or their meaning or their impact on our lives. If we pay attention.

When I think about such moments, it is often not the actors so much that I first recall but the show-stopping beauty of the setting, the theater itself, which imparts such significance to the stories that transpire there and to any characters who may appear. The set, the lighting, the musical score, and the soundscape, the grand arched ceiling of clouds or stars, or backlit screens of skylines all play an essential part. I have remembered for more than forty years a particular sunset on a small, unnamed island on a lake whose name is also now lost to memory, somewhere in the Turtle River country of northwest Ontario.

A small group of us had been out for a week, with another week to go, paddling and portaging, fishing, watching wildlife, fighting whitecaps, running rapids, bantering and sharing and doing all the things that one does on a canoe trip with friends. In truth, I can remember just one dramatic event from the trip—the moment I unsuccessfully attempted to run the canoe through a rock in a small rapid, resulting in a capsized canoe, a gashed shin, and a small scar I carry yet today. But another memory lingers like a favorite photograph to be pulled out and admired from time to time. Yet I have no photograph, no one took the shot, and if they had it could not have captured the scene.

We were seated on a granite outcrop, fifteen feet above the water, supper eaten, dishes done, at the end of a long day of paddling and portaging. We were gazing north. To one side of the sky, on our left, the sun was sliding into the pines in a small bay on the lake's northwest shore. There was a soft skim of cirrostratus clouds, and they were lit with a golden, peach-colored glow—gently, not in a particularly dramatic way. But the color was extraordinarily deep and warm, infusing the sky and trees and lake and shoreline and the entire scene with a luminosity that somehow seemed to be something more than a phenomenon of surfaces and exteriors. Rather, it appeared almost to emanate from within the objects themselves, as though this radiance were always there, always present, but revealed only at this golden moment. Seen only by these lucky observers. To our right, in the east, the full moon crept over the church spires of balsam firs, rising in silent grandeur, itself bathed in the same lambent glow.

Meanwhile, the lake and woods were quiet—no calling of loons, no whitethroats singing their evening song, no aspens rustling in the day's last breeze. It seemed the very silence itself called our full attention to the tableau before us. But it was not simply a scene being witnessed. We were now a part of it, as any audience in any fine theater is called on to be. I can see the six of us clearly still, as if in the nonexistent photograph or some painting of the mind, young men full of the sense of adventure and freedom and exploration, shirts off in the warmth of the evening—stopped short. Caught in the amber of a timeless moment. I suspect I will see it always.

Other sunsets reside in the same mental album, scenes from the grand theater. From countless more canoe trips in the North, from a first evening by the Pacific Ocean, from a beach on the Caribbean, from another wide beach on the German island of Borkhum on the North Sea. But among the most poignant—and sunsets are always poignant—are those from twenty to thirty years ago on our Northwoods island, at the end of our old west-facing dock. In those days the island was still new to us—or we were new to it—and among our most favorite times were evenings spent fishing off the dock, evenings with my dad and young sons and sometimes nephews and our good dog, Sugar. While I don't necessarily recall the details of any one particular evening, it is the very accumulation of them that is the real treasure. Memories of the theater. I see Dad sitting in his old, canvas field coat, his favorite brown Stetson hat tugged low against the horizontal rays. Bryan and Eric with hoodies pulled tight against an errant mosquito. Eyes on bobbers, the background evensong of tree frogs or song sparrows or distant loons. And the sun going down in fiery splendor across the channel. Every twitch of a bobber, every walleye netted, every soft conversation about normal, everyday things—all were enhanced and magnified by the stage, the set, the lighting, the ambience.

Sunrises, too, are a part of the great theater's magic. The fog lifting slowly from some wild lake or river waiting to be explored. Colors just beginning to appear as the house lights come up. From a dark curtain of green we hear the first songs of the day, as from a Greek chorus of old. The veery thrush sings in his familiar, tumbling, downward spiral. A kingfisher rattles from a dead jack pine. A red-eyed vireo repeats its notes as if counting all the leaves in an aspen. Barely pausing for breath, he will count all day, perhaps ten thousand songs by dusk. A raven croaks tunelessly as he flies over. Dipping and tipping from side to side, glossy black feathers glistening, he comments on the prospects of the day and the vastness of his wilderness domain. Along the rocky shoreline, ledges and glacial erratic boulders catch the light, orange lichens beginning to flame. And all the stories of the North Woods begin to be told by the timeless tellers—innumerable dramas—from the blooming of the shoreline iris to the ripening of a wintergreen berry. Even the slow, imperceptible weathering of rocks is taking place.

When folks imagine a theater, many think of entertainment—a show, a lively drama with interesting characters to capture our attention. And to be sure, such moments are well worth waiting for. On any wilderness trip an encounter with charismatic megafauna like wolves or moose, pine martens, lynx or bobcats, foxes and otters, even bald eagles is something to be anticipated and treasured when it occurs but cannot be predicted or counted on.

I remember a particular trip in Quetico Provincial Park long ago. Most of my groups were self-selecting in those days. Whenever I gave a talk or a workshop or concert around the country, I would put out a stack of fliers describing my upcoming season of guided wilderness trips. If someone took a flier and later contacted me about participating, they already had a pretty fair idea of who I was and what sort of experience to expect. But this trip was different, in that a nature center from Michigan had asked me to guide a trip for their members, sight unseen. I agreed, and as always I enjoyed my group, except for one woman who posed something of a problem.

Before the trip began, she wrote to me several times, asking if she would have to eat fish. No, I said, there would be plenty of other foods, although fish would certainly be available. Are you sure? she asked. Yes, I was sure. As it turned out, she tried some fried walleye on the second or third day out and loved it, and ate fish all week, even asking for extra helpings, and then reaffirmed at our last campfire that she was never eating fish again! In any case, Becky (not her real name) had a bit of a problem with . . . many things. On the first morning in our first camp, I asked her how she had slept. “Sleep!” she answered. “Who can sleep on the hard ground like that?! I need some aspirin.” Oh. And so it went during the week, with many complaints and annoyances. I retained my natural patience, charm, and good humor. Mostly.

Until one fine day she accosted me about why she had traveled so far and spent so much money to come to Quetico Park and had not seen a moose. Or a wolf. Or virtually anything else "interesting." I sat down on a rock, a dandy rock that I could have told her all about, just as I had explained many things during the week, but I knew she wasn't interested.

"Becky," I answered, sort of patiently, "there are different kinds of parks, you know. This particular one is a wilderness park. It is not a water park or a playground park or a petting zoo, and it is most particularly not an amusement park, in which everything is arranged and managed for your comfort and entertainment. Here we have to create our own amusement and adapt and adjust to the weather and the wind and the landscape. Most important, the creatures who live here—and there are many—are not placed here to amuse or entertain us. They *live* here. Wild and on their own. We cannot call them out at certain moments when we are feeling bored. This is their home, in which they live their own rich and meaningful lives and fulfill their own purposes and destinies. And sometimes, if we are quiet and lucky, we might get to observe them and learn from them and, maybe for a short time, even feel as though we are *almost* a part of their world."

It was a good speech. I don't think she got it. Although the complaining might have eased up. Slightly.

In any case, my Beckys were few and far between in all my guiding years. And I indeed do remember many an interesting or astonishing moment when one or more of the impressive actors in the great theater made their presence known. The time we heard the moose crashing through the woods for a full minute before he emerged, enormous and grand and majestic and irritated beyond all measure by the mosquitoes and flies that had evidently been bedeviling him. Out of the woods he charged like a freight train, saplings toppling before him, broad antlers tossing, then into the lake with a tremendous splash, water thrown in every direction, a momentary rainbow round his great head. Perhaps we heard him sigh in relief. Perhaps I just imagined it.

But had I ever doubted the precise meaning of the words *magnificent, indomitable, overwhelming,* I now understood them. Yet even the proud monarch had been driven to near distraction by the torment of tiny insects.

I remember watching the hunt, the eternal drama of life and death, between a pine marten and a snowshoe hare, how our entire group observed the chase, circling over and over again through our camp, and then the final moment of triumph and tragedy.

I recall the bald eagle tracking a Canada goose, close behind, just fifty feet above the water, above our canoe, the eagle then rising far into the sky as if giving up the chase, but then folding its wings and plummeting downward to strike a lethal blow, the goose falling, tumbling into the water, the eagle flapping lazily away to land in a tree, sitting there, patiently waiting for the goose to drift closer.

In my mind's eye I see a family of otters coming near the canoe, curious, heads bobbing up and down as they appraise the situation and wonder at the strange creatures in the strange hollow, pointed logs. I see the moments shared with loons, rising suddenly near the canoe, so close we could see a minnow in a beak, droplets of water catching the sun, and the wild, red eye that reflects and manifests the entire meaning of wilderness.

I can see a pack of wolves in the Northwest Territory, the same dusky color as the sandy soil, loping effortlessly along the shoreline through the jack pines, symbol of all that is free and untamed. And I remember the lone wolf I once met beside a wilderness road, how it stayed when I stopped the motorcycle, continued to stay when I climbed off, and then capered and darted and feinted, back and forth, tongue lolling out, all but begging for a game of tag before eventually melting into the woods.

I think of various bears, including the cutest cub I'd ever seen, halfway up a jack pine tree near the latrine; a bigger bear who didn't want to share a blueberry patch; and an even larger one who popped his teeth and mock-charged and insisted that our campsite and food pack were actually his. We reluctantly agreed about ownership of the campsite but grabbed the food pack on our way out.

I remember watching a bobcat, stealthy and silent as death, stalking a family of black ducks among the shoreline cattails.

Such singular moments and many more are burned into memory. But there is another, simple and intimate way of seeing the daily drama of life and feeling a part of it. Perhaps no one I know so exemplifies this way of seeing and being better than my friend Larry Weber, recently recognized with a Lifetime Achievement Award from the Minnesota Association for Environmental Education. In guiding seniors in the Road Scholars program with Larry, I have seen and been reminded of all that so deeply attracted me to the world of nature so many years before as a boy. To Larry, every encounter, no matter how small, is full of interest and fascination. Larry will spend an entire morning photographing orb spiders

and their glistening webs, then hold one in his hand for half an hour—observing, learning, thinking. And then easily entice a seventy-five-year-old woman who has never touched a spider in her life to do the same: to hold and admire the little creature she has probably spent decades thoughtlessly dispatching. It is a privilege and a joy to watch someone—anyone—suddenly rediscover the wonder of nature, to begin to imagine and appreciate all the marvelous characters and dramas that surround us every day of our lives.

And in that drama, we too have our roles to play. Roles compounded of history and ambition, exploration and discovery, commerce and art and poetry, and all the glory and pathos of the human condition. In my earlier years of guiding, I often led trips in tandem with my great friend Denny Olson. Denny was long a professional naturalist at nature centers, colleges, and institutions in Minnesota and Wisconsin, and possessed a near encyclopedic knowledge of the outdoors, especially the North Country. But his gifts went beyond that. Denny was and is a talented actor and has long traveled the country doing one-man shows as The Critterman, Doctor Death, Dr. Avian Guano, and Doc Wild, in each guise skillfully drawing audiences into the realm of nature. On our canoe trips Denny often brought along another character, hidden from participants until just the right moment. Then, while dishes were being washed and camp chores completed, Denny would softly disappear. It was my job to gradually shepherd the gang down to the water's edge—the better to observe a loon, a turtle, a faraway eagle, or some mysterious sound.

As we sat by the lake, waters lapping quietly, we would hear . . . was it really? . . . yes, singing . . . from far away but drawing nearer. The unmistakable sound of a French chanson, sung in a clear, high baritone. Eyes would widen, quizzical looks, all conversation ended. And from around the point, through the mists of time, a canoe would appear, paddled by Denny. But no, dressed in billowing blouse, red sash, tall moccasins, and colorful cap, it was in reality the Lost Voyageur. This poor soul, we would learn, had been separated from his party of North Country traders and explorers 150 years previously and had been paddling and portaging, traveling the Canoe Country and searching for his friends ever since. At first he was all joy and relief at finding us, thinking we were the object of his long quest, thinking that I particularly was his bosom friend, Henri. And indeed there was a resemblance but, no, we were simply who we were. Yet still, to the Lost Voyageur we were objects of wonder, the women with their tight-fitting, painted-on pantaloons. Men with their fancy wrist watches. Our canoes made of metal or some other strange, smooth substance. Our magical torches and our packaged foods. A strange bunch indeed.

After his initial wonderment, our traveler engaged us with stories from the past, from fur trade days, from Alexander Mackenzie and David Thompson, the North West Company, and the brigades of the rival Hudson's Bay Company. He regaled us with tales of wilderness and wildlife and all he had learned from his friends and teachers, the Ojibwa and the Cree. He spoke movingly of the beauties and wonders they had shown him, and that he had come to know so well in his century and a half of wandering the wilderness—from lichens and mosses and wildflowers to the great pines to the shy creatures of the forest.

Then, as suddenly and mysteriously as he had arrived, the Lost Voyageur would get into his canoe and paddle away. Sometimes, unbidden and with no way of anyone knowing or predicting, the wilderness would step in and close the curtain, giving a brief and fitting closure to the tale. A loon might wail from the mists. A beaver might slap his tail in the gathering gloom. Once a wolf howled from the far hills, and on one occasion a meteor lit up the darkening sky. But sometimes there was just the lyrical, whispering swish and gurgle, slow and easy, of the paddle, as the canoe melted once more into the past, offstage and into the wings.

These evening encounters—the gold of sunset blending into moonrise, the gradual appearance of stars—were timed perfectly for theater, of course, when strange stories are a little easier to believe, the line between reality and fantasy a bit harder to discern. At such times magic is in the air, as lighting and staging provide the perfect setting for the eternal yet ever-changing drama of rocks and trees, birds and animals and people, and the mystical ties that bind us all together. At these moments we may feel a part of things that are grander, somehow deeper and more profound than normal everyday concerns. But in truth such moments are always present and always available to us. Anytime, day or night, dusk or dawn, when we stop to look with open eyes and listen with open ears, we can feel a part of the great story. The story of all life on Earth. A story forever told in the theater of the wild.

MAKING CAMP

On this evening we simply toast the lake, a lovely gathering of waters where the river we are traveling pauses and rests before exiting in a short millrace, continuing its journey to Hudson Bay.

We can't be sure. Even with the binoculars we can't quite be sure. Is that an opening in the pines up ahead at two o'clock (using the bow of the canoe as noon)? Maybe. Is that a gently sloping ledge fit for a canoe landing and maybe a water's edge kitchen? And back behind in the pines, rising up from the shoreline, could those be level spots, little open spaces suitable for the tents, our little homes for the night?

All of the answers are maybes. But the opening looks promising. Certainly worth paddling over and taking a look. It's been a good day but a long one, with two portages carried and almost twenty miles paddled. No kind of record, but respectable, with the normal bantering and teasing, birding and wildlife viewing. We spotted a bull moose, big as a garden shed, chewing arrowhead tubers in a beaver pond, and squadrons of pelicans, tilting and soaring, sun glinting off their white wings in an azure sky. And there were plenty of quiet miles, reserved for thinking and pondering. If you like that sort of thing. Which I do. It has been a day like many others, different only in the particulars, but with each of those particulars important, the accumulation of them the whole reason we are here, exploring a patch of wilderness that truly seems to need exploring. By us. Not in the sense of cartographers

charting unmapped territory but in the sense of seekers searching out the essence of the North Woods, of the wild and green and living Earth. Maybe of our own souls. Unmapped territory after all, perhaps.

But those thoughts are not top of mind at the moment. We are tired. We are hungry. The sun is sinking. We need to make camp, and that spot on the shore could be it.

The paddles dig deeper. The pace quickens, almost imperceptibly at first, then faster and faster until there is an unspoken but clearly evident race to the site. I, being a slightly, moderately, comparatively—all right, very—competitive sort, pull with all my strength, encouraging Julie in the bow to do so as well. Why? We are, as I say, tired, and there is no conceivable, earthly reason to do so. We do so anyway.

We don't win. Which is annoying, for two or three seconds. But as Ulysses S. Grant said, "Get 'em tomorrow." For now, there are more important things to consider. The spot looks good. The sloping ledge is indeed wide enough for the four canoes, with room to unload the packs and establish a kitchen and a small dining hall. I climb out of the stern and slosh onto dry land, then continue past the smooth granite landing and a large boulder and into the woods. The spaces between the jack pines and spruces and balsams are level, just wide enough to accommodate the tents, with mossy floors for comfort, and perfectly framed open views between the trees and out to the lake. We'll see the sunset tonight and the offshore islands will catch the first soft rays of the morning. It's a fine place. I return to tell the others. "We're home," I announce with a smile.

AND SO ACTIVITIES COMMENCE. Everyone knows what to do. Packs come out of the canoes, a bit damp on the bottom from an early morning shower. They are tossed unceremoniously onto the rock, the food pack and equipment pack requiring a couple of extra hands. Fishing poles are extracted from sterns and bows, where they had been kept handy for casting and trolling along the occasional weed bed or other likely-looking fishery. Day packs and extra paddles are removed, and the odd pair of tennis shoes and water bottles that had not been stowed away.

In a couple of minutes, all is onshore. The canoes are dumped and overturned, resting side by side. They are, I think to myself, remarkable things, no longer made of birchbark, no longer carrying fur bales or trade goods or voyageurs, but still heir to all the canoe has ever meant, still vehicles of discovery, carrying paddlers through endlessly unfolding scenes of beauty, down boisterous rapids, into secret bays and toward wild horizons.

One canoe is left out to make one more evening excursion, when someone goes out to gather buckets of water for cooking and lemonade. Said lemonade may benefit from the possible addition of an alcohol-enriched Special Ingredient, as co-leader Jim likes to call it. The particular type of special ingredient, its mixing and hour of consumption, are strictly of Jim's choosing, as all agree he must be in charge of such an important component of camp life.

Tent sites are now chosen, carefully but quickly, as no one wants to be left with the worst site. As I was on land first and have seniority and rank, I have already dropped my small day pack on a spot near the water but away from the kitchen, with a fine view and a good place to hang clothes. It is the best spot. No one else complains. At least out loud.

After the personal packs are hauled to the tent sites, and dry camp shoes are put on, most of the crew go to work setting up tents. Each site is cleared of offending rocks and pinecones and sticks, the moss smoothed out to as near-perfect and level a bed as possible. Tents themselves are strung and stretched taut, the better to ward off any night rains, although the air is dry and the sky is clear. Corner stakes to hold the tents in place are pushed in at a shallow angle, for under the moss and bearberry, the soil is mere inches thick on the bedrock, the accumulation of ten thousand years—a very short time geologically—of erosion, frost cracking and rock chipping and lichen growing and the remains of white pines and aspens and birches and wolves and bears and red squirrels since the final retreat of the Laurentide Ice Sheet. An occasional heavy rock—left by the same benevolent glacier—is used to help reinforce and stretch a corner or two. Now air beds are tossed into the tents and blown up and sleeping bags rolled out on top of them. (My old friend Scott once told me, "If you can't sleep on the hard ground, you haven't paddled far enough." He is, needless to say, a foolish man.)

Each site becomes precious and sacred to its occupants, their own sanctum sanctorum, a private little piece of the great wilderness, a home-away-from-home, at least for one night. Homesteaders will soon know each branch and stump, every sitting rock or tripping root on their property, and be able to navigate them even in the dark. Short clotheslines are strung and are quickly festooned with socks and hankies, wool sweaters, and various fashion accessories.

It is time to hang the rain fly. After a bit of careful pondering, a spot is chosen to accommodate a twelve-by-sixteen-foot sheet of ripstop nylon, where all can gather and a camp stove be set if the weather turns foul. Tying off the four corners is not difficult, but in order to elevate the center, creating room for heads, the Doug's Sock Method must be employed. This involves first tying a small rock or a tennis shoe to a slim rope, picking out a stout branch, and tossing the rock and string over said branch. It sounds fairly easy. It isn't.

Once the string is finally up—a matter of throwing and throwing and ducking, and "Let *me* try," and gesticulating and cursing and laughing—then Doug's Sock is retrieved from the equipment pack and deployed. The sock is an old, scroungy, once-white garment that was long ago banished from my clothes bag and relegated to other duties. Its main duty is to be balled up to go under the center of the rain fly, where the string is tied snug around it and the entire operation hoisted into the air, anchored at the four corners. There. Done. It will not rain now.

Thoughts turn to food. Dinner and relaxation. For some.

Three of our crew are still working. They have not been setting up tents and rain flies and throwing and ducking. Instead, they have been busy in the kitchen-dining hall. This is the cook crew, which rotates daily and comprises the head cook (a position of significant authority and prestige), the assistant cook, and the gofer, whose job is to do whatever the head cook and assistant cook tell her or him to do. As all trippers eventually occupy each of these positions a number of times on an expedition, no one complains about being the gofer. Much.

On this evening the crew have assembled a fine fire ring with level stones to hold the grate, and the gofer has already been out in the set-aside canoe and gathered water for drinking and cooking. Such water is always gathered safely away from camp, where shoreline impurities are settled out. Firewood has also been gathered and the cook fire is crackling. Tonight I am the head cook. (Some kind soul has set up my tent.) Gail is assistant cook and Bill is gofer. And on this evening the head cook has decided that the primary fare will be fish chowder. Accompanied by pan-fried biscuits. I most always decide that the main course will be fish chowder accompanied by biscuits, as this is my specialty. I am frugal with my specialties. In fact, this is the only one. But experience has taught me that a hot, easily prepared, filling, and (perhaps) delicious entrée seldom goes wrong on a canoe trip. My fish chowder checks all those boxes. And where a number of walleyes might be required for everyone to get a full plate of fillets, just a fish or two is required for chowder. Plus, I simply enjoy making it. I like making biscuits, too, as there is a fine feeling of accomplishment with each one that emerges from the pan, golden brown, ready to be topped with a little butter or jam.

The chowder, on this night composed of instant milk and some thickener, potatoes, onions, peppers, spices, and two walleyes, is bubbling and of appropriate consistency. The biscuits are ready too. Gail has mixed the lemonade and made the dessert—instant pistachio pudding (which nobody really loves but that I have brought along since my first canoe trip, and we don't mess with tradition). Gail, a better cook than I am, often is more creative, for instance having recently made chocolate cake without the use of chocolate or cake or an oven. (Well, a couple of chocolate bars were pilfered from the lunch pack.) She wrapped the strange concoction in foil and buried it underground, under the coals. When it came out, it was sort of like chocolate cake. I was impressed. Tonight, the pistachio pudding is cooled and set. The dinner bell (spoon on a tin plate) is sounded, with what dignity and ritual can be summoned. It does not take long for the bell to be answered. From whatever secret spaces or shoreline overlooks or tucked-away tents campers might have disappeared to, they now reappear. Looking gaunt. Desperate. Famished. Plates and bowls are held out, plaintively but politely, as much as possible with deference to the needs and sensibilities of others. Chowder is ladled out, biscuits provided. Folks pour their own lemonade. And now stillness descends on the camp and on all the vast North Woods, with only the grinding of molars and occasional soft sighs of gustatorial contentment disturbing the silence of the wilderness.

EVENTUALLY, the first desperate pangs of hunger are satisfied, and as seconds are scooped out, and maybe thirds, conversation reappears between mouthfuls. The level of chowder in the pot steadily falls until, with Bill's final assistance, there is none left at all. A few biscuits remain, which will be saved for tomorrow. Pistachio pudding is served. And now it is time for the evening ritual, in which the insipid lemonade is enlivened with Special Ingredient. Cups are lined up on an overturned canoe in a perfect row, all the handles turned in the same direction. The sun sets low behind the cups, creating a picturesque tableau. With great care and the skill that comes with years of experience, Jim measures into each cup just the prescribed amount of the coveted elixir, then adds the yellow powdered drink mix. Again, quiet descends. There is often a short toast, folks raising their cups to a difficult rapid well run, or a long portage well trod. On this evening we simply toast the lake, a lovely gathering of waters where the river we are traveling pauses and rests before exiting in a short millrace, continuing its journey to Hudson Bay. Here we too have paused and made our home for the night.

Dishes are gathered up and done, a project in which the head cook, by dint of being the head cook, does not participate. Instead, with my work finished, I wander down the shoreline to a comfortable-looking boulder and light up my corncob pipe. I like the vanilla-tinged aroma of the tobacco. I like that the pipe is cheap and Huckleberry Finn–ish. I like smoking it at dusk. And I like that puffing on it keeps mosquitoes at bay. On this night there seem to be no mosquitoes. I light up anyway. Jim strolls down to the water's edge with his own pipe going, smoky tendrils rising in the still air. He carries his spinning rod tipped with a Five of Diamonds Dardevle. He will cast awhile in hopes of hooking another walleye or perhaps a pike. But we really don't need the fish, and I suspect Jim's real motivation is simply to enjoy some private moments and gaze at the sunset.

Back up the shore, the clink of pots and pans and dishes has finally ceased, and packs are being stuffed and stowed. Eventually I wander back that way and find the crew all gathered there, warm sweaters on against the evening chill, staring into the fire. With dinner done, the flames now lick up the sides of fair-sized logs, of no use for cooking but perfect for fire gazing. As minutes pass, the soft tones of idle conversation combine with the crackling fire and the flute notes of white-throated sparrows to form a sort of auditory sedative, although falling asleep is seldom a problem after traveling over the Earth for fourteen hours under your own power.

Eventually the lights of the night sky begin to flicker to life, with Venus dangling just above the pines on the far shore. The sky above gradually darkens, the constellations appearing star by star. It is quite satisfactory to be on our rocky ledge, a part of the great Canadian Shield, looking up at them. It is satisfactory to sit by a warm fire on a cool evening, to smell the woodsmoke, to listen to the fire, to ponder the day just lived, and to think about the one to come.

After a while, someone gets up quietly and heads for a tent. Then someone else. There are soft good-nights and the sounds of zippers opening and closing. By the dying fire, Jim and I pull out the maps, whisper for a few moments about tomorrow's route, then stare for another minute or two at the flames. Finally, the fire is doused and we too make for our mossy beds. In a few minutes all that can heard in camp is the gentle, rhythmic cadenza of snoring wafting between the balsam firs and the tents.

It's a good camp. Probably the best one in all the North Woods. At least until tomorrow night.

IF YOU'RE GONNA BE DUMB

Every time I do something stupid, or painful, it comes to mind.

I have a great friend and golfing buddy named Carroll. He is a good golfer but not quite as good as he thinks he is, which is still better than I am, which is annoying. But Carroll is a wonderful guy and fun to be around, so I put up with it. And once or twice a summer I may beat him for four or six or nine holes—a cause for much celebration and a beer and enough false hope to keep me golfing.

In any case, the golfing isn't really the main deal: it's just a handy excuse to hang out together. And in the course of hanging out there is much banter and storytelling and teasing and trash talking (which I am better at than Carroll, which somewhat makes up for the golfing part). It is quite amazing how many different jokes and stories two guys who see each other so often can come up with without repeating. Hardly. One time Carroll told me a little story that has stuck with me ever since.

We were standing over a putt. Or a drive. Or a 7 iron from the fairway. Or something. I'm not really sure what. And one of us did something dumb. Maybe a swing and a miss. Or a slice. But more likely something that involved physical pain. A shank off one of our shins perhaps. And Carroll said these memorable words: "If you're gonna be dumb, you gotta be tough." Stopped me in my tracks.

"What?" I said, laughing. (Carroll and I laugh a lot.)

"If you're gonna be dumb, you gotta be tough," Carroll repeated.

"Did you just make that up?" I asked, still laughing.

"No, my dad told me that one time when I was growing up, and I was getting taller [Carroll is about six feet two], and I came down the basement stairs and banged my head on a beam, and that's what my dad said to me. 'If you're gonna be dumb, you gotta be tough.' I've always remembered it."

"Well, now I'm going to remember it, too—that's a great saying!" I chuckled. And I've kept my word. I've remembered it ever since.

I AM FOND OF SAYINGS and quips and aphorisms, especially ones that are useful and help me to make some practical sense of a confusing world. And I found that Carroll's saying—that is, his dad's—is endlessly useful. Every time I do something stupid, or painful, it comes to mind. So obviously it comes to mind a lot. It reminds me to toughen up and not complain. It reminds me of another similar favorite saying of Dorothy Molter, the famous Boundary Waters Root Beer Lady, who lived for fifty-six years on an island in the border country and who loved to say to someone who needed to hear it, "Quitcherbellyachin." A profound, one-word reminder to suck it up, tough it out, and move along with whatever needs to be done. A fine saying, especially in the wilderness.

Another favorite of mine and Canoe Country old-timers: "No matter how cold and wet you are, you're always warm and dry." There is a whole wilderness philosophy contained in those thirteen words. Grit. The fortitude to carry on. The concept of mind over matter. The reminder that attitude is everything. And the knowledge that whatever the inconvenience, it is just temporary. As long as you survive.

But getting back to Carroll's particular saying, I have found it to be useful in more ways than the obvious one. I have learned that by occasionally replacing *dumb* with another word, the saying becomes endlessly adaptable, and even more useful. *Dumb* is plenty useful by itself, of course, but as in the case of a good socket wrench set, it never hurts to have other fittings. And the fitting I like best and have found most useful is *sensitive.* As in, "If you're gonna be sensitive, you gotta be tough." Or you could perhaps substitute *tender.* Or *caring.* Or *sentimental.*

You see, some of us in this world are of a personality type psychologists label *highly sensitive,* as in, "She is a highly sensitive person." This is not just an offhand observation or insult but instead refers to a specific way of being—of seeing, experiencing, and interacting with the world. It can cause a sunset to be an occasion for tears, or a particular piece of music to lay us out on the floor, or the song of a cardinal to cheer us up for half a day. Psychological literature says that such a highly sensitive person (HSP) may have an increased or deeper central nervous system response to physical, emotional, or social stimuli. Let's see . . . Check. Check. Check.

As in the case of all psychological models, it's important to remember that it's, well, a model. Not a box in which to fit but a way of understanding oneself and those around you. There are many such models, from the traditional medicine wheel or mandala to modern psychological profiles like the Myers-Briggs Type Indicator. When I took the Myers-Briggs almost forty years ago, I found that I was located very strongly in a quite small percentage of the population labeled INFP, which stands for introverted, intuitive, feeling, and perceiving. Such folks are often idealistic, creative, artistic, shy but good communicators, strongly principled but loathe to engage in personal confrontation. They can often have difficulty getting on in life, until they get their bearings. It was helpful to know that there were others like me, although not a whole lot. When I learned that some of the people supposedly like me were William Shakespeare, Antoine de Saint-Exupéry, J. R. R. Tolkien, A. A. Milne, Helen Keller, Albert Schweitzer, Fred Rogers, and other personal heroes, it helped even more. Someone even added Joan of Arc and Sir Lancelot to the list. Well, geez, sign me up!

Again, it's just a model, someone's best attempt to categorize and make sense of the wide variety of human behavior. When Kathy brought home from her beginning-of-the-year teacher workshops some information on another model about learning styles, I was again interested and found that four descriptors—abstract, concrete, random, and sequential—can be combined in various ways to explain how kids (and adults) learn stuff. Or don't. It was remarkably unsurprising to learn that I was abstract-random. Certainly not concrete-sequential. I didn't even have to be told the definitions. I was reminded of that time long ago when I was told I always had both feet firmly planted in midair. Well, yeah. Where else would you put them? Of course, this was long before I became stable, grounded, organized, and all squared away. Pretty much.

ANYWAY, we have these people who are considered highly sensitive. Not much doubt that I'm firmly ensconced there. Maybe you are too. We occasionally have difficulties, you and I, dealing with the vagaries of life.

If you are the type of person who gets a tear in the eye at the sight of a noble old tree clinging to its last speck of life; who listens to birdsongs and hears notes from heaven; who sees every fresh dawn as an awakening as pure and symbolic as the first morn; or who cannot pass by a flower without stooping to smell it, then you, my friend, have a problem. If you are a person who cares about prairie bluestem and meadowlarks and redwoods, about rainforests and pollinators, who is concerned with whales and green sea turtles and leatherbacks, exploited wilderness areas and coral reefs and glaciers and climate change, and who worries about our grandchildren and our grandchildren's grandchildren, then you are doomed. Absolutely doomed—against all the yahoos, fools, nincompoops, and ignoramuses of this world, who are many and who are often in power, and for whom such concerns are merest rumors. Or frauds. Or mean nothing at all.

You are doomed, that is, unless along with being gentle and caring and sensitive you can also learn to be tough. Tough enough to keep your balance, at least part of the time. Tough enough to get back up when you get knocked down. Tough enough to use those sensitive powers of perception to recognize the yahoos and fools for exactly who they are and deal with them accordingly. And not give in and not give up, no matter how many tears are shed or sleepless nights are endured or blood pressure meds are required. Tough enough to buckle up and help defend the things you love. And those grandchildren's grandchildren.

How do you do that? I don't know. I'm still working on it. Every day. I read somewhere once that it helps to be only a part-time fanatic. To set aside moments or days when you consciously say, "No, this is not the time to think about that. Not the time to mourn whatever it is I'm sad about. I will appreciate what is in front of me. I will engage with this hour, this cup of coffee, this rose blossom, this grandchild. I will appreciate my life." It helps to have interests (at least a few) unrelated to your causes. Bridge or chess or gardening or painting. It helps to read about other times when people had other challenges—terrible challenges—and fought their way through them. Which is, of course, virtually all the times that human beings have lived on the Earth. It helps to find inspiration in other creatures who also face obstacles and difficulties in their daily existence. Which is, of course, all creatures. It helps to not let yourself become isolated (no easy task for sensitive people) but to remain connected to the world around you in many ways, and to a circle of friends and family who support you in hours of need. It helps to look at the stars at night and find perspective in the scale of the universe, or to put your hand on a boulder and try to imagine what it means to be two and a half billion years old. Physical exercise is helpful—the flood of endorphins released as worries of the mind are temporarily lost in the exertions and sensations of the body, as the challenges of one more step, one more lap, one more weight, one more mile are accepted and accomplished. Maybe it helps to take baths in pickle brine, or to walk barefoot across hot coals, or lay down on a bed of nails, or brush your teeth with sand. Though to be honest, I haven't tried any of those therapies.

But the other things help. Sometimes a lot.

It also helps to laugh. Laughter is an antidote to sadness, an inoculation against defeat, and a preventative of despair. So I go golfing with Carroll. And sometimes we hit the ball out of bounds or into a pond. And we tell stupid jokes. And we laugh at our mistakes and our bad putts. Especially when it's the other guy, but sometimes at ourselves. And sometimes—accidentally—someone says something smart. And useful. Like, "If you're gonna be dumb, you gotta be tough."

THE ARROWHEAD MAKER, THE TIGER, AND ME

And the saber-tooth tiger . . . is sneaking around, closer and closer.

I was visiting a school. It had been quite a while, with pandemic restrictions and attendant complications, and it was good to be back among students and teachers once more. As always, I sang a song or two, told some stories, shared my books, and talked about caring for the Earth. As I often do, I also talked a bit about my hard times in school—about being an ADHD child and adult.

After speaking about my difficulties in learning to read, and my special teacher, Miss Little (about whom I wrote a children's book, *Miss Little's Gift*), I also took time for a little aside. I said, as I often do with school audiences, that I have some trouble with one of the words that ADHD (Attention Deficit Hyperactivity Disorder) stands for. I asked the kids to guess which one. They successfully guessed *disorder.* I asked them, "If I have brown hair and someone else has blond hair, does one of us have a disorder?" Shaking heads and murmurs of "No."

"Well, what about brown eyes or blue eyes, or short or tall, or white skin or brown skin or black skin?" More shaking heads. A few louder "No"s.

I went on. "So bodies can be different, and that's okay. Right? Well, maybe brains can be different too?" I noticed a little girl in the fifth row of the gym bleachers, maybe a fifth grader, with her face in her hands. "There are many things," I said, "that ADHD people seem to be actually better at than regular people. We may have trouble sitting still for very long, we may have trouble concentrating or focusing on just one thing. Instead, we focus on lots of things—we notice *everything*! We may have a bit of a problem following directions or behaving ourselves—my wife Kathy says I still don't know how to behave myself." (The little girl looked up from her hands, tears on her face, a slight smile. A friend next to her put an arm around her shoulders.) "But we can be very creative. And energetic. Often we're artistic. We can see the big picture instead of the small one. We can put things together in new ways, ways that there might not be any directions for. We can be explorers. We can find new and unexpected pathways in life. We can be very successful!"

"Do you know that I have written thirty-eight books?" I asked. "That I play the guitar and banjo and mandolin and violin and piano? That I travel and give talks all over the country? And that I draw illustrations and do artwork and lead wilderness trips and paddle canoes and ride a motorcycle and have an island and . . . well, do you know *why* I do all of this stuff?"

Wide eyes, shaking heads.

"It's *because* I have ADHD, that's why!" Laughter. "I can't just sit still in one place and do just one thing!"

"Now I have a little story for you, okay? About a disorder. I've thought about this ADHD stuff a lot. And sometimes I wonder: what if I had been born in a different time and place? What if I had been born in the time of the cavemen? Which seems like a long time ago but really wasn't. And do you know one of the things that cavemen and women didn't have to do? Sit still indoors at a desk for eight hours—that's what! But anyway, we are back in the time of the cavemen and women, okay? And our little group—our clan—is sitting around the campfire one night. And there is a very important member of our group, someone who *is* good at sitting still and concentrating on just one thing. Is that me?" (More shaking heads. Laughter.) "Of course not! But it can be useful and important and a very good way to be. And there is someone in our group who is so good at it—sitting still and concentrating—that we have put that person in charge of a very important job, making arrowheads. Because we are a hunting clan, and if we don't have arrowheads that fly straight and hit their mark, we might starve.

"So one night we are sitting around the campfire, and the arrowhead maker is making arrowheads, chipping and chipping away, concentrating very hard. And meanwhile, sneaking around the camp, in the brush, is . . . a saber-tooth tiger! And it is very hungry. (Because they always are.) And it is sneaking around, closer and closer. Now, think: is the arrowhead maker, concentrating so hard, going to notice the saber-tooth tiger?"

Many shaking heads. Concerned looks.

"But am I going to notice the saber-tooth tiger?"

Vigorous nodding heads.

"Of course! Because I notice *everything*—right?! Now think real hard again: which of us is going to get eaten by the saber-tooth tiger? Me? Or (pointing to my left) *that* guy, the arrowhead maker??"

Laughter. Many shouts. "*That* guy!"

"Right!" I say. "So *now* who has the disorder?"

Crazy laughter.

"I'd say getting eaten by a tiger is a pretty bad disorder, wouldn't you??"

And the little girl in the fifth row looked up, tears streaming, a broad smile, shoulders shaking, the girl next to her hugging her. And I thought: in that moment, that little girl is worth every stupid little thing I might screw up at, or forget to do, or get backwards or upside down or misread the directions for . . . for a good long time. And that she, and maybe some others, just might remember this.

And I thought maybe there's a reason we ADHD people have survived and are still around, contributing to school classrooms. And communities. And the gene pool. Still telling stories and sitting around campfires. And still dodging saber-tooth tigers.

A VALLEY OF LIGHT

Tramping the Hills with the Holy Trinity

What we did see I will never forget. Hovering over the valley floor was a golden blanket, throbbing, blinking, glowing, challenging the infinite dark depths of the universe.

John Muir would be the last to arrive. Henry David Thoreau, Aldo Leopold, and I were already there—had been getting acquainted, sharing a beer or two, and swapping stories. I'll admit it was a bit intimidating, sitting on the front porch with these legends, these giants of American conservation. Immortals, literally. But they made me feel at home, as if I might have something of value to offer as well. Maybe.

The front porch was attached to a grand old three-story house in a tiny town in the back-country hills of Missouri. It had been a long trip, and my journey from Minnesota had been shorter than had Henry's from Massachusetts or maybe Aldo's from Wisconsin. Not to mention the time factor involved. For you see, Aldo had died fighting a grass fire in 1948, and Henry had last drawn breath in 1862. Still, both seemed in good health and good spirits on this summer evening. I wondered about Henry in the June Missouri heat, in his high lace-up shoes, wool trousers, long sleeves, and vest. But he seemed untroubled, and the cold beer undoubtedly helped.

As John had still not arrived and the hour was growing late, we decided to choose up rooms. In fact, it turned out Henry and Aldo had already picked a couple, so I was left to choose between a small one—quite lovely with a single twin bed and a wash basin on a stand—and a large, glorious space with a queen bed and windows facing the morning sun. And a private bath. I thought hard about it and decided that John Muir was used to sleeping in a pup tent on the granite ledges of the High Sierras and would probably be just fine with the smaller room. I took the big one with the windows and the bath. I felt kind of bad about it for a few minutes, but not bad enough to change my mind.

It wasn't much longer when we heard sounds from down below, and the three of us traipsed down the long, elegant staircase to find John of the Mountains, with his long beard, walking staff, and gear, just arrived from California. His eyes twinkled merrily, and a wry smile peeked from behind the white whiskers. But it was quickly apparent that after his long journey John was more interested in sleep than in either beer or conversation. (Again, added to the distance was the time factor: John had last walked the Earth in 1914.) So we showed him to his small room—which I still felt kind of bad about—and off to bed we went. It was not easy to go to sleep. I could hardly wait for tomorrow to arrive, to head out into the Missouri hinterlands and spend the entire day, an entire weekend in fact, tramping the hills with the Holy Trinity of American conservation—Muir, Thoreau, and Leopold.

Wow.

Such opportunities do not come along frequently—as in, never. But this one had arrived in the form of an email. How would I like to come to rural Missouri to host and emcee a series of programs featuring Muir, Thoreau, and Leopold? Would I please consider the idea of introducing each of these revered gentlemen, telling something about who they were and what their important legacies meant, the context of their times, and along the way add a few relevant songs or stories of my own? The audience would consist of environmental and conservation-minded citizens from across Missouri and far beyond, brought together by the once-in-forever chance to see and hear these legendary icons altogether, in the flesh. Or as close as possible.

The fact of their deaths obviously made such an encounter more difficult. This small problem was to be surmounted by the portrayal of each man by a professional actor/reenactor—each of whom has largely dedicated their lives to presenting these icons as authentically as possible, virtually inhabiting their personalities, and returning them to life. Well, how does one say no to an invitation like that? It is not an everyday thing—the chance to spend abundant, unhurried time with lifelong heroes you thought you'd never meet. Particularly if they are deceased.

I had personally known Sigurd Olson, another giant of the environmental movement. Had thrilled at the chance as a young man to visit him at his home, to sit in his writing shack, and to soak up the pipe smoke, the stories, the ambience, the whole feeling of being there with the man who had so greatly inspired me. This would be as close as I would ever get to having the same experience with figures who had similarly inspired Olson. And me and millions of others. Yes, I would definitely be going to Missouri.

So it was that I now found myself trying to fall asleep in the big bed in the big room, with the east-facing windows and the private bath, while John Muir slept in the small guest room nearby, with Thoreau and Leopold occupying similar spaces just across the hall. The whole thing kind of gave me the shivers.

As I lay there feeling shivery and excited, and still a little guilty about the room, and completely unable to sleep, I thought about what I knew about these historic figures, these larger-than-life fountainheads of American conservation and environmental ethics. I knew the basics, that they were different men of different times, despite remarkably similar ways of thinking and feeling about the natural world. These ways of thinking and feeling were unusual—even radical—for their times but would eventually help to transform an entire national ethos, from one of nearly unadulterated materialism and exploitation to at least the dawning understanding and appreciation for wild and natural things, and finally sustained efforts to preserve them.

Henry David Thoreau (correctly pronounced THOR-oh) was first in the lineage. A resident of Concord, Massachusetts, he was famed for having abandoned all the comforts, norms, company, and social conventions of his time (most of them, at least) to live alone in the woods beside a small lake called Walden Pond. He lived in a tiny cottage he built himself, kept scrupulous track of all the natural phenomena he observed, and created a timeless, lyrical, and deeply insightful book titled *Walden.* Within its covers he plumbed his own thoughts, feelings, and personal philosophy on subjects like Economy, Beanfields, Solitude, Higher Laws, and the Pond itself. Thoreau moved to Walden Pond for a total of two years, two months, and two days, famously saying that he went to the woods because he "wished to live life deliberately," and deploring the fact that "the mass of men lead lives of quiet desperation."

He was not a great literary success in his lifetime; it took five years to sell two thousand copies of *Walden,* and he once remarked, as he lived among stacks of unsold books, that he had a personal library "of nearly nine hundred volumes, over seven hundred of which I have written myself." But his little book—deep and thoughtful, but also laced with wit and humor—eventually became recognized as a classic of American literature and for 170 years has been a touchstone for those interested in nature, philosophy, and self-reliance. I first read *Walden* in junior high and had always thought Henry David would be one of those fascinating folks that people have in mind when they ask, "What historical figure would you like to have dinner with?"

For this weekend in Missouri, Thoreau would be brought to life by a man named Richard Smith. Richard was a fascinating character himself—a former punk rocker who developed a keen interest in history, literature, philosophy, and Henry David Thoreau. An interest so deep and encompassing that eighteen years earlier it had caused him to move permanently to Concord to follow his passion. Since then, he had become widely recognized as a genuine authority—writing about, speaking about, but mostly *being* Thoreau, not only for the Thoreau Society at Walden Pond and in the Concord area but across the country. With his short stature, shock of black hair, woolen clothes, and a knack for speaking in the more formal style and cadences of the nineteenth century (along with a rapier wit), he had already given me the eerie sense that I was actually meeting Thoreau. Or at least the ghost of.

JOHN MUIR WAS A SCOTSMAN, born in Dunbar, who as a young lad fell in love with the East Lothian coastline and countryside. When he was eleven, his family emigrated to America, settling in Wisconsin. His father was a harsh and strictly religious man, and young John rebelled early and often against such strictures, fleeing into the outdoor world for escape. But he remained deeply spiritual throughout his life and wrote of the world of Nature with near biblical transcendence. As a young man, Muir studied at the University of Wisconsin and had his first formal lessons in botany, which "sent [me] flying into the woods and meadows in wild enthusiasm." He never graduated but took an eclectic course of study including botany, geology, and chemistry, a foundation of knowledge that served him well in his lifelong pursuits.

As a young man, Muir lost his sight for six weeks due to an accident in a factory. He was unsure he would ever regain his vision, and when he did he resolved to refocus his life, devoting himself to studying and glorying in wild nature wherever it could be found. In one of my favorite scenes from his life, when challenged by a skeptic about his rather unconventional lifestyle, Muir responded by quoting Christ's injunction to "consider the lilies of the field," saying that he indeed intended to spend the rest of his life "considering" them. His considerations took him on a thousand-mile walk from Kentucky to Florida; on to California where he fell in love with the High Sierras and near single-handedly conceived of and saved Yosemite National Park; to Alaska, where he thrilled to the mountains and the glaciers (which he presciently theorized had carved his beloved Yosemite); and to innumerable other wild and beautiful places. He wrote lyrical books and countless magazine articles, founded the Sierra Club, and became in many ways the iconic prophet of environmentalism and wilderness preservation.

For our purposes, John of the Mountains would be inhabited by an engaging, twinkling-eyed fellow named Lee Stetson. With those bright eyes and a ready grin emerging from behind his Muir-like whiskers—along with a thick Scottish brogue he could fall into at the drop of a hat and an encyclopedic knowledge of all things Muir—Lee seemed like the very embodiment of the man. So much so that he had performed as Muir for thirty-four years at Yosemite National Park for audiences totaling hundreds of thousands, had traveled the country and the world in character, and had been featured as Muir's historical scholar and voice in the acclaimed Ken Burns PBS series *The National Parks: America's Best Idea.* Again, it would feel to me throughout the weekend, especially when Lee was talking and gesticulating with impassioned enthusiasm, that I was literally spending time with John Muir.

THE THIRD MEMBER of our trinity was Aldo Leopold. Born in Burlington, Iowa, young Aldo, like Muir, was drawn to nature from his earliest years, exploring the woods and hills of the Mississippi River valley. With a happier childhood than Muir, Aldo was taught hunting and woods lore by his father and took to such pursuits enthusiastically, while also avidly conducting his own studies of birds and wildlife all around his home. An excellent student with a keen mind, Leopold went on to study forestry at Yale and upon graduation was sent by the U.S. Forest Service to the Arizona and New Mexico territory. While there, he was tasked with predator control, among other things. It was upon shooting a wolf and watching a "fierce, green fire" die within its eyes that his personal philosophy and attitude began a gradual but profound shift toward what he would eventually term a *land ethic,* in which human beings are not in charge with rightful dominion over all but are instead a responsible part of something he called a *biotic community.* In describing his ethic within this context, Leopold said, "A thing is right when it tends to preserve the integrity, stability, and beauty of the biotic community. It is wrong when it tends otherwise."

Leopold eventually moved with his family to Wisconsin, taught at the University of Wisconsin, and bought eighty acres of cutover, ravaged land in central Wisconsin's sand country. He spent the rest of his life restoring it. He built a little shack out of odds and ends and flotsam from the nearby Wisconsin River. He and his family would stay there on overnight adventures, and Leopold wrote about the entire experience in one of the most moving, important books in the history of American nature writing, *A Sand County Almanac.* With a gift for writing memorably in plain, clear language, Aldo Leopold produced what became an environmental bible for the twentieth century. He died fighting a springtime grassfire near his land, and his book was published a year later, in 1949. It sold in very modest numbers until thirty years later, when as a paperback it rocketed to prominence in the newly energized environmental movement and became recognized as the timeless classic that it is.

Aldo Leopold would be portrayed on this weekend by a slender fellow, thoughtful and sensitive, with khaki shirt and pants, fedora, and a pair of round, gold-rimmed glasses just like Leopold's, from which he peered at the world with a keen but kind interest. His name was Jim Pfitzer. As a young man, a friend who knew his heart had told him about *A Sand County Almanac* and said that he needed to read it. Jim bought a copy and began reading it and decades later had essentially never put it down. It spoke to him that deeply. He contacted the Aldo Leopold Foundation about his desire to present programs and bring the great ecologist back to life, and he received their blessing and assistance. Though from the South and not Leopold's Upper Midwest, and without any recordings of Aldo's voice to listen to, Jim had worked on getting a flat midwestern tone and the cadences apparent from Leopold's writing. As I would learn, when he became Leopold and stepped onstage, he could mesmerize an audience.

These were the men—historical figures of inspiration and

mythology who had profoundly shaped much of my own thinking, with whom I was to spend some time, through their alter egos. But it was not the chance to learn more facts about them that excited me, that kept me awake that first night. It was the opportunity to meet the personalities themselves, to soak up the intangibles—tone of voice, cock of eyebrow, body language, attitude, offhand remarks, and illuminating asides—that filled me with anticipation. Tomorrow would be a great day. And it was getting closer by the minute. Time to get some sleep.

MORNING DAWNED bright and blue and warm in the hill country of Missouri, and after breakfast we were on our way, the Holy Trinity and I, to the farm where everything would take place. Prairie Star Farm was in reality more nature preserve than farm, restored and renewed from its prosaic, utilitarian days into a gorgeous place where the only crops were wildflowers, tall grass, and woods. This labor of love had been accomplished by conservationists Bruce and Jan Sassman, after Bruce inherited the property from his father. Bruce was the mastermind behind the whole idea of the Holy Trinity conference, and it was the Sassmans' lovely house in town where "the boys" and I were staying. In order to accommodate visitors to the farm and highlight his environmental message, Bruce had built exact replicas of Aldo Leopold's Sand County shack and Thoreau's Walden Pond cottage, widely spaced on the property. And up on a wooded hilltop, as near as Bruce could come to a mountain, was a beautiful, heavy-duty walled tent to represent Muir's dwelling.

Touring the property with Bruce, getting a feel for the rolling landscape, we stopped in at each abode. Thoreau's cottage, neat and tidy and trim, gave the feeling not of a replica but of the genuine article, a place—the place—where Henry David would have felt right at home. Over the course of the weekend, Richard/Henry would spend the bulk of his time at the cottage, greeting the visitors who wandered the farm, with his best efforts at, umm, hospitality. At one point, he could be overheard describing his visiting and seating arrangements, saying, "I have three chairs—one for solitude, two for society, and three for friendship." A curious woman who had been plying him with questions asked, "Did you have many visitors at Walden Pond, Mr. Thoreau?" He didn't miss a beat. "Ahh—too many!"

Jim/Aldo's home for the weekend would be his iconic shack. Having visited the real place in Wisconsin several times, I was stunned at the authenticity. I suspect Aldo would have been as well. In fact, Jim later told me that on first beholding it and walking inside, he had been moved to tears. Visitors to the shack this weekend would meet Mr. Leopold, in his khakis and round-rimmed glasses, discussing his philosophy and land ethic, and just telling stories about happy times at the rustic property, his family's getaway for relaxation, research, and (mostly) hard work. As I stopped by later that day, I heard him explain to a gathering: "You know, the Wisconsin River down here can rush quite high in the springtime, and all manner of things come washing down-river. And that's how we built a lot of the shack—the things that washed down the river and we could salvage."

Finally, there was John Muir's tent on the mountain-hilltop. Without the feeling of permanence of the other two dwellings, it nonetheless seemed perfect—a woodsy retreat, welcoming and homey yet reflecting Muir's peripatetic, forever hiking, always on the move personality. It was clear that Lee/John felt perfectly comfortable there. I stopped by at one point to hear him waxing at length, in his Scottish brogue, about his great friend, President Roosevelt: "Ahh, good, good Teddy. I'd never before had a more interesting, hearty, or manly companion. I fairly fell in love with him! And during our three-day camping trip up in Yosemite, I stuffed him pretty well full of stories about timber thieves and spoilers of the forest." His listeners sat under the shade of the trees in rapt attention.

Meanwhile, back at the entrance to the farm, where the Sassmans had their home, there were plentiful outdoor tables and chairs, booths, and refreshments. There was also a fine old barn, and for the weekend a large and sturdy Chautauqua-style open-walled tent, as from a century or two earlier, where the five hundred or so guests would gather for the evening programs. These programs were to be the highlight of the experience as, in the gloaming with frogs and crickets singing from the pond and the tall grass, and whippoorwills calling from the hillsides, everyone would gather to hear emissaries from another time.

As each man took the stage, after I spoke a bit about them and formally introduced them, a hush would fall over the crowd. What would he say? How would he sound? What would he really be like? In order of time, Thoreau came first. In his wool trousers, vest, bow tie, well-formed, broad-brimmed straw hat, and a rather formal demeanor, Henry David began to speak. He was intense, his speech clipped and direct. Overall, he gave the impression of a rather prickly individual, not likely to suffer fools gladly. He acknowledged that he indeed was seldom found so far from home and his customary seclusion and allowed as how he "certainly never visited 'the territories.'" He hoped that his presentation "would not prove to be too transcendental for the ruffians" before whom he now found himself. Said ruffians took it all with good humor. Henry spoke of arising each morning with the goal of making his life "of equal simplicity, and I may say, and innocence, with Nature herself. I have been," he said, "as serene a worshiper of Aurora as the Greeks. I got up early and bathed in the pond. That was a religious exercise."

But it was when Henry set aside his prepared remarks and responded off the cuff to questions from a curious and delighted audience that his personality, attitude, and eccentricity really shone through. Time and again he had the audience laughing out loud at some clever, unexpected, or not entirely housebroken response. (Richard later told me that for authenticity he indeed tries to respond in Thoreau's actual words or to paraphrase as closely as possible.) When a woman asked in perfect innocence if he had ever married, Henry drew himself up in indignation and huffed, "Certainly not!"

At another point, he expressed surprise, although not necessarily disapproval, to find so many women in the audience and that they had actually read his books (at Henry's time considered "men's literature"). This was all done with humor and wit, but when I later asked Richard about the comment, he said it truly was uncommon in the early nineteenth century for women to attend lectures, and in some places they were even banned from doing so. As it became more accepted in the 1850s, a mixed audience of men and women was still called a "promiscuous audience." In any case, our thoroughly promiscuous group greatly enjoyed Henry and his eccentricities and got a glimpse not only of his philosophy and love for the natural world but of the customs and attitudes of another age. Henry closed with pure inspiration: "If you have built castles in the air, your work need not be lost; that is where they should be. Now put the foundations under them."

NEXT TO TAKE THE STAGE was John Muir. With a warm, engaging personality animated by great enthusiasms, he connected with the audience immediately. It was quickly apparent they felt they were truly meeting John of the Mountains. He moved around the stage energetically, rolling up his sleeves, waving his arms as he recounted "the noble exhilaration of motion" hanging on to a tall treetop in a great storm, "tracing indescribable combinations of vertical and horizontal curves, as I clung like a bobolink on a reed. Oh, happy me!" It was clear that Lee Stetson had found what he called Muir's "eloquent, simple, and lovely truth" and was a master at communicating it to an audience, "helping people understand where we are in the universe" and bringing Muir to life.

There were great joys but also sorrows in that life. At one point Muir addressed them. He detected some surprise, he said, "and perhaps some doubt, that the spirit of old John Muir still wanders upon this good planet. I have heard the rumor that I died—and, they say, long ago!—perhaps of a broken heart, eh? Or a shattered spirit, from the loss of the Hetch-Hetchy Valley that I fought so long and so hard to protect. And I suppose there is some romance attached to the idea of dying of a broken heart . . . . But now, think on it. If we wilderness lovers died every time we lost a place we loved, our species would long ago have gone the way of the dodo bird!" He also sounded a cautionary note but with good humor: "I have no doubt that if all the beautiful wild places were utterly stripped away from us, and there remained only one tree—one tree reserved as the most noble and glorious, eh?—well, it wouldn't be long before you would find a lumberman and a lawyer at the foot of it!"

The audience, by now completely enchanted, laughed along with him. But in their enchantment, they also absorbed a bit of the spirit of old John—deeply in love with life and the natural world, willing to fight for it, and ready to get up in the morning still in love and ready to fight for it all over again.

LAST TO MAKE HIS APPEARANCE would be Aldo Leopold. With a calm, almost studious demeanor, a contrast to Muir's humorous brogue and over-the-top enthusiasm, he appeared in his subdued khakis and wire rims. Knowing that Jim did not have the vast years of experience in performance that Richard and Lee had, I wondered briefly if he could fill the space and hold the audience. Well, that thought was soon dispelled. It was Aldo Leopold himself who took that stage. The University of Wisconsin teacher. The communicator. The writer and thinker. And he spoke with great clarity and deep, if understated, emotion. He talked of his time as a young man in Arizona. He spoke glowingly of a mountain called Escudilla. And he told of the time he and his Forest Service party, tasked with predator control, fired from high on a rimrock into a pack of wolves. "When our rifles were empty," he said, "the old wolf was down, and a pup was dragging a leg into impassable slide-rocks." He paused. Blinked. "We reached the old wolf in time to see a fierce, green fire dying within her eyes. And I realized then . . . and have known ever since . . . that there was something new to me in those eyes—something known only to her and the mountain. But I was young then and full of trigger itch; I thought that because fewer wolves meant more deer, that no wolves would mean hunter's paradise." Leopold paused again. Swallowed hard. "But after seeing the green fire die, I sensed that neither the wolf nor the mountain agreed with such a view."

A sense of pathos hung in the humid air of the big tent. From the darkness outside, the voices of frogs and crickets throbbed—the songs of nature and of wild things. If not for them, you could have heard a pin drop into the soft, green grass. You could have heard the assembled audience breathing. Maybe. Or perhaps they were holding their collective breath. For there was no other sound. No movement. Nothing to destroy the spell. For spell it was. Aldo Leopold was on the stage, calmly commanding the moment. With Henry David Thoreau and John Muir watching from the wings.

The applause eventually came in waves. For Aldo and Jim, for Henry and Richard, for John and Lee. For the entire immersive experience. People stirred and spoke and returned to their own time and place. Part way. But not completely. What they had heard and felt and known that day, that evening, would stay with them. As it has stayed with me.

Later when the guests had said their goodbyes, wiped away their tears, and said their thank-yous, Bruce took us—the Holy Trinity and me—on one more starlight tour of the backwoods farm. Across the meadows we went, fording a stream, climbing up into the hills. Here under the stars in rural Missouri, in mid-America, far from any city, town, or highway, it all seemed fitting. Perfect. Timeless. A fine occasion for Henry, John, and Aldo to come together and gaze into the night sky.

Eventually, we came down from the hills. On emerging from the wooded trail, we entered an open valley and breathed in the rich, damp, earth-perfumed air. The valley was full of prairie wildflowers, but at the midnight hour we could not see the blossoms. What we did see I will never forget. Hovering over the valley floor was a golden blanket, throbbing, blinking, glowing, challenging the infinite dark depths of the universe. They were fireflies, of course—hundreds of thousands, perhaps millions of them, who could say? Certainly far more of the brilliant little beings than I had ever seen in all my life. Standing there with John Muir at my elbow, inhaling the fragrance of the night and absorbing the sight before us, with Thoreau and Leopold to either side, I thought of Muir's beloved mountains—his famous "range of light."

Light comes in many forms, I thought. Internal and external, mental, spiritual, and physical. It can come through the written or spoken word, the flash of a whiskery smile, or the gleam of an impish eye. And it can be found in many places. In the High Sierras. In a shack in Wisconsin or a tiny cottage in New England. Or in a valley—a valley of light—deep within the hills of Missouri. Hills I once had the chance to walk in the company of the Holy Trinity.

THE FIRST AND ONLY NATURALIST-GUIDED MOTORCYCLE TOUR OF NORTHERN MINNESOTA

The road is full of curves. Lean into them.

At least we figured it was. The first and only, that is. If someone else indeed accomplished the feat before, I apologize. But when Bryan and I decided as naturalists to lead a group of nature-minded motorcyclists down the twisty, snaky backroads of the woods and prairies of the northern half of Minnesota, we reckoned it was a new idea. Nor have we heard since of any groups of bird-watching, tree-hugging, flower-sniffing bikers repeating the journey. So on that first day, as we lunched with ravens at Jay Cooke State Park, as we rode the high rocky eminence of Hawk Ridge (the great midcontinent birding landmark), as we wandered up venerable old Highway 61 with balsam breath and lake breezes in our faces and the miles rolling by beneath the wheels—well, I had the feeling of being a kind of pioneer. Sort of.

To be sure, I was not the lead rider or scout—*l'avant,* as the North Woods voyageurs of old would have said. No, I was riding in the sweep position, meaning last. Which is not to say it was not a position of significant honor and esteem. I was, after all, the elder and emeritus guide on the trip. And in the back of the pack, I was responsible—for keeping careful watch, for taking care of any problems or pullouts or mishaps or dawdling that might occur. Although in truth, throughout the journey I was the only dawdler, a fact one of the female members of our party would regularly explain as, "Doug's just having a moment." Again. Meanwhile, Bryan was in the lead, charting the route and setting the pace. As I had taught him to ride only a few years before, helped him stand the bike up after he bumped into a tree by the driveway and fell over, and patiently explained many vital aspects of motorcycling, from tight corners to tar snakes, and still thought of myself as the expert motorcyclist in the family, I was continually surprised—and annoyed—at how quickly he set that pace. How deftly he leaned into the curves and corners. And how hard I had to work to keep up. But more about that later.

That first evening, after taking off in morning fog from Bryan's Osprey Wilds Nature Center near Sandstone in wool sweaters and full leathers, after riding through the pines along old Highway 23 past the Nemadji watershed and putting on a couple hundred miles with stops at Palisade Head, Split Rock, and Gooseberry Falls, we pulled in tired and hungry to a little streamside campsite by the Baptism River. The Baptism is one of those dozens of brooks and small rivers that, brown with tannin, come wandering lazily out of the bogs of the Superior highlands. But their casual attitudes change as they reach the steep North Shore slopes of old Glacial Lake Duluth, whence they all commence a wild race to their ultimate release in the vast blue expanse of Kitchi-Gami. Ours was a primitive camp, with tent sites and pit toilets, a fire ring and table, and hand-pumped spring water. With the stream tumbling and singing, washing over shining stones and gurgling through eddies, it seemed perfect for our purposes—just the right scene to set the tone for a nature-focused expedition. Bryan had chosen well. It was a pattern that would continue for the whole trip, as I would admire how he had picked just the right roads and destinations, overlooks and pullouts, each one an opportunity to connect with a particular facet of Minnesota's kaleidoscopic landscape.

As the stream sang its cheery song, accompanied by evening robins and veery thrushes and chickadees, camp was established.

Bryan's old friend Nick had pulled in with the van carrying extra camping gear and groceries so the riders could travel lightly. Now tents were set up, clotheslines hung between balsam firs and jack pines, with damp sweaters tossed over them. Dinner preparations were begun. It was a familiar and comfortable routine, one I'd repeated numberless times on scores of wilderness canoe trips. But it was also different. Rather than canoes turned over by the water's edge, lying there sleek and prone in the fading light, painter ropes snubbed around trees in case of a nighttime blow, paddles tucked carefully underneath, there were instead motorcycles. Red. Black. Silver. Gold. Shiny. Steel. Latent power and speed implied in every sensuous curve and glint of chrome. Balanced on their kickstands nonchalantly, as if ready to roar to life and hit the road again on a moment's notice. Ready for a rider to throw a leg over the saddle and head for Wyoming. Or Albuquerque. Or Bozeman. Or one of those places. With hardly a thought.

I have long loved the romance of the canoe. Have thrilled to the feel of the paddle, the lift of a hissing comber racing in from behind, or of the bow slicing through on-rushing whitecaps, climbing the slope of a big wave, pausing at the crest for a moment as if poised at the lip of disaster, then sliding down the smooth back side and into the trough, then rising and beginning the process all over again. I have loved the quiet of mist-shrouded mornings and golden evenings, the sense of being embraced by the wilderness and the entire natural world, the canoe and its paddler a part of every aspect of the landscape and the waterscape, the wind and the sky and the weather. I have gloried in the freedom of it all, of a craft so simple and light and versatile that it can be carried on the shoulders from one waterway to the next, can be dropped into new blue waters, and in just moments have its bow set and underway to another horizon, another island, another headland, another campsite. I have marveled at how the same craft can be sent hurtling down the snowy froth of a surging rapid and, with skill and luck, bring the paddler safely through to the eddy pools at the bottom, where with a turn of the head and a look back one can marvel at what has just been accomplished. And I have gazed with feelings of appreciation—no, deep affection—at a canoe, or two or three, tipped over and resting as if in sleep on some glaciated ledge, smooth bellies ghostly in moon-and-starlight, awaiting the rising of the sun and the promise of a new day's journey. There is not very much about a canoe and the waters it is meant to ply that I am not in love with.

But I love things about riding motorcycles as well. I am not the sort who enjoys traveling in a pack, although for this special group I was happily making an exception. And I do enjoy riding with a friend, or sometimes with Bryan. But usually I ride alone. Not particularly fast. The ADHD kid in me loves the feeling of movement—constant motion—while actually sitting motionless, meditatively, just leaning a bit this way and that, twisting the wrist for a little more speed, or less, small motions of the feet for the brake or the clutch, otherwise completely still. Meanwhile, one hurtles through the air, through a constantly changing landscape, a moving, gliding part of it all, vastly different from the cocoon-like automobile, with every scent and aroma accessible, all the surroundings visible, the breezes felt, the wind in the face. And I love the freedom to just throw a leg over the saddle and . . . go.

I once sat down to write out a few of the basics of motorcycling, at least the way I do it. The things one does, or feels, or knows, or learns:

The road is full of curves. Lean into them.
Smell the air.
Breathe the wind.
Feel the sun.
Be a little scared.
Keep your balance.
While riding, talk to yourself. But be interesting.
Take roads less traveled.
Keep your windshield clean.
Keep your bike polished.
Bring a good map.
Wear good boots.
Remember, stopping is as important as going.
Your mother was right—be careful.
But have fun.
Try to look good—it's a kindness to others.
Keep your wheels on the ground.

Make sure the wrench fits the nut.
Don't leave things loose, but don't twist too tight.
Know your bike.
Know yourself.
Expect the unexpected.
There are certain things to be keenly aware of.
They are . . . everything.
And remember—it's all one trip.

So as I lay in the tent that night, listening to the little stream gurgling nearby, I thought of these things. Some of them. For a little while. But the stream sang its insistent lullabye, and before long . . .

IN THE MORNING we were up early in the chill, making breakfast, breaking camp, checking the bikes, donning leathers, packing gear. And then back on the road.

Highway 1 from the North Shore toward Ely is nearly legendary—the gateway for countless wilderness adventurers through the decades, into the wonderland of the Canoe Country. But for a motorcyclist, without canoes on the top rack or pulled in a trailer, it is somehow even more remarkable. Constant rises and falls, twists and turns of the narrow road. Tall white pines looming atop one ridge after another, aspens spangling the hillsides followed by dips and descents into tamarack and black spruce bogs and meandering, beaver-dammed streambeds. All of it somehow close, more real and accessible than in an enclosed car. But Bryan was taking no extra time and setting a swift pace—we had a schedule to keep—and I constantly found myself falling behind as I dawdled momentarily over one wonder or another.

One of the few complaints heard on the trip thus far was of the previous evening's marshmallows. Too glommed together and gooey was the consensus, to make proper s'mores. On any of my own trips I would have ignored such a complaint—in fact, we've never had s'mores on any of my trips. But Bryan, more contemporary and progressive, more kind and thoughtful than his dad, stopped at Zupp's Grocery in Ely to remedy the faulty marshmallow situation. The new and properly floofy confections were tossed into the van. Back onto the road once more. We cruised past the turnoff to Burntside Lake, where my friend Nancy Jo Tubbs runs a family resort, Camp Van Vac, that dates back to the nineteen-teens, and where iconic Listening Point lies tucked into the pines and the rocky shores. But we would not be stopping at Burntside today.

Eventually, as we headed down Highway 169 toward Virginia and the Iron Range, we encountered what would prove to be the only rain of our trip. And it was a hard rain. I've never liked riding in the rain—not for the discomfort so much as for the decrease in perceived safety. Traction is reduced by whatever numeric factor on those two rather than four tires. Goggles or glasses or helmet visors become coated with raindrops or possibly fog, reducing visibility. And because most motorcyclists, like me, do not like riding in the rain and thus avoid it whenever possible, we don't have as much experience dealing with it. But sometimes it is unavoidable, and with no shelter or convenient place to stop we continued on carefully, over slick and sloppy pavement, finally taking refuge under a picnic shelter in Virginia where lunch was consumed, stuff dried out, spirits revived, and the rain thankfully ceased.

So on we went, toward what was for me one of the most anticipated parts of the trip—Northwoods Highway 38 and the Edge of the Wilderness Loop, with our planned stop at Scenic State Park. How I have always loved it there, with three-hundred-year-old white and red pines towering over a 1935 log lodge built by the Civilian Conservation Corps (CCC). Such places always give me a feeling of peace, of perspective and timelessness, and of shared values between the decades. It was there at the park that JoyGenea magically found her husband, Tom, his number-one goal of the trip—a beautiful cluster of showy pink ladyslippers, which Tom had never seen. A nature walk yielded other common miracles and wonders, from wild sarsaparilla to cornhusk lily to bearberry to Canada anemone, and I had the feeling—as I often did in canoe trip guiding—of leading a group through a living poem. Each plant, every tree and shrub, with an evocative name and a story to go with it. We also found and hiked an esker—a onetime upside-down river that flowed through the bottom of a glacier, leaving a winding river *mound* of rock, sand, and gravel rather than a normal river *bed* carved into the earth.

The days and miles, campsites and overlooks kept flowing by. On the bikes it was an opportunity to really soak up and savor the northern Minnesota landscape. And as the miles accumulated, with the roar of the wind and the rumble of the engine, an uninterrupted chance to think. I recalled other rides, particularly a solo ride to the Badlands and Black Hills not long after my dad passed away. How it felt like the whole trip was an extended recollection and conversation. How I felt as though Dad, who had never touched a motorcycle that I knew of and certainly wouldn't approve, was somehow sitting right there with me, seeing, feeling, hearing, experiencing all that I did. That we did. We talked of things we'd never spoken of, subjects never quite broached, and sorted out some difficult stuff. And at the end of the ride, I somehow felt closer to him than I ever had.

And I thought of my own sons: Bryan, who was leading this trip and with whom I had frequent opportunities to share adventures and outdoor experiences; and Eric, whose life had taken a somewhat different path, leading to a home in Florida. Eric too had become an impressive young man, a doctor and author in the field of personal wellness. Though Eric and I hadn't had the chance to share as many outdoor adventures, he seemed in recent years to have become the prime motivator and facilitator for connective family ties and ongoing communications, fascinated with family history. The year before he had dreamed up, planned, organized, and helped Kathy and me take a grand trip to Poland and Germany, her ancestral homelands. A trip we would likely have never taken otherwise. The trip was a great gift to Kathy, rekindling her love for and understanding of grandparents she hadn't seen in decades and great-grandparents before them. And I had the chance to tag along, to share her emotions, and to see parts of old Europe I had only read about, including my one request—a side trip to the great medieval cathedral in Cologne, six hundred years in the making and the largest in Europe.

Now there was a new grandchild in Florida, and Eric was eager that Sofie get to share future outdoor adventures with her granddad in the years to come. A fine thing to look forward to. So as I rode, I thought about these two boys, about their growing skills and abilities and responsibilities. I thought about passing lanes and the passing of torches. I thought how motorcycle trips are not so very different from the Big Trip—the trip of life—with bends and curves, rainstorms and sunrises and unexpected challenges, and with new horizons always approaching. I thought, as I'd often mentioned to canoe trippers on some wild river, that no matter what trip you're on, it's all one trip.

THE MILES and hills and streams kept rolling by. We skirted the shores of big Lake Winnibigoshish and its fertile wild rice beds, on to Lake Bemidji State Park and then my old friend Itasca, where we walked awestruck beneath countless magnificent trees and stood under what was until recently the state's largest white pine. A windstorm had robbed it of some of its height, but it was still overwhelming. Then we leaned our way through glacial moraine country, down some of the windingest, snakeiest, twistiest two-lane roads I ever saw. Fabulous for motorcycling. Once again, Bryan had chosen well.

But once again, I fell a bit behind, more than once. On reaching a gas station I touched Bryan's elbow and guided him around back of the station. I thanked him for his excellent leadership, then said, "You know, Bryan, I don't know when you got to be such a better rider than me—but there are times when I'm having a little trouble keeping up. I think other people might be too." As usual between Bryan and me, one gentle mention was all it took. The pace eased up a bit, and I felt more comfortable. JoyGenea later told me that she and Tom felt the same way as well. We camped that evening in the rolling hills of delightful Maplewood State Park, where loons and coyotes serenaded us through the night.

Next day the cycles took us out onto the prairie, where a Big Wind was blowing as it often does. As we rode our way toward Minnesota's west coast, the bikes danced across the asphalt. We made Lake Traverse and the birth of the Red River of the North, and just south of it Big Stone Lake, and the hauntingly beautiful Big Stone National Wildlife Refuge, where the Minnesota River begins its journey toward the Mississippi. We gazed across the gorgeous prairie landscape, undulating in the wind, and I imagined famed newscaster Eric Sevareid pausing there as a seventeen-year-old boy more than ninety years before on his epic adventure to Hudson Bay, chronicled in his classic book *Canoeing with the Cree.* Here two great rivers began in virtually the same place, flowing in opposite directions—one watershed to Hudson Bay, the other to the Gulf of Mexico. Our journey—our stops and hikes and overlooks—were providing just what we had hoped: a full sense of the sweep and topography, the landscape and history of much of the northern half of the state. A feeling for the land. As I stood there looking at red granite outcrops and boulders, at wetlands and tallgrass prairie in what was once the bed of mighty Glacial River Warren, I had the sense that I so often sought but that could never be predicted or controlled—the sense of somehow being a part of it all. Of the great and timeless story. Watching the others, hands resting on handlebars, eyes cast to the distance, no words spoken, I knew they felt it as well.

Back on the bikes, we battled the prairie wind toward Glacial Lakes State Park to camp beneath its grove of burr oaks on the grassy slopes. When the sun rose, we were on our way once more, this time to Little Falls and Charles Lindbergh's boyhood home by the Mississippi. Then on past a wildly windswept Lake Mille Lacs, where kite surfers were having a field day on the gale-tossed waves. Then back into the eastern Minnesota woodlands through tamaracks and spruces, past marshes filled with redwings, and suddenly, after a week on the road, we were somehow back where we'd begun. At the beautiful nature center under the pines.

As with every trip, with the saying of goodbyes, the packing of gear, it seemed almost impossible that it was done. That the next morning would not bring cowboy coffee, scrambled eggs and bacon cooked over a crackling campfire, and a gathering over maps to discuss the day's route and what our trip might hold in store. But then I remembered: it's all one trip. And I slung my leg over the saddle to head home. Or Bozeman or Laramie or one of those places.

BEETHOVEN IN THE PINES

A log cabin with aged wooden walls, a stone fireplace, and a high ceiling is evidently an excellent acoustic environment.

I took a break from the windfall I had been clearing for an hour. It was tiring, noisy, backbreaking work—lifting, carrying, and stacking heavy logs and running the chainsaw—and I still had many more limbs and trees to clear, the residue of a fierce summer storm.

Pulling off gloves and soundproof earmuffs, I found a stump to sit on—an old mossy favorite I had met long ago and named Dr. Woodrow F. Stump. (The F. stands for Forrest.) Dr. Stump, I had learned, was something of a woodland psychologist, blessed with a special knack for listening, for putting things into perspective, for calming a restless mind, and making life seem a little more manageable—like any good mental health professional. But on this day I didn't really need any counseling or advice. I just needed a stump to sit on. That and a pause from wrestling fifty-pound logs and manhandling a whining, growling, smoking chainsaw.

Sitting there with Dr. Stump, my ears grew accustomed once more to the gentle music of the forest. A soft autumn breeze played its tune high among the pines. A pileated woodpecker laughed uproariously at some private joke from somewhere deep in the woods. A jay shouted its name. A red squirrel scolded. In the interludes all was quiet.

Almost. Gradually, so gradually I barely noticed it at first, I became aware of another tune, another sort of music. It lilted and drifted lyrically among the pines, almost disappearing at times, at others becoming clear enough that I could almost make out the notes, the rhythm, the harmonies. The music seemed familiar. Straining to hear, I finally recognized the tune—Beethoven's "Für Elise."

Beethoven in the pines. Not a bad sound. In fact, a lovely sound, perhaps much the way old Uncle Ludwig, who loved pastoral settings, had meant "Für Elise" to be heard some 220 years earlier, when today's big pines were small seedlings. In the gloom of the forest among the boles of the old trees, the music seemed fitting and appropriate. It was not being played perfectly: there was a small stumble every now and then, a moment's pause to find the right note, then the melody would continue. Clearly, the music was being played by a student—a student, I knew, who was playing a Steinway in a log cabin for a piano lesson.

Music has been a part of my family's life for as long as I have been around and long before that. The two are inseparable. Music. Life. The two so intertwined it was hard to imagine one without the other. I'm sure that some of the earliest sounds I heard—after I was born and maybe even before—were melodies and chords and harmonies.

Because we had two musicians for parents—Dad was a composer, teacher, and choir director; Mother, a pianist, accompanist, and piano instructor—music was in the air my brothers, Bruce and Tom, and I breathed. Coming home from school in the afternoon, we were greeted by the wafting sound of Mozart or Bach on the piano as we walked in the back door, grabbed a chocolate chip cookie, and headed out to play football. Or if the weather was bad, sat down to read a book or watch afternoon cartoons. Piano lessons were being taught, and the cartoons had better not get too loud. Scuffling and roughhousing in the house? Not a chance.

In the evenings we boys had our own piano practice to do, at least as important as homework, probably more so. And often later in the evening we heard from downstairs the rich tones of Dad's baritone voice as he practiced for a concert or a recital, accompanied by Mother. The instrument yielding all of this practicing and teaching and accompanying was a classic 1921 Steinway, my mother's pride and joy. With a shimmering ebony sheen, punctuated by shining black and white keys, it was a presence as real and constant and as much a part of the family as brothers or pets, and certainly not a mere piece of furniture.

When I went off to college to study (music, of course), I fell in love with (who else?) another music student. A talented pianist and singer named Kathy. The prettiest girl in the music department. Smart, too. Too smart to be interested in me. But I persisted for four years and eventually wore her down. After marrying and purchasing a tiny house of our own, Kathy began teaching piano lessons on a small, upright Sohmer—a college graduation gift from her parents—building a large and enthusiastic studio of dozens of students in little Cherokee, Iowa. In a few years we moved to Minnesota, first to Morris out on the western prairie, then to the St. Cloud area, where again she built up large classes of students. Eventually, Kathy changed tracks to teach public school music and did so for about thirty-five years, while also singing and performing in countless community choirs, plays, and musicals. And all this time my mother kept on teaching as well, ceaselessly, racking up what I still assume to be an uncontested world record of seventy-three consecutive years of piano lessons, if anyone keeps records of such things.

A few years ago, Mother, with an aching back and arthritic fingers, reluctantly accepted early retirement at age eighty-nine. She moved to a nearby senior home where she faithfully cheered on the Minnesota Twins. Kathy retired from her school teaching at about the same time. And as we took on the job of clearing Mother's house and helping her to move, the old Steinway, refurbished and refinished and still a gorgeous old dame, called to Kathy. In truth, it had been calling for many years. And it had always been Mother's wish that Kathy would have it. So after working out the financial arrangements, that is exactly what happened.

The upshot is that our small cabin in the woods is now made significantly smaller by the presence of a shimmering, black grand piano in the cabin's great room. There, it is the centerpiece of a going enterprise called the Log Cabin Piano Studio, modestly but appropriately designated by an artistic hand-lettered sign nailed on a pine tree at the end of our long, winding lane. And by a swirling treble clef on the cabin door. The studio is now the site of a lively class of students, all learning scales, triads, theory, Bach, and Mozart. And Beethoven. Taught by Kathy, of course.

After decades of study, teaching, and performance, Kathy finds that the teaching comes easily, from a vast well of knowledge. And going to work no longer involves donning coat and hat and boots and starting a cold car in the dead of winter and dealing with principals and superintendents, but simply greeting a bright young face at the door with a warm smile and saying, “How are you, and how was school today?” Followed by a few short steps to the piano bench. Sometimes, for a special recital day or when the lane becomes a muddy mess or the stone sidewalk to the front door becomes a lake, the caretaker and forester of the estate (me) lends a hand as shuttle driver or wetland manager so that footsteps to the door are not too much of an adventure.

The Steinway doesn't seem to have lost any steps over the years. If anything, it sounds better than ever. A log cabin with aged wooden walls, a stone fireplace, and a high ceiling is evidently an excellent acoustic environment. The kids love the big sound. Our cats, Simon and Koda, don't seem to mind the activity: in fact, they appreciate all the extra attention. And despite the occasional cock of an ear or the twitching of a tail, they are fairly easygoing music critics. Moms and dads often stay for the lessons; they too like listening to music in a log cabin, so they say. And in the warm months, parents and grandparents sometimes migrate outdoors onto the deck, to watch the Father of Waters (the Mississippi River) flow by under the tall pines, to listen to cardinals and chickadees and the music of the woods. They often mention how peaceful it all feels, a small break from the daily rat race.

Mother has passed away now. But we feel her presence and influence every single day. I know Kathy hears it in every note and feels it as she sits with her students at the same keyboard where my mother taught for so many decades.

And I, the forester, in my office adjacent to the studio, working on a new book perhaps, am sometimes transported in time to long-ago days when the same old piano sang from a house on the Iowa prairie. It was a part of the family then. It still is. And the sounds of Bach and Mozart or "Twinkle, Twinkle, Little Star" are a fine and fitting accompaniment to the typing of words on a page.

Sometimes I take my life into my hands and risk a stern look from the Teacher by poking my head in the door and offering an unsolicited comment: "That sounds really good! What piece is that?" Sometimes I quietly stroll through the Log Cabin Studio on my way to the kitchen for a chocolate chip cookie. Just like fifty years ago. And sometimes I just slip outside and sit under an old pine with my friend Dr. Stump, the two of us listening to the pleasant wafting of piano music from a cabin in the woods. Listening to the strains of Beethoven.

The echoes—from cabin walls, from pine trunks, from Iowa, from long ago—are beautiful.

A CHRISTMAS WALK

I tried to comprehend the truth that all we have ever known, all our species has ever been, all the history we've ever written, and all the sacred stories we've ever told have taken place on one infinitesimal speck of dust circling a grain of sand in one galaxy in a thirteen-billion-year-old universe with more grains than are contained on all the beaches and all the deserts of all the world.

It was Christmas Eve, and it was cold. It had been ten below zero in the brilliant sunshine of the short day, with sundogs bracketing a cold and distant orb. It was now thirty below out on the groaning, cracking Mississippi ice near our cabin under the timeless, watchful gaze of Orion. Snowshoeing along that winding white road in the starlight, I followed mink tracks near the shore. And I listened to the silence. I wondered about those burning stars above, the constellations, the same sky pictures that a certain Teacher and his followers had gazed at twenty centuries earlier. The same ones that local shepherds, according to the old tradition, had seen on the night he was born.

I thought about that long-ago night. About the account of a strange and different star somehow brighter than all the rest. About the stories, legends, and lessons I had heard since before I was old enough to listen. About all that we know, or think we know, and all that we wonder at yet today.

We know that approximately 2,023 years ago an infant was born (skeptics who doubt that he ever really existed advance a weak case, with more faith in skepticism than in evidence) likely in a cave-like space under a simple stone dwelling, to an unwed teenaged mother, delivered into poverty in a troubled corner of the world. About thirty-three years later he died, put to death by the powerful, the clergy, and politicians of his day.

Some said the infant was holy; others said the man became holy through prayer and selflessness, through the overcoming of temptation, through exquisite empathy and concern for his fellow human beings. Some have said he performed miracles and feats of magic. Others have said that the real magic, the truest miracle, was the inexplicable way he touched and elevated the souls of those with whom he came in contact—as if their eyes and ears and hearts were opened. Even the mere telling of his story, long after his death, can still have this effect. Although the story is widely known, it is almost certain that the man at the heart of it has been grossly misunderstood through the centuries by billions who have quoted his name. That name was Yeshu or Yeshua, known to most today as Jesus.

People have killed in his name. People have fought wars in his name. People have bought and sold uncounted trillions of dollars' worth of merchandise in his name. People have bought and sold slaves and defended the practice in his name. People have burned crosses in his name. People have been burned at the stake in his name. Genocide has been conducted in his name. People have destroyed Creation in his name. People have hated in his name. And they still do.

People have also taken vows of poverty in his name. People have devoted their lives to the sick and the weak and the poor in his name. People have fought against slavery and exploitation and every form of injustice in his name. People have become brave and merciful and generous, to the point of giving their own lives, in his name. People have found hope and meaning, beauty, love, and salvation in his name; they have fought for the beauty of Creation in his name. And they still do.

What seems clear from these stupendous contradictions is that the mere claiming and reciting of the story and the name lead to no preordained values or attitudes, acts of goodness or compassion. Rather, it is those open eyes, ears, and hearts that are key in trying to truly understand the story and its meaning. It is the story of a person whose very essence came to be understood as goodness, as truth, as courage and mercy and compassion—to the extent that many who saw him and came to know him had the feeling that they were witnessing the very nature of God Himself. They were seeing—and believing—that there was a goodness at the heart of the universe, a light in the heart of darkness that could ultimately triumph over evil, over suffering, even over death.

The need for those open eyes and hearts was often referenced in the Teacher's own stories. Stories like the Good Samaritan, the Adulteress, the Mote in the Eye each illustrated that every listener must first and always look inward and take into account his or her own mind and heart, own weaknesses and flaws. For only in doing so can we determine whether our actions, words, and lives are truly reflective of the revered name so often invoked—or, as is all too often the case, simply demonstrate our own selfishness and pettiness, our all-too-comfortable customs, fears, and prejudices. This is and always has been the case. And it is a difficult thing to attain such a piercing inward view. But that is the space that the Teacher, this Holy One whose birth so many celebrate, always claimed and said he inhabited—the space of the innermost heart and soul, the "Kingdom of Heaven within."

So we retell the old story and try to imagine a time and a world so very different from our own. And yet the same. Christmas is and has always been a time to reflect—on our inner worlds and the greater world we share—now bound together more tightly and seamlessly than ever before. It is a world, as the Teacher taught, in which there is no "them." There is only "us." It seems that the deep, dark dead of winter is a good time, as it has been every winter for two thousand years, to examine that kingdom within in each of us, to ponder the mystery of a humble birth and a single life lived long ago, and of the one great Life we all share. It is a good time to see if we are truly honoring the old, familiar story, and the extraordinary person at the heart of it.

THAT NIGHT ON THE RIVER I thought about these things, wondered and pondered as I have all my life. My mind drifted back to the church pews where I sat for so many Sundays as a child, listening to the choirs my father directed, the reverberation of the timeless hymns, the grand chords my mother played on the pipe organ. To the sermon the minister had chosen for the week. The details of those sermons were now lost to memory, but the feelings and insights were still embedded in my subconscious. I walked on, pondering, listening to the shush-shush of the snowshoes on snow-covered ice, following a wandering mink track on the edge of a starlit road of white, which seemed to reflect the Great White Road of the Milky Way high above. I tried to remember, to imagine that even though that faintly glittering swath of stars seemed impossibly far away, it was actually our own galaxy, our own particular home in the universe. I tried to comprehend the truth that all we have ever known, all our species has ever been, all the history we've ever written, and all the sacred stories we've ever told have taken place on one infinitesimal speck of dust circling one grain of sand in one galaxy in a thirteen-billion-year-old universe with more grains than are contained on all the beaches and all the deserts of all the world.

Was it possible, I wondered, for any earthly story, any event, no matter how important, to have a significance, truth, and meaning relevant in some way to the trackless infinity of such a universe—and even possible universes beyond? That it can speak to our humble, human place within it all? Is it possible that the concept of a universal Christ, a timeless, cosmic spiritual entity of profound love and acceptance, temporally manifested in the person of Yeshua but always present in all of creation, could be an answer? Could it place human belief, experience, and narrative within the vast context of the cosmos?

Most of our sacred stories—touchstones and guideposts for cultures, civilizations, and religions—are from long ago, most of them from the Axial Age, a time of unprecedented thought, reflection, intellectual and spiritual growth, but a time when any advanced knowledge or understanding of the universe was as far away and beyond human vision as the dark side of the moon. I love many of those stories. I was raised within the one celebrated at Christmas. Was raised for the most part within the river of traditions and teachings flowing from one man's birth, life, and death. It is impossibly strange, I thought, how sometimes, rarely, a single life can begin in some unknown humble place—a small room, a teepee or seasonal shelter, a cave or stable, or on the bare earth itself—and in the gathering of its days flow on to affect all of history, to impact billions of lives, and in doing so change the world. Just as one single raindrop, falling to Earth at the right place and time in geologic history, can gather other raindrops to itself, gather brooks and streams and tributaries over the course of time and space, and become a great river. Become an organizing, determining force on the landscape itself, a story that will be forever told.

I followed my own snow-covered river and in the faint light saw the mink tracks I was trailing veer into the tall grass along the riverbank. The little hunter had heard a mouse perhaps, or a vole and, instincts aflame, had darted from the open ice into the grassy, labyrinthine world of the tiny rodent. I could not follow there in the dark, could not see how the story turned out. Pulling my hood back and stretching in the cold, I gazed once more up to the twinkling heavens and saw the navigation lights of a jetliner, perhaps 35,000 feet high, blinking against the cold stars. It made no sound audible on the river far below. What did the world of the mink and the mouse have to do with the modern world of sky-walking airliners, of intercontinental travel? Perhaps as little as our small planetary world of modern human technology and achievement has to do with the vast realm of the stars, with intergalactic distances, the mysteries of dark energy, dark matter, and possible multiverses, all far beyond our reach. Perhaps as little as a time of shepherds and primitive stone-walled huts and inns—with cattle living below the human quarters and poor infants lying in mangers—now has to do with our modern world of glass-walled skyscrapers, luxury hotels, computers, internets, and interstate highways.

And yet the world of the mouse and the mink, the world of the manger, the infant, and the shepherd are still worlds of blood and bone, sense and sinew. As is our own. Presumably, as are other worlds in other galaxies, beyond even the white river in the sky. Was it possible that some great soul who lived in the days of the shepherds and stone huts—someone of deep and penetrating insight, wisdom, and empathy—could know this one world as well or better than anyone today in a high-flying jetliner or a glass-walled tower? Perhaps even understand the essence of life as it might extend to some other planet, circling some other distant star? People on our own planet live in simple stone huts and tend sheep yet today. The constellations, the pictures in the sky, shine down now in nearly identical form to the pictures of a night some 2,023 years ago. Mink leave their tracks on the snow yet today, for a tracker, a seeker, a questioner to follow, wondering at the stories in the snow as well as the stories in the sky.

And the inner world—the world the Teacher spoke of—remains as mysterious and holy and consequential as it ever was. All that happens in the great, external world comes first from some impulse somewhere within. Every action, word, and deed, every track in the snow or spaceship to the stars begins somewhere in the mind. And it is in that inner realm of self-reflection and self-knowledge that we must examine our own heart and conscience and determine how best to conduct our lives in the context of our small planet among our fellow beings.

Walking on the frozen river, following my own tracks back to their source on the riverbank, near the old cabin under the pines, I continued to think about the world of twenty centuries ago. The world of shepherds and flocks living under the same stars I gazed at now. The world of an infant in a cattle stall, and later of a Teacher carrying his shepherd's crook and guiding his flock, a Teacher whose words and thoughts are honored yet today. It is all one world, I thought, one universe, one realm of light and darkness, mystery and beauty, bound together by the world within—what the Teacher called the Kingdom of Heaven within.

NEMESIS

When the great attack came, Little Boy Man launched arrow after arrow, thousands of them, and struck great blows with his war club.

Gail was losing it. I had never seen Gail lose it before, and it was a strange thing to behold. At first I didn't understand what was happening. Busy with canoes and gear on the riverbank, I became aware of yelling. The yelling then seemed to escalate into something more resembling a prolonged wail, even a scream. It did not sound like playful roughhousing or teasing—often a part of our trips. Concerned, I looked up from packs and paddles to witness a seemingly headless figure careening through the camp, arms waving wildly. I could almost make out the despairing words. Something like, "I can't take it anymore! I just can't take it!"

Concern immediately became fear, and I dashed up the slope from the river to see what terrible calamity had befallen our group. Someone said, "Gail is in her tent, and she said she's not coming out."

"Why not? What's wrong?" I asked, suddenly remembering the pack of wolves we had seen running through this site just before we had pulled in and camped here.

"I don't know. She just started yelling. She said she can't stand it anymore."

Gail had been fixing supper. It was her turn on the rotating schedule, and she was our best camp cook. In fact, she was best at any number of things—an experienced, knowledgeable, and always dependable canoe camper, a strong paddler and portager, who had been on a number of trips with me, including several major expeditions. She was a great person to have along on any trip, self-assured, skilled, and reliable. What in the world could have happened?

I headed for Gail's tent. She didn't want to talk. But after some patient prodding, I learned the source of her despair. It was the black flies. They had been bad through most of the trip, and none of us had enjoyed them, often wearing head nets and gloves when in camp, which was unusual for us. But with her quiet stoicism, I had not really noticed how much more seriously Gail was impacted than the rest of the group. For some reason, bites that for me were a somewhat worse nuisance than mosquito bites, lasting a little longer and itching more noticeably, were for Gail a source of unrelenting misery. Her welts lasted for days, some becoming raw and bleeding. To make matters worse, her head net (the reason she had resembled a headless figure running through camp) had developed several small holes, probably from campfire sparks. The tormenting little flies found their way in through the holes but did not find their way back out. And the whole biting, buzzing, itching mess had eventually, suddenly become too much for her to bear.

I felt bad for not noticing, not seeing what a tough time Gail was having. But an evening spent in the safety of the tent, with some hot tea and supper, gradually improved the situation and Gail's normal ability to cope. That and a roll of duct tape from the bottom of the equipment pack, applied strategically in small bits to the head net holes. We made sure a tube of strong anti-itch cream, some Benedryl tablets, and an antibiotic cream were employed and kept readily available as well. By morning she was the Gail we all knew once more, a match for any situation.

Her episode of the night before, particularly in light of the way her body's particular histaminic system responded to the biting flies, was not unheard of. Many are the tales of people stranded or lost in the North Woods without proper clothing or protection, driven to distraction—or worse—by insects. A truly vicious allergic reaction can even result in black fly fever, wherein a person can develop a high temperature, headache, nausea, and swelling of the lymph nodes. A wilderness camping manual I consulted before guiding my first far north trip had stated plainly, "The mosquitoes and black flies can drive strong men mad."

The explicit warning had worried me—another worry to add to a packsack full, including rapids, storms, injuries, and becoming lost, among others. But as the years and trips and miles, the rivers and lakes accumulated, most worries had eventually subsided into a small, manageable lump in the pit of my stomach, almost forgotten. Dealing with insects, as with many things, became mostly a matter of common sense and experience: trying to schedule far north trips later in the summer after black fly season was past; understanding that open water was usually a safe haven from biting pests during the day; that areas around waterfalls and brisk rapids created their own moisture-laden wind currents that discouraged insects; that black and dark blue clothes (like blue jeans) are the most attractive colors to mosquitoes; that rocky outcrops were better for camping than low, sandy, brushy, or marshy areas; that the mosquito hour around dusk was generally the most problematic; and that windward rather than leeward points were always preferable. A good, smoky campfire smudge could be helpful, too, and I acquired the habit of often puffing on a pipe in the evening hours around camp.

Such precautions eventually eliminated bugs as a major concern on my wilderness canoe trips. Out of habit I always kept a small container of bug dope handy in my day pack but almost never used it. And head nets and gloves were always on the packing list but again were seldom pulled out of the pack. Until the trip on the Fond du Lac River of northern Saskatchewan with Gail's group, when we discovered black fly season was not quite over. For the first week of that trip, bare skin was kept carefully covered whenever in camp or on the portage trail. And we learned to be careful about little holes in the netting.

THROUGH ALL MY GUIDING YEARS, I have found that one of the best ways to take the sting out of many situations was with a story, a trailside or campfire tale that might be a tad short on scientific data but long on meaning, perspective, humor, or some other worthwhile quality. And one of the situations amenable to storytelling was every camper's nemesis—bugs.

Out of the myriad stories dealing with insects, I had found two that I became especially fond of, both of them Native American tales. It has never been a mystery to me why Native American stories are the most effective and most appropriate of any when sitting beside a campfire under the stars or beneath the shadows of trees. These are the stories that comprise the original owner's manual for life on this continent—a place traditionally called Turtle Island—from the peoples who have lived here for thousands of years and have come to understand its moods and meanings more deeply than anyone.

The first insect tale I learned from an old book, *The Soul of the Indian,* published by the University of Nebraska Press in 1911. It was written by a Mdewakanton Dakota man named Charles Alexander Eastman (1858–1939), whose family name was Ohiyesa. Trained out east at Dartmouth College and Boston University as a physician, Ohiyesa returned to his land to serve his people as their first medical doctor and tried hard to bridge the divide between the original inhabitants of the country and the new arrivals. In his book, he told the ancient story of First Born Man and Little Boy Man.

In the old story as he told it, the warmth of the sun entered into the body of the Earth and eventually produced a being known as First Born Man, Ish-na-e-cha-ge. First Born Man was something more than a man and was able to roam at will among the Animal People, understanding all of their ways and many languages. They beheld him with awe and could do nothing without his knowledge. But eventually he became lonely and created for himself a human companion, Little Boy Man, by withdrawing a sliver from his great toe.

Little Boy Man was created as an infant, innocent and trusting, and learned everything about living on the Earth from his Elder Brother. The Animal People loved Little Boy Man for his friendly and playful nature. But Ik-to-me, the Trickster-Spider, began to sow distrust and fear among the animals, saying that this young man was becoming too powerful and clever and would one day come to dominate them. Eventually, Ik-to-me instigated an attack by all the Animal People on this first Human Being. Little Boy Man learned of the plot and returned to First Born Man heartbroken, for he loved his animal friends. But his Elder Brother told him that the battle must be fought and won: this was the first separating of the path between Human Beings and the Animal People.

First Born Man armed his Little Brother with bow and arrow, war club and spear, and created for him a stone fortress. When the great attack came, Little Boy Man launched arrow after arrow, thousands of them, and struck great blows with his war club. Attacks came from across the prairie, from the climbers scaling the stone walls, and even from underground by the burrowing creatures, but all were repulsed. Finally, the Little People of the air, the insects, attacked mercilessly, filling his eyes and ears, tormenting him with their poisoned spears. But First Born Man had his little brother strike a stone with his war club, producing sparks that kindled a great fire, filling the air with flames and smoke and driving the insects and all the attackers away.

The Animal People finally sued for peace, and an agreement was reached whereby the animals would give to the Human Beings their flesh for meat and skins for clothing, but not without effort and danger and sincere gratitude on the part of the People. But in a final act of defiance, the insects refused to abide by the agreement and continue to torment Little Boy Man's descendants to this day. And the Bird People, in turn, punish the insects for their intransigence.

In an interesting postscript, the Dakota elders of Ohiyesa's day insisted that the many prehistoric arrowheads and spear points found and ploughed up throughout the country were not of their own design: they were in fact totally unknown to them, too large and unwieldy to fit their arrows, and were instead the ancient residue of the great battle between Little Boy Man and the Animal People.

ANOTHER TRADITIONAL STORY—this one from the Anishinaabe (Ojibwe) people—told of a great cannibal monster of the North Woods, the Windigo. This fearsome creature, able to disguise itself as a tree or boulder or any object of the forest, caught and devoured the People mercilessly. Until finally a little girl came forward with a clever plan.

Following her directions, the People dug a deep pit in the woods. They then placed venison as bait in the bottom, along with sticks, branches, and birch bark. Covering the pit with grass and leaves so it could not be seen, the people retreated to hiding places nearby and waited for the Windigo to come. That night they heard the great, stone footsteps approaching and cowered fearfully in the dark. Hearing a loud crash, the People followed the little girl's instructions and, carrying flaming sticks and twigs from the village fires, quickly threw them into the pit. The birch bark and branches in the trap soon burst into flame and the awful Windigo was engulfed in flames and destroyed, but not before screaming a terrifying curse: "I will return again and again with every generation!" it howled. "And I will eat you all, and your children and grandchildren, forever and ever!"

After the fire was out, the People, fearing the awful curse of the Windigo, gathered up all the ashes in the pit. Then carrying them to the top of a high hill, they flung them into the night winds, scattering them far and wide.

For a long time—all through the long, dark moons dominated by Kiwedin, the North Wind—the Windigo did not return. But one day in early summer, when the little girl and her grandfather were out in the woods, they were attacked by a cloud of what appeared to be . . . ashes. The tiny ashes buzzed and whirled and whined, and wherever they landed on exposed skin they bit fiercely, raising bumps and welts that itched and itched and itched. And so it was, the old story tells us, that the Windigo returned in the form of mosquitoes and returns every summer to this day, keeping the terrible promise it made so long ago.

And so we suffer still, when we take canoe or pack into the wilderness, when we do not choose our campsite carefully, when we walk a portage trail among the thick spruces and balsams where cleansing breezes do not reach. But in return, we have stories. Stories that speak of the past, of ancient cultures that have long lived close to the Earth, stories that speak of the mysterious relationship between Human Beings and the Animal People, and even the Little People of the air.

For Gail on that trip in the far north, the duct tape was probably just as helpful as a story. Perhaps.

A CHANGING OF THE GUARD

And recognizing, absentmindedly at first and then suddenly very clearly, that all the sights, sounds, and sensations are essentially unchanged from what you remember from twenty or thirty or fifty years ago. This is a rare sort of thing. A rare and fine and comforting thing.

Traditional North Woods family vacations at the lake are composed of many things.

Sunsets are important. (Sunrises less so, because of the necessity of arising early to view them, a hardship on any honest vacation.) Stars are nice—both the shooting and the stationary varieties. Tall pines are a requisite. Blueberries. Pancakes. Campfires. S'mores. Cattails. Boats and canoes and all manner of watercraft. A cabin. Lawn chairs. (Old but still functional.) Docks. (Old but still functional.) Board games. (Old and held together with yellow Scotch tape.) Grandparents. (Old but still functional, Scotch tape occasionally required.) Uncles and aunts and nieces and nephews and cousins and grandchildren. Fishing tackle. Fish. Traditions. Memories.

Things that are not required: Televisions. Computers. Cell phones.

That last notation is important, for if a traditional North Woods vacation gets mucked up with too many modern artifacts, well, then it isn't anymore. A traditional, North Woods vacation, that is. And this is not the grumpy opinion of an old, fuddy-duddy, Luddite grandparent. It is a plain fact.

It is almost always the case that a few simple guidelines can help us to more fully enjoy ourselves in the true spirit of a North Woods vacation:

Wear pants you can wipe your hands on.
Wear a good hat, preferably ugly.
Keep soda and beer in a cooler.
Keep worms in a cooler.
Don't drink worms.
Listen to loons.
Don't try to keep your feet dry.
Don't leave your tackle box open in the boat.
Don't step in your open tackle box.
Or sit in it.

Make sure you have simple rules:

Anyone who brings a cell phone on the dock gets thrown in with it.
Talk softly when you're fishing.
Always watch your bobber.
Make a list of the many things you'll never accomplish on docks, in boats, and in cabins.
Burn the list.

AND SO, NOT LONG AGO, another summer came along and with it another family vacation to our little cabin on Fawn Island in Rainy Lake. We did a fair job of following the guidelines. The sunsets were lovely. The stars burned brightly. Contentious games of Parcheesi and Scrabble and Chinese Checkers were played nightly, on boards held together with yellowed tape. The loons did their part, providing well-orchestrated concerts—complete with preludes, overtures, concertos, arias, and cadenzas. Tubing and water-skiing were accomplished, with a minimum of physical trauma and mayhem, except to one of the grandfather's knees. Sympathy was requested but very little provided. Rather, a firm

"I told you so" was the response from the grandma. Traditions were observed. Memories were recalled.

Best of all, everything was done with family. Younger son Bryan, my longtime First Mate at the lake, was there with all his family. My cousin Terry, who grew up with me as my third younger brother, was there for the first time in several years, accompanied by his son Michael and two small granddaughters, Grace and Riley. The girls, from Washington, D.C, were excited about everything that was new and different. And *everything* was new and different—from beach to kayak to mallards to minnows to frogs to chipmunks to going out in the boat on the Big Lake. And the girls had a chance to get acquainted with our grandchildren, Maya and Henry. As a parent or a grandparent, for us few activities are more rewarding, in an unambitious sort of way, than sitting lazily in the sun in a lawn chair, cold drink in hand, watching and listening to the splashing and giggling of children on a small sandy beach. And recognizing, absentmindedly at first and then suddenly very clearly, that all the sights, sounds, and sensations are essentially unchanged from what you remember from twenty or thirty or fifty years ago. This is a rare sort of thing. A rare and fine and comforting thing.

Other child-oriented activities, equally unrelated to the aforementioned and offensive modern artifacts, were accomplished as well. With Oma (Grandma) Kathy's guidance, small rocks were painted and decorated with great panache to resemble birds and frogs and dinosaur eggs. Stepping stones were made, complete with handprints à la Grauman's Chinese Theatre Hollywood Walk of Fame. Oma Kathy's splendid Fawn Island blueberry pies, universally acclaimed as the most delectable food on all the planet, were created and consumed. An amazing long-distance, open-water swim, similar to an English Channel crossing, was organized and executed—all the way from the dock to the little beach and back—with life jackets or floaties, of course.

One particular evening stands out within the panorama of happy memories. As our family prepared to head out across the

Big Lake in the Big Boat to meet Terry's family and get a hamburger at the lakeside restaurant, four-year-old Henry was having a hard time with . . . something. Perhaps but not obviously related to some interaction with big sister Maya. Tears were flowing.

"Henry, would you like to help me drive the boat?" I asked. Tears stopping. Vigorous blinking. Sniffling. Nodding.

"Okay, buddy, well, come up here and sit in my lap." Henry immediately dived into my lap. Henry had never before been in the driver's lap with the Big Boat running, with the powerful old inboard 8-cylinder engine growling and rumbling, with everyone sitting behind him in the passenger seats. With only the Wild Blue Yonder stretched out before him. We chugged away from the dock and I placed Henry's tiny hand on the throttle lever, mine on top of his.

"Okay, Henry, push," I said. Henry pushed. The boat growled more loudly, rose up on its tail, the bow in the air. "Push harder, Henry," I said. Henry pushed harder, the engine roaring, the boat beginning to plane out on the water, across the great wide-open lake. The bow settled, the boat skimmed, the wake foamed white behind us, and for the next five minutes Henry did not blink. At all. He gripped the steering wheel tightly with both hands. "Turn a little bit this way, Henry," I would say. "This is called *starboard.*" Henry wrestled with the steering wheel and the boat turned a little. "Now a little bit that way, Henry. That's *port.* Now, see that red buoy up ahead? We're going to go far around it—because there's a rock there, buddy. Good. Now, steady as she goes . . ." Steadily we went.

As we neared the dock in Thunderbird Bay, I said, "Okay, I'll take it now, Henry." And Henry slowly unclenched his white-knuckled little fists from the wheel. He blinked. Perhaps twice.

"Was that fun, buddy?" Vigorous nodding.

"Shall we get a hamburger now?" More nodding.

Henry seemed happy. Very happy. I was happy too, because it was abundantly clear that somewhere during the crossing of the Big Lake, there had been a changing of the guard. I had acquired a

new First Mate, an assistant that I could patiently guide and mold to eventually fill in for Bryan, who since Maya and Henry's birth and the start of his own household and career had in all honesty become noticeably lax in the many duties he had performed so long and so well.

But perhaps best of all? Big sister Maya had not said a word all the way across the lake. No "It's my turn now!" No "This isn't fair! I'm older!!" Not a word. Nor at supper, either. A completely patient and understanding Big Sister.

But as we climbed into the boat after dinner for the return trip home, I heard a soft, little girl voice: "Opa, can I drive the boat on the way home?"

"Why, sure, sweetie, climb on up here."

So now with a little girl in the grandfatherly lap, we had a repeat performance—the same no-blinking, blue-eyed laser focus, perhaps even more intense. The same iron grip on the wheel. The same turns to starboard and to port, the same, "Steady as she goes." All of it in the soft, rose-tinted ambient glow of a northern sunset. The same sort of glorious sunset our family had been enjoying for decades of gatherings at the lake. And when we reached the Fawn Island dock, when I asked Maya and Henry to toss me the ropes and help me tie up, I knew that my good fortune had doubled. I now had two First Mates, for many North Woods at-the-lake vacations to come.

One never knows exactly when such defining, life-altering moments will arrive. When the past will unexpectedly give way to the future. Perhaps in only a moment. When the able assistant of so many years—from fetching hammers and nails and lemonades to helping fix the dock to tying up boats to occasionally piloting the ship safely to harbor—will pass the baton to a new and capable generation. It might happen as we sniffle and dry a few tears. It might happen on the way to get a hamburger. Life is funny that way.

COMPUTER CLASS FOR THE BRONZE AGE

My computer learning curve has been steep (really more of a cliff than a curve), but I have persisted and learned a great deal. Well, that may be overstating it.

On my desk, in the Writing Office (which is really just a room but I like to call it the Writing Office) is a small, brass . . . thing. On the front of the thing are little open windows that show the day of the week, the month, and the date. On each end of the thing are little twisters that you turn by hand to rotate the day, date, and month. This technology is perhaps a thousand years old. But it suits me, and I like it. I like turning the little twisters to start the day. It helps me to feel in control of . . . something. It is a feeling I know will not last, but it is a good way to begin the day.

The little brass thing sits directly to the right of the computer. By way of contrast, the computer is responsible for helping me to feel in control of . . . nothing. Absolutely nothing in this world. As I am now the author of somewhere north of three dozen books, one might assume that the computer and I would have developed a somewhat close, perhaps intimate (or at least businesslike) working relationship. This assumption would be wildly incorrect. Of the thirty-eight books, thirty-four of them have been written on a yellow tablet with a pen. Again, this basic technology is thousands of years old, and it suits me. And it is the way Miss Little taught me to write in the second grade, and I don't like change.

It is odd perhaps that I have had this uncomfortable relationship with the computer and its smaller siblings, the laptop, the tablet, the cellular telephone, and whatever other digital what's-it that's popped up lately. Odd because my childhood hero, my granddad, was a whiz at all things mathematical and modern in his day. A favorite family story tells of the time, probably in the late 1950s, when Granddad was called from his troubleshooting and personnel office at McDonnell Douglas Aircraft Corporation. The company had a new widget. A giant, bells-and-whistles, mathematical widget called an "electronic brain." It filled a very large room. Maybe several. Maybe a whole building. None of the muckety-mucks in the high-concept technology departments could get the thing to work. There were jet engines and planes and rockets and eventually spaceships to build, and it really needed to work. Could my granddad make it work? was their question. He did. I have no idea how, as no one in the family could tell me, and my mathematical, abstract-thinking capabilities still top out at about 7 + 9, and I don't like dealing with multiplication or fractions very much, or long division at all. But my granddad did it. He made the widget work. And we put men on the moon. And that story always made me proud.

Unfortunately, although I did inherit Granddad's love of fishing and the out of doors, I inherited none of the genes involved with fixing widgets or electric brains or making friends with computers. Still, in the interests of joining the twentieth century (the twenty-first is still a murky horizon, far beyond me) and in order to stop being a terrible embarrassment to my grandchildren and the rest of the family, I have lately taken to working on the computer. Sort of. I get stuck a lot and need to repeatedly holler to Kathy for help, or when she is gone or stops responding or strikes me (gently, usually), I call friends or my digital guru, JoyGenea. Needless to say, this messes up my day, and probably theirs, and pretty much wipes out that small feeling of control I had briefly in the morning. With the brass thing on my desk.

My computer learning curve has been steep (really more of a cliff than a curve), but I have persisted and learned a great deal. Well, that may be overstating it. In fact, my then eight-year-old granddaughter Maya one day commented, "Opa learns, but he doesn't learn much." Ouch.

In any case, I have thought that perhaps as a service to others who might also be stuck in the Bronze Age, or who have occasional arguments or physical altercations with computers, I would share a few of the things that I have learned.

IT ALL BEGINS with terminology, and the terminology—at least in my case—begins with a mouse. In the computer world a **mouse,** for those unfamiliar with the term, is a little plastic dingus that you push around with your hand on something called the **mouse pad** (this is where the mouse lives), which in turn pushes around another little dingus on the screen (also called a **monitor** but we'll get to that later). The little what's-it on the screen looks like a tiny Indian arrowhead and is called a **cursor.** (We don't know why it is called that.) Eventually, the little arrowhead stops in various random places and magically turns into a hand. A Mickey Mouse-type hand with some sort of a white glove on it. If you then click the hand with the mouse, the hand will take you to some entirely new place in the digital cosmos. This is all disconcerting and mildly frightening, but we are getting ahead of ourselves. Back to the mouse.

One fine day my mouse stopped working. Or more accurately, the mouse kept running around on its pad but stopped moving the little arrowhead. I took the mouse to Best Buy. To the Geek Squad counter. I described the problem as best I could to the young (very young) guy at the counter. He looked at me. He looked at the mouse. He thought for a minute. He said, "You have a defective mouse."

"I do?"

"Yes."

"Have you ever heard of anything like this before?"

"No."

"Then how do you know?"

"Because it's not supposed to do that."

"So the mouse is . . ."

"The mouse is defective."

"Right."

He went on to say that I should send the mouse back to the manufacturer and get a new, nondefective one. It perhaps bears mentioning that we have had through the years any number of mice in our log cabin in the woods—deer mice, white-footed mice, jumping mice, big mice, little mice—but never before a defective mouse. Oh well, live and learn.

Meanwhile, back to my digital studies. It has been a slow and tortuous process, but I have continued to educate myself on many other interesting facets of computer terminology/technology. Here are a few of the basics:

There is a box next to the computer that is called the **modem,** or the **router,** or possibly both. The router is nothing like a Roto-Rooter, which I at first imagined but is instead a device through which the **Internet** (an amorphous dimension not precisely understood but akin to a digital universe with its own mystical laws) is made accessible to the computer. What or who lives inside that box, the router? Don't ask. Whatever they are, they are small and devious and can be easily turned to the dark side. The box has blinking lights, which if they don't blink properly means something is broken, and then you go to Best Buy to the Geek Squad counter, or call the telephone company.

The keyboard sits in front of the screen and is similar to an old acquaintance beloved by many generations called the **typewriter.** This old friend has now been hopelessly corrupted by the computer, the Internet, the modem, and the mouse.

The wireless network is something I've heard of but we don't have because we live in the woods under tall trees and wireless evidently does not like the company of squirrels and birds and leafy tree limbs. So instead we have the telephone company.

The telephone is an anachronistic device that sits near the computer. It is somewhat related to the modern **cell phone** but by contrast was once used to make actual telephone *calls,* wherein one person speaks to another. The telephone does not take pictures or function as a flashlight. It does not **Tweet** and it does not have **apps.**

The monitor next to the telephone is the most obvious part of the computer. In fact, I often call it the computer but am informed that it is not really. It is also not related to the magnificent monitor lizard, which lives in places warmer than our woods.

Icons are little tiny pictures that live inside the monitor screen that are supposed to tell you how to do stuff, most of which I can't do. I really don't know what the majority of them represent, and I am in general afraid to find out.

The minimizer is a little yellow button that when you click it (with the mouse-cursor) makes everything go away into a kind of computer purgatory, a netherworld that is not quite here or there. Stuff is supposedly retrievable from this purgatory, but in fact, you will never be able to find it again.

The maximizer is another button you push that makes everything HUGE. At first this was startling, but as I get older and my vision gets worse, I like this button more.

The browser is a poorly named something-or-other in the computer that helps you *find* virtual stuff in the virtual world. More or less. It has very cool nicknames like Firefox and Safari and Chrome. Varying sorts of browsers live in the virtual world, just as different species of animals browse in the real world. It all depends on what sort of browsing animal you want to be.

Add-ons are things that you add on to the browser. I guess. I don't know why.

Plug-ins are sort of like browsers too, maybe—sort of—but cause more trouble.

Updates are the software company's automatic suggestions that arrive uannounced from nowhere to scare you and to fix problems that haven't happened yet, but probably will. Which is also scary. Think of Hannibal Lector whispering to Clarice in *Silence of the Lambs.*

Social media is the black hole in the computer, or in the cell phone, that leads to a parallel universe where everyone is anti-social, angry, paranoid, envious, and crazy. Don't go there—you'll be happier elsewhere. Unless you find the kitten videos. Or the guilty dog ones.

The credit card is perhaps the most important item of all. This of course is the slim piece of plastic kept near the computer so that you can respond instantly to advertisements for every kind of product or service that the browser, the plug-ins, the add-ons, the pop-ups, the extensions, the router, the mouse, the monitor, and the entire Internet seem to think you need. This is a wonderful thing. Pretty much. Maybe. I have never actually used my credit card in this way, but every so often I take it out of my wallet and look at it and think about it. Then I put it back. Quickly.

And here, my friends, we may have essentially reached the limit of my computer knowledge and expertise. In fact, we probably reached it quite a few paragraphs ago. But there is always more to learn, and I'm just the guy to learn it.

Oh, one more thing. Just to the right of my computer desk is a shelf full of things called **books.** They don't have any add-ons or plug-ins or routers, although there sometimes is a mouse in the vicinity of the bottom shelf, near the corner logs of the Writing Office. The books don't try to sell me anything or scare me with updates, and they never annoy me to the point where I want to throw them in the river. They are friendly and quiet, and they suit me.

I believe I'll go and read one now.

A CIRCLE OF SOULS

I had long believed that external landscapes reflect inner ones and vice versa, and that to travel the wilderness is in many ways to traverse an inner world just as real and daunting and just as mysterious.

We had been paddling and portaging through the Canadian bush for a week and a half. We were well into our trip, and through the daily panorama of rough trails and big lakes, storms and rapids, winds and waves, campsites established and taken down, we had developed the closeness and deep-seated comradeship that often come to those who travel the wilderness together.

The times we had shared were unbroken by entertainments or distractions and were instead focused by challenges, brightened by sunrises and sunsets, and illuminated by beauty. I read somewhere once that "beauty unshared is a dagger through the heart." At least I thought I had read it. But I have repeatedly looked up the quote and cannot find it anywhere. If no one ever said it, they should have. Maybe I made it up myself and wrote it in a notebook somewhere. I think I will assume that I did and take credit for it. Because it's a good quote.

To see the last fiery rays of the sun descend behind a silent wall of pines, to watch an eagle snatch a fish with barely a ripple stirred, to listen to the mournful wail of a loon and then to raise an arm to point and begin to say, "Did you see . . . ? Did you hear . . . ?" but to find no one there to share the experience? Such moments can feel, if not like a dagger at least painfully poignant and lonesome.

But we had few such lonesome moments on our trip. Although we were alone and surrounded by wilderness—by thousands of miles of unbroken and mostly unpopulated wild country—our little band had re-created, or rediscovered, a human condition known through the millennia. We cared for and supported one another in everything. We shared everything. And through our shared journey we developed the strong interpersonal bond that intensity of experience often creates. It was not something we really talked about or even noticed at the time. It just happened, through the accumulation of moments, miles, and daily events.

And so one night, as the washing of dishes was nearing completion, as last dips in the lake were taken, a few clothes hung out on cords strung between spruces and balsam firs, and the final touches put on the evening camp, it seemed a good time to gather round the campfire together. It often is, of course. But sometimes the weather is foul or the wind is strong or the mosquitoes fierce or people are just too tired. This evening seemed perfect. True, we had paddled many hours and covered many miles, but we were rounding into shape and no one seemed exhausted. In fact, the tiny, spruce-covered and somewhat mysterious island on which we had camped, where it seemed as if nary a soul had ever trod before, along with a lingering sunset and emerging stars, seemed to have had the opposite effect. We felt awake, aware, and energized. The lake was still. The air was cool and dry. No one was in a hurry to head for the sleeping bags. So we gathered around the fire. We talked about small things and the events of the day, until we lapsed into quiet. Then silently, a great gray owl landed, like a spirit of the North, in a pinnacled spruce top just thirty feet away, and the spell was complete. We would sit awhile longer and share a North Country evening, in the land of David Thompson, Alexander Mackenzie, and Sigurd Olson.

We had arranged a suitable fire ring of loose stones found scattered about on the bedrock, pushed up above the waterline by the expansion of winter ice. Someone had found a sparking slab of schist, someone else a square-edged chunk of feldspar, a hunk of granite with a vein of rose quartz running through it, and several others. Enough to make a fine stone circle. Now in the gathering gloom, with a faint light still streaking the northwest, a leaping orange flame danced within the rocks, and faces were illuminated by the flickering glow. They were faces I had come to know. People I had come to know. I wondered if it might be a good time to get to know them better.

"How would you guys like to play a game?" I asked. I had in mind a little exercise Kathy had brought home from school one day from a teachers' workshop. She had tried it out on me, and I had been intrigued, even smitten. It had elements of psychology and a gentle spirituality, combined with a feel for the natural world around us. Not remotely the usual fare from a school workshop. I had jotted down the essentials in my journal and determined that someday I would try it out when the time seemed right. I had pulled it out on a few one-week Quetico trips and other occasions. But this place and time seemed especially propitious.

"What sort of game?" someone asked. And so we began.

The game was really a kind of quiz, a question-answer exercise meant to gently illuminate the psychological landscape within the participants. I had long believed that external landscapes reflect inner ones and vice versa, that to travel the wilderness is in many ways to traverse an inner world just as real and daunting and just as mysterious. The game, in the context of our wilderness island, was a way to view the two worlds together and perhaps examine that reflection.

I had everyone reach into their pack and pull out a scrap of paper and something to write with. "I'm going to ask you three questions," I said. "Without thinking too much about it—strenuous thinking seldom helps—give your best, honest, short answer. Remember, it's just a game, no grand claims or predictions, but I think it's very interesting. Are you ready to give it a try?" Everybody affirmed that they were ready.

"Here's the first question: what is your favorite creature in the world? Give three reasons why." After a moment the soft scratching sounds of pencil on paper could be heard. The campfire cracked and sizzled. Otherwise, all was quiet.

When everyone was finished, looking up a bit quizzically, I went on. "Next, write down your favorite color and three reasons why." The same scratching sounds, the same process. When all were ready, I said, "Finally, imagine you are in a very dark place. Pitch-black. All alone. Suddenly a beam of light pierces the gloom. What are your first three reactions?" More scratching, which seemed to go on a little longer this time.

Finally, everyone was finished, and faces again looked up with that half-expectant quizzical expression. I said, "Okay, thanks, everybody. Wasn't that fun?"

"What? Wait! Aren't you going to tell us what it all means?" came the chorus.

"Oh, yeah, I guess we could do that," I chuckled. "Would someone like to share their first answer?"

No immediate replies. Then Diane piped up. "Wolf," she said. "My favorite creature is the wolf." She gave her reasons, which I can't recall, but they seemed apt.

Gail spoke up. "I love the whale," she said and explained why. Again, it made sense.

Marlene, with her free spirit and wild mane of blonde hair, answered, "Mustang."

Mary, a pleasant, quiet, and gently steady young woman, said, "Dog."

Mike, sturdy, stout, somewhat of a loner but with twinkling eyes and always quick to help with any physical chore requiring muscles, said quietly, "Bear. I like the bear."

Jim, big and strong and my co-leader on many a trip, a man whom I knew well (yet somehow not so well) answered, "Grebe." Hmmm, I thought. I think we'll come back to that one later.

At some point I shared my creature, the chickadee, and gave three reasons for my admiration, the same I had given Kathy when she first sprang the game on me years before. "Small but tough," I said. "Good cheer, strong spirit." I remembered that Kathy had laughed.

Finally, it was Ted's turn. "Wolverine," he said. And he gave his answers.

At this point, the clamor was insistent and unanimous. "What does all this mean?" came the chorus once more.

"Well, remember that it's just a game," I said, "and it doesn't necessarily mean anything. But I have found it quite illuminating. And usually pretty accurate. So according to the game, the answers you gave, the creature that you chose—especially out here where you have plenty of time and space to think and feel—is the way that you see yourself."

Gasps. Nods. Chuckles. Laughter. Then silence. "Well, what do you think?" I asked. "Does it fit? Does it work?" Nearly all piped up and agreed, not only for themselves but for each other, that indeed the names fit. For that is what the creatures that had been chosen would soon become for us. Names. Names in the wilderness. Or at least nicknames.

I then explained what the other two questions meant. The favorite color and the qualities it represents are the sorts of people you most like to be around, I said. Someone answered blue. Calm, serene, tranquil. Someone else, red. Bold, bright, exciting. For me, green symbolizing life, growth, change.

And the first three reactions to the beam of light in a dark place? One's feelings about God or the world of spirit. I remembered the three answers I had once given. Curiosity. Curiosity. Curiosity. In truth, I cannot now recall who among our group gave which particular answers to the last two questions, but I never forgot the names. They seemed to fit so well, illuminating something about the character and personalities of my traveling companions.

Except for two. The first was Jim's grebe. Jim is a big, strong fellow. Former college football player. A great man on a portage or in the stern of a canoe. A fine and knowledgeable birder. Quiet and efficient around camp, self-sufficient, good sense of humor, wonderful as a co-leader. But as many times as I had taken trips with him and all the time we had spent together, there was always the feeling that some part of him was somewhat inaccessible, just beyond reach, beyond knowing. I knew that he had served in Vietnam but had learned no details. Nor did I ask. All that I knew about Jim was all I needed to know. But now in the flickering campfire light, I asked, "Jim, why a grebe?" He answered, "Because he only shows as much of himself as he wants you to see."

Ah. The pied-billed grebe, a diving waterbird somewhat between a loon and a small duck, was known to pioneers and woodsmen as the helldiver and has the remarkable ability to not only dive in an instant but also to partially submerge, leaving only its head or beak above water. Jim. Partly hidden. The grebe. Of course.

Still, I wondered about Ted the wolverine. Of all the folks I'd had on wilderness trips, Teddy was one of the gentlest. Self-effacing. Sweet. The Cree children on our journey flocked to him whenever we came to a reserve or village. With his round wire rims, soft voice, and a smile like the sunrise, he was a joy to be around. But a wolverine? It seemed completely out of character.

I had not yet had the chance to spend much private time with Ted on our trip. But a day later, I made sure that we were paddling partners. Although I didn't ply him with questions, it gradually emerged that we shared an interest in psychology, had in fact both had counseling, in which Teddy was still immersed. As the hours and paddle strokes went by, I learned that Ted had experienced a rough, emotionally abusive childhood with a domineering and frightening father. Ted had never had the chance to spread his wings, to truly be himself, to find that part of himself that could be strong, free, even fierce, if need be. The wolverine was, I realized, an aspiration. A spirit animal maybe. A creature of the North Woods we now traveled that could symbolically perhaps lead Ted toward a more balanced, more assertive, and healthy way of being. It made perfect sense.

Now these years later, whenever I think of our trip—the sunrises and sunsets, rapids and rainstorms, the vast and silent sweep of the wilderness—I know that as always it was the ideal opportunity for exploration and discovery, not only external but internal. And I clearly remember the names of my friends. Bear continually impressed us with his strength, with his strange habit of lifting and carrying heavy packs not by their straps but by wrapping them in a bear hug. Mustang was her wild, free-spirit self, always ready for fun and laughter but serious about the adventure of life. Whale dived into everything with grace and full commitment. Grebe began perhaps to let us see just a little more beneath the surface. Everyone lived their lives—or at least a month of them in the great North Woods—in accordance with their own strengths and weaknesses, challenges, and aspirations. Including the Chickadee.

And along the way, from time to time, we glanced at—or pondered—one another with a just bit more curiosity, insight, and understanding. Treasuring a nickname, noticing a certain way of being, of approaching the world. And sometimes, around an evening campfire, we saw in the dancing light not just friends and companions, but something more, something deeper—a circle of souls, each one separate and unique but traveling together through the wilderness. Through this journey of life.

FROM THE WILD HORIZONS

It was a place where two worlds once met—or actually three. The world of the Ojibwe and Dakota, of the advancing white civilization, and of the original and timeless wilderness.

Our sons and grandchildren tell us we live in a museum. They say it in kind voices tinged with forbearance. True, old stuff is everywhere. Old furniture, old books, old knickknacks, old musical instruments, photos, paintings, mementos, mantle clocks and grandfather clocks. And rocks. You name it, it's old. Kathy and I are the eldest children in our families of origin, and we both grew up with a sense of responsibility toward and interest in history—especially family history and heirlooms. And our cabin in the woods was built in olden days (about 1930) out of logs from old red pines, with a double-sided twin fireplace of rocks (primarily St. Cloud granite) that was quarried (long ago, of course) out of bedrock deposits approximately 2.5 billion years of age. That's old. Geez. We do live in a museum. We should charge admission, even for kids and grandkids.

Many of my personal keepsakes are reminders of something else, though, something other than the mere fact of great age. They are symbols of places and times when the wild world was nearer at hand for most folks, close enough to see, to smell, to touch. As such they are tokens, reminders of wild horizons—places that were at one time the limit of vision, the edge or meeting place of the already known and of the beckoning unknown. The sorts of places

I have had the chance to visit or explore, paddling and camping and living close to the heart of the Earth for a spell.

About five feet from my writing desk is the rib bone of a woodland caribou, whittled, smoothed, and shaped. It was harvested from a campsite on the Churchill River in northern Saskatchewan. The camp was on a broad and lonely gravel bar reaching out from the west shore of big Lac Île-à-la-Crosse, and it was there that my friend Mike found the bone on the first night of a three-week expedition. I know just when and where Mike found it because he came to my tent, too excited to sleep that first night, and started scratching softly at the nylon, speaking urgently in a stage whisper. “Hey . . . Bourgeois . . . Doug . . . Doug! Bourgeois! Hey! Doug! Are you awake?!”

It was about 2 a.m. We had just completed a 1,500-mile drive, a day of organizing, planning, stashing of vehicles and trailers, checking in with the local Royal Canadian Mounted Police, unpacking and repacking and getting people and gear into canoes and out on the water—all the semi-organized chaos that accompanies the first day or two of any major expedition. We had then paddled about ten miles, made camp, cooked supper, washed dishes, and finally hit the hay. I was excited about our trip too. But not too excited to sleep. I was pooped. But Mike was relentless. In response to his repeated overtures, I may have groaned. That was a mistake. Mike took it as an affirmation of his efforts.

“Yeah. Hey, Doug. Great, you’re awake! Hey, you’ve got to come out and see this!”

Another groan. The effort to form words. “See what, Mike?”

“The northern lights. They’re incredible!”

“I’ve seen ’em before, Mike. I saw them before we went to bed. They were great. But I’m tired.”

“Yeah, but they’re even better now. I can’t even describe it—they’re just—wow—you’ve got to come out and see them!”

A final groan. I drug myself out of the bag and the tent. The northern lights were out. They were pretty good. They looked much as they had before.

"Mike, what's the . . ."

Mike was holding out his hand. He had his penlight out, pointing at the outstretched hand. In the pool of light was blood. A significant amount of blood. Not good.

"Mike, why didn't you say—"

"I didn't want anybody else to hear, to know what happened."

"Well, what did happen, Mike?"

It turned out that Mike had been whittling. Carving. What, he wouldn't say. At one o'clock in the morning. In the dark. Well, by the glow of the northern lights. We went and found the equipment pack with the first aid kit. I got a better flashlight. We pulled out the hydrogen peroxide, some antibiotic ointment, and several butterfly closures. I got the cut cleaned up, rinsed, closed, and wrapped. We were quiet, and no one else woke up. Mike was embarrassed and wanted it to stay just our secret. The next morning, he explained the bandage with some little white lie I can't remember now. But . . . first night out. A bad cut. Blood in the sand. Not a good start, even a bad omen perhaps.

Except it wasn't. It turned out to be no kind of omen at all, except maybe a good one—for trouble out of the way, for big lakes to be safely crossed and rapids successfully run, for eagles and moose and bear that would be seen and fish caught, and laughter shared, and the great joy and satisfaction of a group of people growing ever closer to one another and the wilderness that surrounded them. At the end of the trip, around a little campfire of fragrant birch and pine, closing words and thoughts were expressed and a few simple gifts exchanged. Small items, gathered or handmade—things to jog a memory—to remind a person of an extraordinary time in an extraordinary place. Gatherings from our wild horizons. I no longer remember all the gifts. But I remember mine. It was from Mike. And it rests in my writing office—the caribou rib bone, carved and crafted into a small bone knife. And of course I remember the place where Mike found it, and the night he began working on it.

Such mementos surround me in my work space, as I recall

trips taken, landscapes, lakes, and rivers explored, and the people who were there with me. Nearby hangs a tiny, handmade wooden yoke, as though for miniature oxen. The attached note on a scrap of birch bark declares it to be a Mammaygwessy Portage Yoke, made by a delightful trip participant named Jim on a journey through Quetico Park. I had told the story of the Little People of the Ojibwe and the Cree, who hide among the trees, rocks, and shorelines. They have magical powers and abilities and are sometimes tricksters, but traditionally they are also protectors who guard against the serpents and monsters who live in the darkness below, preventing them from coming to the surface and harming people. The tales made quite an impression on Jim, as such stories will in the evocative context of the wilderness.

In a corner near the door is a beautifully shaped hunk of driftwood, white pine with picturesque knots and a small protruding branch. It has been smoothed to a satin finish by nothing but the washing and tumbling of waves on a wild northern lake, the little branch making it a fine hat rack. And so it is as I reach over and grab a ball cap or fedora when going out the door.

A lovely little dream net, woven just so within a delicate hoop of white cedar festooned with a bit of duck down, dangles and twirls from the center beam of our old Fawn Island cabin. It has hung there for nearly thirty years, an original cabin-warming gift, a wish of good luck and happy times from a friend in our first summer there. We have never moved it.

Photographs make great reminders of meaningful places and experiences. Many of us keep them now on our smartphones and other devices, but my favorites are framed and hung around the office and house, even in my "branch office" in the carriage-house garage where I like to write in the summer. Wilderness waterfalls and rainbows and grand landscapes. A shot that someone took of me, sluicing down a brawling rapid, solo, bow in the air as I powered through a haystack on the Bloodvein in northern Manitoba. I feel an echo of adrenaline when I remember the time and place, and the curious combination of fear and unbound freedom I knew in that moment.

A particular favorite is simply a shot of a large, flat-topped boulder, chest high, at a camp on a big northern river. On the boulder is a shallow tin plate about twelve inches around that I used to fondly refer to as Rachel (she had an identical partner known as Ralph). On the plate is an instant Jello-mix cheesecake generously topped with blueberries, raspberries, and saskatoons—a favorite camp dessert. Next to this delicacy is half a summer sausage, a chunk of cheese and a box of crackers, a large jar of peanut butter (with hand-carved, wooden spreading paddle protruding), and a plastic quart bottle three-quarters full of some red liquid, most likely Kool-Aid. Though not particularly profound in any aesthetic sense, this single photo immediately brings to mind innumerable beautiful places, on innumerable expeditions, and old paddling friends who shared countless lunches or dinners consisting of exactly this fare.

Another shot shows my old buddy and frequent co-leader Jim Fitzpatrick and me, leaning back against day packs in the sterns of our two canoes just a couple of feet apart on a northern lake. Blue sky above, pipes clenched in our teeth, paddles trailing in the water. It doesn't look like we are working very hard, and we aren't. We are simply ruddering, glorying in our indolence, as our bow partners hold tight to their raised paddles, between which is stretched a nylon tarp as we sail happily north on a brisk south wind. A fine day.

Among the photographs are manifestations of another, more artistic eye and hand. Francis Lee Jaques, the famed illustrator who created the masterpieces of art and nature in the famed dioramas of the American Museum of Natural History in New York and the James Ford Bell Museum in Minnesota, occupies places of honor in our cabin. Elegant scratchboard prints depict a moose climbing a snowy slope into the pines, a portager carrying a wood and canvas canoe along a rocky ledge, and a scene of the artist himself with his wife, Florence, in a canoe riding big waves past a looming headland. As is the case with truly fine art, each of these depictions seems to touch a place within the viewer and for me brings beautifully to mind images of similar moments from my own wilderness journeys.

I am ever surrounded by rocks, each one a reminder of some wild and lovely place, from ocean coasts to painted deserts to roaring rivers to distant continents. Each stone evokes a scene and perhaps the faces of others who shared it with me. Out in the yard are two stone benches, one from a Minnesota limestone gully. It is chock-full of fossils, dozens of brachiopods and gastropods, the residue of life from an ancient midwestern sea, where now green and wooded hills abide. The other bench contains no signs of ancient life forms and is instead a nearly perfect rectangular hunk of silvery schist, subtly sparkling and beautiful. And heavy. The

fact that it rests now in my yard and that I sometimes rest upon it is the result of a small, inconsequential wager on a long-ago canoe trip. Well, not entirely inconsequential. The loser of the bet paddled and portaged that rock around for me for a week, and every time I rest on it now or watch a blue jay or red squirrel enjoying lunch there, I remember. And feel a touch of contrition. But not much—it's an excellent bench.

THERE WAS A TIME when our own Pine Point woods, where I write these words and observe my bench, was the edge of the wilderness, the wild horizon—a time from which we are not so very far removed today. A couple of years ago, a young man called. He had a request. Would it be all right, he asked, if he came out to our riverside woods with a metal detector and searched for logging-era artifacts? Well, I wasn't sure. I could think of any number of things I might like better than a stranger tromping around in my woods with a metal detector, digging holes, and messing things up. On the other hand, he sounded okay, and I knew that our century-plus pine forest had been logged once during the nineteenth century and again in 1929 (the smaller trees left standing, now become our old grove). Normally I would have said no. But I was curious. Why don't you come on out, I said to the young man, whose name was Jake, and we'll get acquainted and talk it over. A couple of days later, Jake arrived right on time, and he was a revelation. It turned out that Jake knew a great deal about our particular spot on the river and the history of the entire local area.

I was already aware that this was a region of some historical interest. In 1805, after Jefferson's Louisiana Purchase, Zebulon Pike had come up the Mississippi on an expedition to shore up the American position in the fur trade and to assert ownership of lands in the great Northwest. Also, if possible, to discover the source of the Mississippi. As a trip leader and explorer, Lieutenant Pike was evidently everything that I would not want to be—a pompous, imperious little popinjay of a man in search of glory, indefatigable, yes, but who abused and drove his band of twenty men relentlessly, made countless missteps with the Native peoples, and was lucky to eventually make it back alive. Still, he is a part of history, and he did pass our very point on the river, possibly camping on the flat ground under the pines, on about October 11, 1805. He then continued upstream only another thirty miles or so, where he made a winter camp at the mouth of the Swan River, just south of today's Little Falls.

After the river completed its freeze-up in December, Pike went on with a small group as far as Leech Lake, where he ceremonially shot the British flag from over the Northwest Company post, replaced it with an American one, obtained dutiful assurances that the post would now abide by American rules and interests (the British flag was unsurprisingly rehung as soon as Pike left), and decided that he had indeed succeeded in finding the main source of the Mississippi, which was incorrectly—but conveniently—claimed as Leech Lake. Pike then headed back down the frozen river to his winter camp, making his return to St. Louis in April.

In 1832, another white explorer came upstream on the Great River. Henry Rowe Schoolcraft was an explorer and ethnologist who again was in search of the source. Passing our bend in the river, he named the prodigious granite outcrop just across the channel from our pines Peace Rock—this honorific denoting the de facto border between the often-warring Ojibwe to the north and east and the Dakota to the south and west. Schoolcraft was by all accounts a more agreeable man than Pike, and with the help of an Ojibwe guide named Ozawindib (Yellow Head) he succeeded in finding what is still widely considered the headwaters of the Mississippi, a small, clearwater lake he christened Itasca—short for *veritas caput* (Latin for true head).

A little later, in the mid-1800s, another activity was opening up this portion of the frontier. The famed Red River Trails wound from St. Paul six hundred miles north to Red River Colony, now Winnipeg. One of the main routes (the Woods Trail) snaked along the east side of the Mississippi, across from our Pine Point and near Peace Rock, roughly where a rail line runs now. The trail in its heyday was clogged with Red River carts, rough but effective two-wheeled, oxen-pulled vehicles developed by the Métis (the mixed blood French–Indian traders and trappers) to carry fur bales and trade goods, and later all manner of necessities for farmers and settlers headed to and from the northwest. The carts were made entirely of wood and rawhide and squeaked so loudly that they could be heard for miles.

I was generally cognizant of these aspects of the Minnesota story and their near intersection with our little acreage. But Jake was a real history buff with a depth of knowledge beyond my own and seemed genuinely excited about the opportunity to dig up a few items that might illuminate the past. So Kathy and I gave him the go-ahead. What he found shocked us all. He turned up no logging artifacts, the prize he initially said he was after, but after a day or two of patient searching he came upon an old and well-used Indian campsite just a few hundred feet from the cabin—hidden among the pines and covered with inches of duff. In that campsite over the next few weeks, Jake and his metal detector discovered the following: several tinkle cones or jingles, for a Dakota girl's buckskin dress; seven musket balls; a horse bit; a musket frizzen and butt plate for a flintlock rifle; four knife blades; a beaver trap base; a decorative bracelet; two fur bale seals; several buttons; and two musket barrels, one exploded on one end. (A very bad day for someone.) And more.

A number of these items I didn't recognize, and Jake had to explain them to me. In the course of that explanation, Jake shared the fact that directly across the river from us and just upstream from Peace Rock had been a frontier trading post, the Watab Fur Post, owned and operated between 1844 and 1852 by a man named Asa White. In later research I found various references to the site, including in Grace Lee Nute's *Posts in the Minnesota Fur Trade Era: 1660-1855.* In learning more about Pike's expedition, I also found that in the early nineteenth century this area was teeming with bison and wolves and herds of elk numbering in the thousands. I should have known or suspected, with nearby Elk River so named. But I'd never really thought about it. In fact, it turned out that old Zeb Pike had actually shot an elk, after many fruitless attempts with a musket too small in caliber, tracked it to the banks of a then-marshy Little Rock Lake, just a couple of miles upstream from our point, and salvaged half the carcass, leaving the rest for the increasingly assertive and intimidating wolves.

As Jake proudly showed his fur trade artifacts that day in our cabin, he explained that he had originally hoped he would actually find such items rather than just later evidence of logging days but had not wanted to get his (or our) hopes up too high. He was thrilled with what he had found and further explained that a few of the items dated to perhaps a half-century before the historical fur post across the river. And that the Indian campsite—the level ground beside the river near which our cabin now stands—was likely a well-used site far into the past, though no artifacts were found from those earlier days.

Wow. Kathy and I were impressed. Very. And we immediately realized that our feelings, our understandings of our little cabin in the woods would be forever transformed. Our forested point was the site of historic events, witness to the procession of time, the passing of explorers, the era of nation building, and the life of Native American First Nations, still an ongoing part of Minnesota history today. It was a place where two worlds once met—or actually three. The world of the Ojibwe and Dakota, of the advancing white civilization, and of the original and timeless wilderness.

Now when I cast my eyes over mementos from a lifetime spent exploring wild places, a life of journeys and adventures, I bear in mind that here beside the river where we paddle our canoe, where we walk our woods and feed our birds and squirrels, here was once the wild horizon. It was not so long ago. And when I ponder a fur trade musket barrel or a jingle or a nearby bone knife from the Churchill River and consider the meanings they all bear, I think what a fine and lucky thing it is to live in a museum. For a good museum is not just about the past. It's about the flowing river of life we all share, from horizon to horizon.

BOULDERS IN THE RIVER

The current was swifter than I had imagined, and . . . .
in a twinkling we were capsized and tossed downstream . . . .

I have known a good number of boulders—and rivers—over the years. The Canoe Country, and all the North, is a land of rocks. The last glacial epoch left them pushed and scraped and strewn across the landscape—rocks, stones, and boulders of all kinds and sizes. It is one of the most recognizable (and to me delightful) features of the landscape. The larger of these boulders are called Glacial Erratics because of the unpredictable nature of their distribution. They are often found far from where they originated, and because of their composition or content, they look out of place where they now reside. In my guiding years on a geologically focused outing, I would often point them out to a group and refer to them as Glacial Eroticas because it seemed to help the idea stick a little better. Well, that was one of the reasons. It also elicited interesting reactions, ranging from shock to disapproval to laughter.

These erratic boulders can be found almost anywhere. On hilltops or overhanging cliffs, in the deep woods, along shorelines. And in the rivers and streams that lace the Canoe Country together. These waterways are also erratic in a sense because they are so young, geologically speaking—only ten thousand years old rather than hundreds of thousands or millions. This means they have not had time to sort themselves out, to become a fully mature drainage system as in other parts of the continent. And within these young rivers we find, as everywhere else, boulders. I can still see some of them in my mind's eye, looming suddenly in the middle of a rapids, causing concern, consternation, and some fancy maneuvers by the bow and stern paddler in order to avoid disaster.

I remember a pair of them near the foot of our first big rapids on the Churchill River, how they seemed to be rushing swiftly upon us rather than the other way around; how the current swept us toward them with seeming irresistible force, until at the last moment, with a twist from the stern paddler and a cross-draw from the bow, and the powerful assistance of a standing wave created by one of the boulders itself, we sluiced down between them with barely a moment to glance and breathe a sigh as we careened past.

I recall a small pillow rock in the Turtle River country of Ontario, almost invisible under the smooth flow of current but present nonetheless, how the bow struck it head-on, tipping the canoe, spilling the paddlers, and somehow leaving a gash on my shin whose scar I carry today.

And I particularly remember a boulder on the Fond du Lac River of northern Saskatchewan. The river was in flood, but we ran all the rapids carefully, stopping to scout them from shore whenever possible. On this occasion the other canoes went first, as my paddling partner, Bill, and I watched and shouted encouragement and instructions from the far shore. It seemed to me from that distance that the last canoe wasted too much time on what appeared to be a not-very-difficult run, certainly easier than some we had taken earlier. They climbed out twice and lined the canoe through the alders along the shoreline, awash in high water. I became a bit impatient with the lost time on our trip schedule and waved them on, shouting with a note of irritation in my voice. Finally it was our turn, and Bill and I ferried across above the rapid. Anxious to make up lost time and seeing no great difficulty, I eschewed lining as the other canoe had done and instead directed the bow downstream in what looked to be a clear channel. It was not. The current was swifter than I imagined, and we struck another underwater pillow that Bill, in the bow, never saw. In a twinkling we were capsized and tossed downstream in our life vests, floating feetfirst and in no real danger.

But the canoe was not so fortunate. After the spill, it immediately filled with water, then wrapped itself around a large, angular boulder just left of our clear channel. When co-leader Jim and I made our way back, we found the boat hopelessly lodged, with tons of water force making a mockery of our efforts to move it. Try as we might, even to the point of cutting a midsized aspen tree to use as a lever, we made no progress. Then, serendipity. Half a day back we had crossed Black Lake, on whose far shore was a fly-in fishing camp. We had seen no boats or any other travelers on our entire journey on this remote river, but at this moment a big resort boat powered by a 50-horse outboard came roaring upstream, directed by a Cree fishing guide with two customers in the center and bow seats. Seeing our predicament, the guide stopped. And over the next few minutes, he accomplished the seemingly impossible. With just a modicum of assistance from us and his fishing party, wearing no life jacket and scoffing at the concerns we expressed, he ran back and forth on the gunnels of his boat, rapids tossing it wildly, tied a stout rope to the canoe, swung his boat around, gunned his motor, and hauled our canoe free. An incredible display of boatmanship.

The odds of that encounter were mighty low, and even less for a successful outcome. We tried our best to express our profound gratitude, but within moments the guide was gone with a wave, roaring up the rapids with his fishermen once more. We saw no more boats the rest of our trip. Meanwhile, our canoe, made of a heavy and nearly indestructible plastic compound, had floated downstream into the pool below the rapids where we were able to retrieve it, bend it back into some sort of serviceable shape, and replace the shattered cane seats with a rope web somewhat resembling a hammock for a paddler's posterior. The canoe and the seats served us well for the remainder of our journey. And the canoe guide (me), suitably chastened, never again shouted an impatient “Hurry up!” at any canoe navigating treacherous waters. Nor was I tempted to hurry up myself and ignore less-than-obvious dangers. On our return home weeks later, I wrote a letter to the resort, saying what an extraordinary gentleman they employed, and asking that our deepest gratitude and a modest financial reimbursement be passed on. I certainly hope they were.

A LIFETIME OF HIKING and paddling canoes and kayaks has brought me into contact with countless other boulders. On our Fawn Island are some of which I am especially fond, including a flat-topped granite rock by my sitting bench near the dock, on which I like to set a morning cup of coffee. And on the east side of the island stands a great speckled erratic that had a serious crack in it when we acquired the island some thirty years ago. I used to like to examine that crack, about four feet from top to bottom, to gaze through it at the lake, and to sometimes use the natural framing to take picturesque photos. I had done just that one recent summer day, examining spiderwebs within the open space, finding a hollow dragonfly nymph casing. On my return just two days later I was stunned to find the great rock split completely in two, with half of it resting in the shallow water of the shoreline. The boulder had stood there motionless for probably ten thousand years, since the retreat of the last glacier. Who knows how long the crack had been present, widening infinitesimally decade by decade, century by century, perhaps for millennia. How I wish I had been present at the very moment in those forty-eight hours when something that had never moved *moved.* To see and hear the splash. But unlike the occasion of our fortuitous canoe rescue on the Fond du Lac, the timing wasn't precise, the moment of serendipity not quite at hand.

Of all my recollections of encounters with boulders, it is a rock I never met and never saw that is one of the clearest in my mind. Another moment of serendipity.

Years ago, I was writing a manuscript that would eventually

become my second book, *Paddle Whispers.* I thought the spare and simple text would go well with Canoe Country photography, and as I was yet an unknown and unpublished author, I wrote to J. Arnold Bolz, whose brilliant photos often graced the cover and pages of the *Minnesota Volunteer* and numerous national publications. He had also written a lovely book I was fond of, *Portage into the Past* and had provided luminous photos for Sigurd Olson's book *Wilderness Days.* Surprisingly and very kindly, Dr. Bolz—probably forty or more years my senior—wrote back, inviting me to the lakeside northwoods home he shared with his wife, Belva, where we might brainstorm and discuss the idea.

We hit it off wonderfully, sharing many common interests, and tentatively made plans for him to send me photos that might accompany different portions of text. We met several more times, even going into the woods together where Arnold took new shots with me in the frame. We also had the opportunity for more delightful conversations. At this point (and still today) I was very taken with the scratchboard art of F. Lee Jaques, creator of famous dioramas at the New York Museum of Natural History and the Bell Museum, and illustrator of many of Sig Olson's books. Lee was married to Florence Page Jacques, who was also an accomplished author of nature, travel, and children's books.

One day, at Arnold and Belva's kitchen table as Jaques's name came up, Belva told an almost unbelievable story that I've never forgotten. Not so surprisingly, the Bolzes and the Jaqueses became very good friends when they met later in life. Belva recalled a time when the four of them were attending some gala event. Lee cut quite a dashing figure and was (as seemed often to be the case) surrounded by admiring women. Someone asked Florence casually if this fact ever bothered her in any way. Florence answered, no, not really, that there was only one instance that caused her any consternation.

It seems that Lee had told her more than once of a time when he was a very young man. He and a good friend were on a journey through what later became known as the Boundary Waters Canoe Area, at that time not well known or heavily used. As Lee and his friend came paddling downstream, going fast with the quick current, and slipping around a bend in the stream, they saw an extraordinary sight. "There on a boulder in the middle of the river," said Florence, "was a young woman, beautiful, and completely nude. Her long blonde hair thrown back, she glistened in water droplets, sunning herself in the wilderness. There was no one else around, no canoe, no tent, and before the two boys could say or do anything, or imagine what they might say or do, they were swept away, downstream and around the bend. Well, Lee has never gotten over it! Like a Lady Godiva of the wilderness, or a freshwater mermaid, he's remembered that girl all his life, the gorgeous image of her on that rock in the river—wondering who she was, if she was even real or a fantasy, and what her story might have been."

At this point in Florence's telling of the story, Belva said she had gasped and caught her breath. "Why, that was *my mother!*" she exclaimed. "She also remembered that day all her life. She was on her first-ever canoe trip. She had slipped away from camp for a swim, feeling she was quite literally at the very ends of the Earth, taking a few adventurous moments to feel the water, the wind, and the sun on her bare skin, on a boulder in the river, never dreaming that there might be anyone else around or that anyone would appear. Then suddenly, there were these two young men, appearing as if from nowhere, their paddles suspended in the air, mouths agape, silent, as they floated by and then disappeared downstream. She never forgot it, the embarrassment, the risqué thrill, never imagined she would ever learn who they were or where they came from. And now, here we are and, my goodness, what are the odds!?"

Indeed, what are the odds? It's hard to imagine. But it's not hard to imagine the image of that single moment of astonishment, burned into the memories of all concerned. Of a beautiful lady on a boulder in the wilderness. It is a wonderful story of coincidence, mystery, serendipity.

In a sad coda, Arnold and I never got to do that book together. He and Belva were taken from us in a car accident before we finished. But I have always cherished the opportunity to get to know them. To meet and receive the guidance of another older mentor. And I have never forgotten the image in Belva's story. It's burned into my brain too, even though I wasn't there. Meanwhile, I eventually finished writing the book and in the end decided I would illustrate it myself with pen-and-ink drawings, in the style of F. Lee Jaques, as I have done in many books since. Although I only got indirect instruction from poring over the books he illustrated, Lee became a mentor too. And Florence in her writing as well.

So here's to beauty and mystery. To the unexpected. To mentors and to good stories. And to boulders, wherever they may be found.

SLOWING DOWN?

Life is short, no matter how long we live.
So, we had better live.

Over the past couple of years, I have sustained torn cartilage in my wrist, a ruptured shoulder tendon, rotator cuff and bursa problems, a broken rib, torn knee cartilage, a detached retina with vision only partially restored, a painful (!) kidney stone, and a very near heart attack (99 percent blockage in one artery). Among other annoyances.

Some years ago, I went to see an orthopedic specialist about a sore wrist (yes, the same wrist). He employed X-rays, MRIs, and other sorts of photojournalism and returned to give me a cortisone shot in my wrist. I have small bones, small wrists, and somehow the experience of that ridiculously large needle delivering its cargo into that tiny space was not nearly as much fun as I thought it might be. I yelped. Maybe twice. And accused the doctor of negligence in not having .45 caliber bullets in his office for abused patients to bite on. Or to be shot with. During this consultation, the doc looked me in the eye and said earnestly, "You know, you might have to accept the fact that this level of activity may not be sustainable."

Well. I thought hard about what he said, for a couple of minutes, then left the office and went back to *this level of activity*—also known as my life.

For a long time now, without giving it a whole lot of deep thought, I have subscribed to some core theories about aging and living. Theories that are somewhat interrelated and mutually sustaining. I developed these theories myself, although I claim no copyright or trademark ownership and may in fact have been influenced by conversations over a beer, a putt, or a bowling ball, in a fishing boat, or thoughts from the internet, Hallmark cards, TV commercials, or other less-than-gold-plated sources of information. Among the theories, that fifty-five is the new thirty-five; that sixty-five is the new thirty-five; and that seventy is the new—well, thirty-five. That age is just a number. That age is just a state of mind. That you're as young as you feel. That you can be young at heart, no matter how old you are. That . . . well, you get the idea.

And in truth, I still believe most of my theories. Most days. My long-suffering and caring wife, Kathy, often interrupts my activities, or my sessions with ice packs, salves, creams, braces, and other impedimenta, by saying in a slightly annoyed but still loving (sort of) tone, "Douglas, you are not twenty-five anymore!" I answer with, "I know, but I'm still thirty-five . . ." This answer has the advantage of being true, as I am indeed thirty-five, at least. And other numbers can be added as needed. But it seems to have few other advantages, at least in terms of marital harmony or physical indestructability in the face of time. So that theory has been called into question. The others are still operational. On most days, as I say.

RECENTLY, KATHY AND I were visiting Fawn Island, hosting another couple, when I traipsed around to the northeast end of the island to move a canoe from the old dock where it rested. It was about time to go, and I wanted to hide the canoe back in the brush, as I often do when we are away. So with a little extra planning and effort—it is not quite as easy as it used to be—I hoisted the canoe onto my shoulders and started up the gangplank and onto the island. I had only towed the old dock to its new resting spot a few weeks earlier and was not yet intimately familiar with the ground, although I knew that rocks, moss, roots, and a few steep steps were involved. At a precarious moment—just as I was climbing the slope and balanced on one foot with the other in midair—the tail end of the canoe firmly hooked the stub end of a small spruce I had cut for the path. And down I went, backward onto my back. It happened startlingly fast, as such episodes do. The canoe landed on my head, and I felt a sharp pain in my lower back. Very sharp.

I lay there for a few moments, catching my breath, trying to determine exactly what had happened. I had never fallen with a canoe before, ever—over thousands of wilderness miles paddled and portaged. The entire situation was quite surprising. And the pain in my back was . . . painful. Reaching around I discovered a knife-edged rock jutting out of the duff: my unlucky landing place and the cause of my discomfort. After determining that I could still move my feet and legs, and that my head was still attached and bleeding only slightly from an offending bolt on the portage yoke, I tried to slide out from under the canoe. Each small effort at pushing, lifting, and sliding resulted in more pain—a burning, excruciating jolt in my back and down my legs. Finally, with one more push and a slight roll, I was freed and managed to stand up. I bent down to grab the bow handle to pull the canoe to safety. That didn't work. A fresh jolt told me that any canoe moving would have to wait. So I started walking back up the trail to the cabin.

It took a long time. With each passing minute, my steps grew smaller and shorter, until they settled at about three to four inches, and I was shuffling along like Mr. Tudball, Mrs. Uh-Wiggens's boss in the old Carol Burnett TV series. I eventually made it to the cabin. Barely. I tried to sit down. That didn't work either. Much concern was expressed as Kathy and the nice couple bustled around, closing windows and locking doors in hasty preparation for departure. I was virtually carried down the old stone steps to the new dock and the waiting boat. I was able to grasp the tiller and run the boat to the landing, slowly, standing all the way. Then, with much assistance I exited the boat and rolled into the SUV, and off to the small International Falls medical center we went.

At the center, X-rays were taken, which showed no fractures, and it was ascertained that I had a deep and painful bruise near the spinal cord, and other stuff that I can't remember. The diagnosis was quite believable. Some very nice drugs were administered, which I really can't remember either. Kathy drove us home after grateful goodbyes to our helpful friends, and I spent the next several days in bed, followed by trips to a chiropractor and a massage therapist. It took quite some time—longer than I figured it should have—before lingering problems in my back and butt were put behind me. So to speak.

At some point during my convalescence I put out a Facebook post to my kind followers describing the whole misadventure. I got much sympathy, which was nice and the main reason I put up the post. But one fellow seemed to take umbrage. "Doug," he wrote, "when are you going to learn that risky behaviors have consequences!?"

Oh. Wow. Risky behaviors? Carrying a canoe. On my own dock on my own island. Just like I've portaged canoes a thousand times before. Now a risky behavior? Since when? Why? It made me stop and think. And I've been thinking ever since, more or less, with frequent and lengthy breaks. And I have decided that my Facebook friend may have a point. Possibly—a small one. It appears that activities that were once not risky now are. And things that were once moderately risky are now more so. I have no idea why this may be the case, but Kathy, as I've said, often mentions age. As do other folks. And I thus bump into my aforementioned theories on the subject and questions about their continued usefulness.

Each of us has our one life to live and, so far as we know, only one. Therefore, it is incumbent on us, after the demands of duty and responsibility are satisfied (within reason), to try and live that life in the way that we find most agreeable and rewarding. This is another of my theories, and I am not giving it up. For me, this agreeableness is best achieved by spending a lot of time outdoors, breathing pine-scented air, admiring wildflowers, listening to migrating geese and yodeling loons and scolding squirrels, and doing a number of at least moderately physical things. None of these pursuits requires an extraordinary amount of athleticism (except golf, which is no doubt the source of my endless frustration with it). But going for hikes and long walks, riding bicycles and motorcycles, paddling and portaging canoes, working in the woods, clearing trails, running chainsaws and planting trees, building stone walls, captaining a fishing boat, and occasionally going deer hunting with my son and grandson, these are things I am unwilling to give up. Yet.

So. What is the answer? What is risky and what isn't? And how much risk is tolerable or even advisable, and how much is just foolish? Good questions. Probably with no standard answers. Each person has to pretty much figure it out for himself or herself. Just like the rest of life. With help perhaps from caring spouses or friends who remind you (frequently) of your current list of ailments and your age. Of course, age is just a number, and you are as young as you feel. Right?

So I hew to my theories and to my roll of admirable forebears, taking note of how they did things, as I have all my life. I note that my grandmother still played catch with me—with a hardball—into her seventies. My mother taught piano lessons to her beloved students to the age of eighty-nine, teaching for seventy-three consecutive years. I note that Sig Olson was wearing a pair of new snowshoes when he died in a snowdrift, having typed that very morning these words on his old Royal typewriter: "A New Adventure is coming up, and I'm sure it will be a good one." I note that Marjorie Stoneman Douglas lived to the ripe old age of 108, did not take up her vital role in the protection of the Everglades until she was seventy-nine, and lived for her last seventy-two years in a small south Florida cottage with no dishwasher or air conditioning. I note that nearly everyone I particularly admire did things in their own idiosyncratic and original way, encountering and managing the attendant risks.

I also note that, truly, life is short, no matter how long we live. So, we had better live. And make the best choices we can along the way. For now, I still ride a motorcycle, but I don't jump it anymore. I still go fishing and hunting. I still work in the woods and run chainsaws, with a cell phone, chaps, a hard hat, and proper precautions. I still wade streams and tromp up and down hills, catching the good tidings of trees and birds and wildflowers. I still love to paddle canoes, and will continue to do so, but will probably not take long, solo trips anymore. Snowshoeing and skiing are still definitely part of the plan. I might even do other stuff I haven't thought of yet.

And I will still carry my favorite canoe off the dock by myself. But I'll probably go a little slower, being careful of that nasty little spruce stump. In fact, I think I'll get over to that side of the island and trim it off. Right to the ground. Soon as I find the liniment. And get this wrist working again. And my shoulder. And my knee . . .

THREE TROUT AND A BOY

Far below . . . sparkling, frothing, tumbling . . . was the stream. As pretty as any I'd ever seen.

To visit a trout stream is to visit a sort of heaven. To visit a *brook* trout stream is to visit one of the finest, freest, clearest, flowing realms in all of heaven. And to do so in May, when the wild cherries and plums bloom along the country roadsides and marsh marigolds spread their golden bouquets beside the purling rills is . . .

Well.

And so we were off, son and grandson and grandfather, to catch a trout. Which is not the only, or even primary, goal when trout fishing. But on this day it was high on the list, because grandson Henry was going to show me, Opa (the grandfather) how it was done. Henry had just the week before caught a brookie all on his own, fulfilling a New Year's resolution. His father, Bryan, had not made the cast or handed Henry the pole or reeled in the fish. It was all accomplished independently. So now Henry was eager to show Opa the place, the technique, and the skill required in this amazing feat.

When I pulled into the driveway, Henry ran to the car and jumped up and down beside it, as though on a pogo stick, beaming and shouting, "We're going trout fishing! We're going trout fishing!" Poles and reels and lures and spinners were quickly gathered, and the creel I had given Henry for Christmas. Into the car we piled.

There was one short stop to make before we traveled to the trout stream, and that was the dock on the small local lake a quarter-mile away, where springtime crappies and sunfish could be caught. These were more modest, pedestrian fish than a brook trout, yet still wonderful—the friendly fish of my own childhood. And on this day they were cooperative and willing, as they often are, and in very little time we had several. But the brookies were calling, and we were soon on our way.

In the world of fish, the brook trout is a different order of being, a living flame that somehow burns beneath the water. Not even a trout exactly, it is a native fish belonging to the char genus of the salmon family. But to all who admire it, it is known as the brook trout—or simply, the brookie. Or sometimes squaretail, due to the conformations of its tail fin. It does not grow very large, and as its name implies, mostly lives in small brooks and rivulets. But they must be of the clearest, coldest water, with few impurities and a high oxygen content, the water falling and tumbling over rocks and logs, cutting deeper under the banks where the stream bends, curling into eddies, and occasionally gathering into small ponds or pools—perhaps provided by beavers—for a short rest.

In these places the brookie can be found, and when seen it is something to behold, speckled sides, deep red-orange streaks along its flanks and lower fins, a fiercely curled upper lip—the perfect, spectacular predator, it would seem, for the lovely places it inhabits. Although small, it boasts an aggressive mien that belies its size, and one can imagine that for the insects, crustaceans, macroinvertebrates, and the other tiny water creatures it devours, it is plenty large enough to be terrifying. In its world, the brookie is top of the food chain—and acts like it.

For these reasons, it is not extraordinarily difficult to catch, certainly easier than its larger and warier cousin the brown trout, and is therefore a near-perfect quarry for a small boy with a spinning rod.

So we were off on our drive across the spring countryside to a stream or two Bryan had identified and scoped out. In his excitement, Henry regaled me from the back seat with what seemed to be an endless supply of second grade knock-knock jokes and what-do-you-call-it-when riddles. In accord with long-standing grandfatherly tradition, I got a grand total of zero correct answers. Henry seemed okay with this: in fact, my inability to decipher seven-year-old humor appeared to add to his delight.

Finally, shortly before my head exploded, we arrived. Not at the trout stream precisely, but at a small impoundment—a little pond—where I was told that brook trout were to be caught, had in fact been caught the week before. Henry took one side of the pond, Opa the other, with Papa in between. We all casted for several minutes with our little double-aught spinners. (No fly rods on this day, in deference to a small boy just learning to cast.) I tried a couple of likely looking spots on the bank. Mostly, I watched Henry across the pond. He casted well for a little guy, flinging his spinner easily, but it soon became apparent he had expected to catch a trout by now, to show Opa how it was done. He became more antsy, moving here and there on the far shore. He ended up balancing on a not-very-large or stable-looking boulder a couple of feet offshore. I watched more closely. Then the inevitable happened. Henry leaned a little too far with a cast, lost his balance, and slipped off the rock, ending up on his feet but nearly waist-deep in the water. He was wearing his life vest, so it was nothing dangerous, but in an early May trout stream, plenty cold, and startling. I tossed down my pole and started over, but before I got more than a few steps, Bryan was already there.

Henry had already climbed out and managed to hold it together for a minute or so. But then the cold really hit, and a tear or two may possibly have fallen. (Although in retellings of the story Henry assures me this was most certainly not the case.) In any event, Papa scooped him up and said calming things while I gathered up the fishing gear. Then Bryan said something about the fishing trip being over for today, and I said, of course. The car got loaded and we climbed in, Papa turned on the heater, and emotions began to ease up a bit. We drove away from the pond. I mentioned to Henry the time I fell off a log at a trout stream when just about his age, landing headfirst not feetfirst, getting drenched from head to toe. And that I did cry. Henry sniffed and said, "Really?"

"Sure, it happens all the time, to every trout fisherman," I answered.

THEN THE UNEXPECTED HAPPENED. Bryan said, "Hey, Henry, should we stop real quick on our way home, at that winding little meadow stream where we caught a few last week—just to show Opa and make a couple of casts?"

"Oh . . . oh . . . okay," snuffled Henry.

Arriving at the spot, I saw that it was a tiny, lovely, winding brook in a flat, wildflower meadow, the sort of place you might see pictures of under the caption "Brook Trout Stream." We climbed out of the car and I noticed for the first time that Henry was wearing light, nylon pants, the sort of material that dries quickly. Bryan said, "Hey, Henry, why don't you show Opa that good spot where you caught one last week?" Away Henry went, picking up speed as he marched along with his pole. Henry and I soon stopped at a likely-looking bend in the stream, with a nice undercut on the opposite bank. I had left my pole in the car, content to be an Opa-helper-observer at this point. Henry flipped a short cast. Then another. Then a third. And there was the brookie—right where it should have been, under the bank.

It was not a long battle. But for a seven-year-old with damp pants, and his Opa watching, it was a very fine moment. In came the eight-inch fish, sides and belly all aflame, a gorgeous thing to behold. Opa helped with the hook removal and in went the fish into the creel. It is a great thing to practice catch-and-release on a trout stream, as we often do, but there are times when a fellow needs to keep a fish or two. It turned out there were no more lurking under the bank and we started back, to find that Papa had caught a couple off the little walking bridge Henry and I had crossed.

"Henry, should we go ahead and go home now, or would you like to show Opa that beautiful spot on Rock Creek?" asked Bryan.

This time there was no hesitation. "Let's show him!" said Henry. His pants were nearly dry.

Rock Creek, it turned out, was even more brook-trouty-postcard-looking than the meadow stream. Parking the car, we headed into the woods and down a steep bank, with Bryan saying, "Now, Henry, you hold Opa's hand, and don't let him fall!" I didn't feel in much danger of falling. But I got the idea and was very happy to hold Henry's hand. And the trail indeed got steeper and more challenging all the way down. While far below at the bottom, sparkling, frothing, tumbling, like something out of the classic movie *A River Runs Through It,* was the stream. As pretty as any I'd ever seen.

Along the way we stepped carefully over hepatica and spring beauty, wild ginger and trout lily, and when we reached the end of our descent, close beside the stream, we found marsh marigolds and bouquets of the lush but unfortunately named skunk cabbage. We also found a fine-looking little pool that after a number of casts yielded no fish. Then Opa—the old guide, the grandfather—said, "Hey, guys, see that fallen log across that little side channel, with the water falling over it, just upstream? I'll bet you there's one under there."

And I was nearly right. For there was not one trout but two. Beauties. And Henry caught them both.

Soon it was indeed time to head for home. We would return as fishermen had for countless generations—skilled and triumphant, providers for the family larder. And although the grandfather had caught no fish, I had caught something even better—a glimpse of a small boy's joy and accomplishment, and a firsthand view of a gentle, caring father who knew just how to rescue a situation and help his son to feel brave and strong and successful. And, I thought to myself, there aren't many sorts of outings better than that.

Partway home Henry piped up. "Hey, Opa, what do you call it when a dinosaur farts?"

"I don't know, Henry, what do you call it when a dinosaur farts?"

"A blast from the past, Opa!" Uproarious laughter.

Yes, Henry was just fine. I, however, would have to sit through twenty more miles of second-grade boy humor. Oh well, I thought. I can handle it. Maybe.

A FLOWER ON THE FAR SIDE OF THE WORLD

Lucia said that I was very much like a newborn in a brand-new world, trying to understand and absorb everything that was so strange and wonderful.

We stood on a narrow trail on the steep side of an impossibly green and misty mountain. From the trail the ground fell away precipitously, into an even more misty chasm yawning below. The damp sandstone cliffs dripped slowly, as they had for eons. And on those cliffsides were some of the most compelling figures I had ever seen. They stood there before us and they towered above us, many painted in riotous colors, some just the gray shades of the sandstone. One after another they confronted us, more than ten thousand of them, representations of ancient Tantric Buddhism, Taoism, and Confucianism, all dating from the ninth to thirteenth centuries. The enormous Sleeping Buddha was there beside the path, reclining serenely on his bed of stone, and in a hidden grotto stood the golden Avalokiteshvara Buddha of a thousand hands and eyes, seeing, understanding, and helping all beings through limitless compassion. In another site, the great Chinese teacher Lao Tse gazed down on us. The intricately carved Great Wheel of Life imparted its implacable lessons as it had for centuries, while innumerable guardians or teachers warned of potential missteps on the path of life or welcomed us into the dimensions of the mystical. The entire effect was extraordinary. Overwhelming.

And all stood within the context of the misty mountain near Chongqing, China, near the great gorge of the Yangtse. These Dazu Rock Carvings, a World Heritage Site, were just one of many wonders I was experiencing on this, my first trip to China. It was not a journey I had envisioned or ever planned to make. It all began with a private Facebook message, the kind I often don't look at—at least not regularly. But I had looked at this one. It said something along the lines of "Douglas Wood, would you please answer our emails? Please! We really want to bring you to China!" But the syntax was a bit confusing. And besides, what emails?

It turned out there had been a number of them. Coming from an account I didn't recognize and with slightly odd word choice or punctuation, I must have dismissed them. I shouldn't have. For Yunjia Hai, a wonderful young woman I would come to know simply as Yun, was trying very hard to reach me on behalf of her boss, Mr. Ao, entrepreneur and publisher of King-in Publishing in China. Mr. Ao had first discovered my children's books at the big Frankfurt International Book Fair in Germany—the *Old Turtle* trilogy, *The Secret of Saying Thanks, A Quiet Place,* and *Where the Sunrise Begins.* Ao had acquired translation rights and had begun to publish some of these books in Mandarin. I had heard about such goings-on through some of my American publishers—Simon and Schuster, Scholastic, Candlewick—and occasionally received a complimentary book printed in beautiful calligraphy, but I had not paid a lot of attention. I should have.

Now I stood on a mountain trail halfway around the world, trying to absorb the impact of historical stone representations of teachers, sages, and philosophies I had been reading about for decades. I had long been taken with the ancient way of Taoism, a teaching that emphasizes a gentle force or essence within all things and all people, called the Tao, and represented by its two founding figures, Lao Tse and Chuang Tse. Through some combination of fate and serendipity, my first book, *Old Turtle,* had been illustrated by a Chinese American practicing Taoist, Cheng-Khee Chee. His deeply spiritual art was surely responsible in large measure for the success of the book, which was widely praised and translated and sold well over a million copies. I was also at least marginally familiar with Confucianism and various strands of historic Buddhism and had long been interested in Joseph Campbell and his life's work on religion and mythology.

But there is a difference between reading about things in books (however much one loves books) and standing before a thousand-year-old Buddha in a faraway land you never thought you'd visit, breathing the cool, moist air of a deep mountain gorge.

The Dazu gorge was far from the only natural marvel I witnessed. My Chinese hosts—well aware of my lifelong inclination toward rocks, woods, and waters, green and growing things—had made certain to include a number of such nature-oriented stops, as well as more business-centered visits to major cities with their schools, bookstores, and other venues. With my travel-wise brother Bruce accompanying, providing welcome company and assistance in a strange and distant land, we had experienced many a wonderment. We'd traveled the valley of the great Yellow River, gazed at the iconic spires and parapets, eroded over eons from the dusky-colored loess—calling card of the retreating glaciers ten thousand years ago. We were reminded of vaguely similar topography near our childhood home of Sioux City, Iowa, by the Missouri River, one of the few other places on the planet where this wind-blown glacial dust was deposited in such vast accumulations. We visited the fabulous Kaifeng Chrysanthemum Gardens near Zhengzhou, climbing the steps of a great pyramid and viewing forms and fields of color as far as the eye could see. Upon the pyramid and its high overlook, Bruce, with his Indiana Jones fedora, and I in my khakis and traveler's vest, were quickly surrounded by curious young people anxious to have their pictures taken with the visiting Western celebrities.

We had visited the timeless Shaolin Kung Fu Temple, established in the 400s and made famous in America through references in movies and television shows. Every inch of the grounds was spotless, manicured, tended with love and discipline, including a gnarled cypress tree more than 4,500 years old. That night under the October stars, we saw an incredible display of martial arts, theater, and choreography on the side of a mountain and began to get some sense of a mysterious tradition passed on for centuries upon centuries.

One of my favorite stops (arranged by Mr. Ao after he learned of my interest in bonsai trees) was a tree garden on another misty mountain. The bonsais were older and more impressive than any I had ever seen. Ao and his top assistant and our translator, Lucia, laughed as I ran from one tree to another, behaving, they said, like a delighted little child. At one point in our trip, Lucia said that I was very much like a newborn in a brand-new world, trying to understand and absorb everything that was so strange and wonderful. I couldn't argue. Bruce, meanwhile, more adventurous in culinary matters than I, had a grand time sampling every Chinese delicacy and liqueur, more than once egged on by our generous hosts.

But our tour was about more than seeing fascinating sights and enjoying ourselves immensely. Ao so loved my books, he said, and had long wanted to bring me to China, for a very particular reason. In spite of ancient ways of wisdom and philosophies that had long connected the Chinese people to the natural world, Ao feared that such ties were rapidly being lost, especially to younger generations. Were in fact disappearing in the urgency and haste of a people trying to catch up and get ahead. Everywhere we went in the major cities, the scenes were similar. Tall buildings going up, construction everywhere, enormous earth-moving machines moving in virtual parades. Cars, motor scooters, bicycles, electric and gas-powered carts, rickshaws, and vast numbers of pedestrians—all moving, moving, moving. An entire country in motion.

Meanwhile, in all these busy places—cities and schools, bookshops and auditoriums and lecture halls—I gave talks. And in every location I met wonderful people. Lovely, generous, gentle, and considerate people who wanted to make Bruce and me feel comfortable and welcome. Mr. Ao, Yun, and Lucia, and another lovely young lady whose English name was Jade and Beauty had arranged everything carefully. Wonderful posters and billboards, lavish introductions, beautiful dinners and receptions. At the programs, as I read from my books, or told a story, or sang a song, there were images on big screens, with Lucia meticulously translating the words. Every face was attentive, every eye and ear focused on me. Never had I experienced such a book tour.

YET I FELT A VAGUE SENSE OF FAILURE. Of somehow not quite breaking through, successfully communicating what I was trying to say. About Nature. About our human connection with the green and living world, and all the beings with whom we share our journey among the stars. It was hard to put a finger on, with such wonderful attention, but it had something to do with what is often my most favorite part of talks and lectures, the question-and-answer period at the end. Time and again I would get questions, excellent, thoughtful questions, often referencing points I had made in my presentation—so clearly listened to and considered. And so often the question was followed with the word *but*.

"But Mr. Wood," someone would say, "I think I understand what you are saying about making sure our children spend time with Nature, or learn something about plants and flowers and trees and birds, or learn about the phases of the moon or see the stars at night, but how can we do this? We want the very best for our children, we want them to get ahead in life, want them to go to the best school and get good grades and compete in the world. How is there time to do these other things? The nearest park or wild place is far away. And besides, we parents often do not know how to teach these things you are talking about." And every time I would answer as best I could. Good answers, I hoped. Reassuring answers about not needing to know everything, about simply making friendly introductions, spending time together in the natural world. Maybe the answers were effective. I hoped so. And hopefully the books and stories would continue to communicate after I was gone. But there aways seemed to be another question.

Near the end of our tour, our wonderful sojourn in China, we visited one more big city—the most modern, most beautiful, most bustling one yet—Shenzhen, a metropolis of 12.6 million in Guangdong Province. More gleaming skyscrapers, more traffic, more parades of earth-movers, more than we had yet seen anywhere. The effect was overwhelming. As we drove down a main thoroughfare in our minivan—Mr. Ao, Yun, Lucia, Bruce, and I—on our way to my last big talk—my face was pressed against the window. I craned to see the tops of buildings, some newly completed, some still under construction. I watched as scooters and bicycles, cars and trucks whizzed by, as pedestrians bustled in never-ending streams along the sidewalks. All familiar sights by now. But then something different caught my eye. Only for a few moments, as we stopped at a traffic light. A little girl, perhaps ten or eleven years old, dressed in a school uniform and carrying a red backpack, had stopped on the busy sidewalk. She stood beside a flower planter. And as I watched, she bent down until her face was close to the blossoms, stayed there a moment, and breathed in their fragrance. Then she straightened up and smiled. A beautiful smile. And the light changed, and we were on our way.

She never knew I saw her, that little girl, or that anyone had. But in that one moment, a visitor's trip to China was changed. A journey was redeemed and fulfilled. Because in that moment I saw the truth. I knew the answer.

We went on to our destination, and I gave my talk, told my stories, sang my songs. I spoke about our home in the natural world, about trees and birds and the wisdom of sages. The audience was kind and attentive as always. And then came The Question: "But Mr. Wood," it began. I listened closely. And when it was time to answer, I didn't talk about my books or about my experiences in the wilderness. I didn't try to explain something that had perhaps not been clear in translation. Instead, I told a little story—just a minute or two long—about a little girl I had seen that morning.

A small child, who with no adult around to guide or show or explain, had simply stopped—on a busy day on a busy street—and smelled a flower. And smiled. There is always time to smell a flower, I said. For any of us, by ourselves or with a child, a student or a grandchild. And that moment, of understanding that this flower and this fragrance are as important as all the rest of the great and busy world—that moment is everything. That moment is always available and within our grasp. And it may lead to unimaginable consequences. To other moments and other times and other places, to a lifetime of engagement and belonging and understanding.

Or not. It may just be one flower, one moment by itself. But that eternal moment—of aliveness and belonging, of being who and what and where we are—well, we owe that to ourselves, and especially to our children. No matter how busy we may be, or what our goals and aspirations are. It is not important that we be experts or authors or botanists or nature guides. It is only important that we share such moments with our children, whenever we can, imparting the perhaps unspoken lesson that this flower is important. It matters. *As do we all.* And it was not me, a visiting American, saying these things: it was their own little girl.

And . . . for once . . . there were no more questions. None. Only smiles.

Our trip was soon finished after that. One more lovely dinner, a chance for Bruce and me to thank our wonderful friends for all the beauty they had shared with us, for the gift of their own time and attention. There were discussions with Mr. Ao about future books to be published in China. There were hugs and tearful goodbyes, especially from sweet Yun, who had worked so hard to make it all happen.

And then Bruce and I were soon winging our way back across the Pacific, the great ocean I had discovered decades before when I had sourdough bread and strawberries on the beach and fell asleep to the chanting of the waves, imagining faraway lands across the rolling sea. As we flew above the clouds, the whole journey began to seem almost unreal and hard to comprehend. I thought about the Buddha of a thousand eyes and hands, about the Yellow River and chrysanthemum gardens and mountainside bonsais. And then I thought about a little girl, whose name and story I would never know, a beautiful child with a red backpack, who reminded me how important it can be to simply take the time to smell a flower.

THE FRAGRANCE OF JASMINE TEA

Such dark thoughts sometimes come in the night.
They come perhaps when we are alone under the stars.
When distractions are gone and the black forms of trees
loom in silent vigil.

I sat beside the small campfire, feeding it twigs of spruce and balsam—little, dead, light-deprived branches I'd gathered from the lower trunks of nearby conifers. This is always the best and easiest place in the forest to find dry wood, no matter the weather. It's a small secret that has been known for millennia by indigenous peoples and those who live close to the land, who have needed to quickly gather firewood and tinder. I have countless times sent canoe campers out to forage for such supplies of an evening, in many a wilderness camp. And if they did not already know the secret, they were inevitably delighted to learn this small tidbit of woods lore.

The little fire crackled merrily. The water along the shoreline whispered, wavelets lapping, occasionally chuckling in some tiny cleft or hollow at the water's edge. Overhead, the Big Dipper poured its invisible contents over the spruce-steepled landscape below, and into the lake, and onto all the hundreds of square miles of wilderness surrounding me, and over the cities and towns and strongholds of civilization far beyond. As it always had. For anyone who ever sat by a small campfire far below and noticed.

The forest was dark around me. The black silhouettes of trees stood framed in the soft light of the stars. Other constellations were there as well, high above the trees. Draco the dragon. The Corona Borealis. Cassiopeia. The Summer Triangle composed of Deneb (the bright light in Cygnus the Swan's tail), Vega in the upper-right corner of Lyra the stringed lyre, and Altair borne on the outstretched wings of Aquila the Eagle. These were old friends familiar from many a wilderness night under the stars, although my feelings of friendship and affection flowed only in one direction. Probably.

By the light of the fire, I could almost see those many generations of wood gatherers who had come before and sat around similar fires. The Abenaki, the Anishinaabe, the Menominee, the Cheyenne, the Lakota, the hundreds of other native tribes and nations of North America; the frontiersmen and frontierswomen, the voyageurs, the trappers and traders, the immigrants and homesteaders and farmers and pioneers, the loggers and the prospectors and the railroad laborers, and all who had struggled to open up a continent, simultaneously struggling to glean a meager living and to simply survive. I could see a wider swath of humanity as well, individuals of differing skin tones and statures and facial appearances, squatting on their haunches beside a flickering source of warmth and security, even as mile-high ice fields covered the earth and chilled the air. And I could see familiar figures from the more recent past, too, old friends and family members gathered around campfires that were strung like beads of light decades into the past, along lakes and rivers now hazy in the mists of recollection.

But I sat there alone. And fed twigs into the fire. Beneath the Big Dipper. I watched small sparks rise toward the treetops, toward the stars, then lose their brief glow and fade into the night. I thought about the little sparks we call life. About all those generations of human beings, and other beings, all that they had fought to overcome, to last just a little while under the stars. I wondered, as I often had before, about happiness, purpose, and meaning.

I thought about an article I had recently read about the extinction of virtually all life on Earth with the impact of a city-sized asteroid some sixty-six million years ago on the Yucatan peninsula, leaving only a few of the smallest, burrowing shrew-sized mammals surviving, beings from whom we eventually descended. Such a catastrophic collision would surely occur again someday, and there is no saying when. One has only to understand something of mathematical odds, or gaze on the many craters of the moon, to know it. I thought of what that meant to our many confident philosophies and religions, to history and to art and literature, to our human dreams of legacy, of something somehow permanent and lasting, here on our tiny planetary lifeboat adrift on the seas of time and space. I remembered a line I had once read about the pages of Shakespeare someday blowing across a dead and empty plain.

I thought about other uncomfortable parameters of our earthly existence: the fact that at any given moment billions of creatures the world over are suffering and dying, many of them being eaten alive. And I thought about the countless human-inflicted agonies in this world: cruelty and carelessness and ignorance and torture and abuse and war. Things that are far more endemic to human life than we often care to ponder.

SUCH DARK THOUGHTS sometimes come in the night. They come perhaps when we are alone under the stars. When distractions are gone and the black forms of trees loom in silent vigil. And yet on this night, beside my crackling fire, another unexpected thought occurred as well: the curious idea that still, in the midst of this sometimes brutal, always difficult, always threatened, and always terminal existence, we human beings do something strange.

We enjoy life.

Perhaps much of the time. In the midst of manifest meaninglessness, we seek meaning. Persistently. And often find it. In truth, it is in no way strange or anomalous that we are sometimes depressed. Or anxious. Or wracked with feelings of dread or hopelessness. No. Those would seem in the face of all evidence and circumstance to be perfectly appropriate responses to this earthly existence.

The real question is, why are we not always so? All of us? All the time?

Other questions then follow. How is it that we have humor—the ability to laugh and to feel buoyance, silliness, even giddiness? Why empathy? Why tenderness? Grace? How is it that human beings are endowed with this odd capacity to experience true enjoyment—the sensations of satisfaction and comfort, well-being, delight, even bliss—when listening to a piece of music, when smelling a flower, when viewing a sunrise, when holding a child? Why should this be, when with our large brains and active imaginations we know early on exactly what the future holds? As Ernest Hemingway wrote, "All stories, if continued far enough, end in death." One hundred percent of the time. Always. For everyone. Not only for ourselves, but for all of the people and other creatures we will ever know. And not merely death. Along the way, and almost certainly at the end, there is also suffering. And great loss.

That is what we call *life*—the plain and true nature of it. And no one is wrong, or ill, or out of their minds, to see it that way.

And yet tens of millions, hundreds of millions, billions of our fellow travelers on this mortal coil, on this lovely blue marble—the merest speck of dust in the cosmos—do not curl into helpless balls of anxiety and perish in despair. Why not? Why is it that we retain this strange ability to enjoy life, and how do we continue the elusive search for meaning?

I looked at the dark trees around me. Each one of them a picture, a portrait of the act of reaching, reaching for the sun. It's the way trees are made, the way they live. The human mind reaches too, toward growth, toward fulfillment, toward harmony and beauty, toward that something we call meaning. This seems to be the way that we are made. It is well worth noting, I thought, that there really is a sun that trees reach for, that they do not climb toward some imaginary goal that is not there. And in our own growth and reaching, likely we don't either. It would indeed be a strange way to be made, an odd way for evolution to progress—to reach for things that are not there.

I got up from the fire, felt in a corner of the Duluth pack, and pulled out a small packet of jasmine tea—my favorite, infused with the impossibly sweet fragrance of jasmine blossoms. I poured some hot water over the tea bag and caught the aroma. After a minute I took a sip. It was, as always, delightful. I closed my eyes and breathed in the fragrance. I thought of a short passage from the Buddhist teacher Thich Nhat Hanh, in which he explained the simple idea that in order to be enjoyed, tea must always be sipped in the present. That one must be present in the moment, discarding ruminations about the past or worries about the future, in order to enjoy it. "Only in the present," he said, "can you savor the aroma, taste the sweetness, appreciate the delicacy." Without that awareness, that presence in the moment, you will soon look down at the cup and the tea will simply be gone. Life is a lot like that cup of tea, said the revered teacher.

How is it that human beings, in a world that often seems defined by struggle and loss, can yet be happy? Can enjoy life? Maybe it has to do with the very fact that we are indeed small and humble beings in a trackless universe. That despite all our ambition and mental capacity, our ability, our need to explore and comprehend that vast and implacable cosmos and our existence within it, we are yet able—and are meant—to live as creatures of small and personal needs and prospects as well. Physical, mental, spiritual needs that when fulfilled from time to time in simple ways can bring us happiness and contentment.

I took another sip of tea, still fragrant but beginning to grow cool in the night air. The fire was dying low. I tossed on a few more twigs and it flared to life. Standing up, I shuffled out of the campfire's small circle of light and down to the water's edge. I gazed down the dark shores of the lake and heard the yodeling of a distant loon. The wavelets still chuckled softly among the rocks. With a slight shift in the breeze, I could make out the barest, whispering undertone of a small rapid at the north end of the lake. Tomorrow I would nose the canoe over the lip and run it. I'd slip past the boulders and the sweepers and the souse holes and the standing waves and would safely reach still waters. I had done it many times before.

It was a beautiful evening. Tomorrow would be a good day, a day to simply be alive. A day to enjoy. I cast one last glance down the long, dark shore, then turned and walked back into the circle of light.

ACKNOWLEDGMENTS

I am grateful for the assistance of my unofficial personal editor and advisor, Nancy Jo Tubbs, in the preparation and polishing of this manuscript. Her keen eye and good ear for the sound and meaning of the words has been invaluable. Equal thanks to my University of Minnesota Press editor, Erik Anderson, for his belief in the book, his literary acumen, and his assistance in accomplishing the flow and feeling of the text and illustrations. I am also grateful to all the staff at the Press for their skill and assistance.

Thanks to friends and family members who are an integral part, not only of my life, but of many of these stories, particularly my brother Bruce, who helped make my trip to China not only possible but more enjoyable and meaningful.

Thanks to Emily Anderson for her artistic sense of the North Country and the beautiful cover illustration.

Especially, thanks to my wife, Kathy, best friend and first reader and listener, for patience, love, and kindness over a lifetime. She has made this writing life possible.

Douglas Wood is an author, artist, musician, educator, wilderness guide, and creator of thirty-nine books for children and adults. His books include *Old Turtle,* the *New York Times* bestseller *Grandad's Prayers of the Earth,* and the memoir *Deep Woods, Wild Waters* (Minnesota, 2017). He has read his books at the White House and at the Lincoln Center in New York. He lives with his family in a log cabin on the Mississippi River in Minnesota.